SCHE HONGI
RA-VLOOT.

# Drake's Island of Thieves

# *Drake's Island of Thieves*

## *Ethnological Sleuthing*

WILLIAM A. LESSA
Foreword by Fred Eggan

*THE UNIVERSITY PRESS OF HAWAII*
*Honolulu*

**Library of Congress Cataloging in Publication Data**

Lessa, William Armand.
    Drake's Island of Thieves.

    Bibliography: p.
    Includes index.
    1. Pelew Islands—Discovery and exploration.
2. Drake, Sir Francis, 1540?–1596. 3. Ethnology—
Micronesia. 4. Ethnology—Mindanao. I. Title.
DU780.L47      919.6'5     74–81140
ISBN 0–8248–0333–7

Figure 1 (title page). Francis Drake. This portrait was engraved by Freeman from an original painting by J. Houbraken. Source: Arch'd Fullarton & Co., Glasgow. (*Courtesy The New York Public Library*)

to Blake Clark

# Contents

# *Illustrations*

# *Tables*

# *Foreword*

THERE ARE FEW ADVENTURES in history more dramatic than Francis Drake's voyage around the world in the *Golden Hind*. Almost four centuries ago he entered the Pacific by way of the Straits of Magellan, cruised northward to the vicinity of Oregon, and then headed westward across the Pacific, guided by maps and navigational charts that he had taken from a Spanish pilot whose ship he had captured off Panama. The first landfall occurred on September 30, 1579, and the behavior of the native population during the three days they tarried led him to designate the place as the "Island of Thieves."

Historical scholarship has agreed on many details of Drake's voyage but there has been wide difference of opinion as to the identity of this island. It was clearly a high island rather than a low one. Some authorities have favored various locations in the Carolines, including four atolls, while others have argued for the Marianas, to which Magellan had earlier given the appellation Islas de los Ladrones, based on his experiences there. A recent scholar, Andrew Sharp, has rejected Micronesia and suggests that the Island of Thieves is none other than Mindanao, but this turns out to be a more complex solution than he envisioned.

William A. Lessa has entered this controversy with the aid of a relatively new tool, ethnohistory, and has not only solved the main problems but has also provided us with a fascinating account of navigation in the Pacific in the sixteenth century and of the cultural complexities of Micronesia. Ethnohistory employs the chronological and documentary methods of conventional history, but also utilizes ethnographic data and oral accounts of people without written history to provide a more rounded account. The major contributions of ethnohistory have been to the study of the American Indians, where the collaboration of historians and anthropologists is resulting in a more adequate and satisfying historical account, but the method has many potential applications. Dr. Lessa is here using ethnohistory for a more specific purpose—testing the clues furnished by the various accounts of Drake's landfall against the accumulated knowledge of different Micronesian, and Mindanaon, cultures, which have been obtained by ethnologists in more recent periods.

Dr. Lessa's credentials for such testing derive from extensive field research on Ulithi and neighboring islands of the Carolines beginning in the late 1940s and a subsequent detailed study of the peoples and cultures of the western Pacific. He has also become thoroughly familiar with the whole corpus of exploration in the Pacific, since the brief accounts available at present for Drake's voyage are not only secondary but often conflicting. Hence, it is important to be aware of the state of the art with regard to contemporary knowledge of navigation, as well as to pay close attention to the various ethnographic clues. Thus, in Drake's time it was possible to determine latitude with considerable accuracy, whereas longitude could only be roughly estimated, an important factor in deciding between the Carolines and the Marianas as the locale of the Island of Thieves. To narrow the choice further, Dr. Lessa examines such problems as demography, types of canoes— including their decorative techniques, outriggers and their methods of attachment—clothing or its lack, betel chewing and tooth blackening, weapons, and the behavior of the inhabitants that led to the designation of the island. As an ethnological detective he tests each clue against the available evidence and gradually narrows the choice to two island groups. Then, by comparing the two groups in detail, he finds the preponderance of evidence in favor of one of them. Not content with this demonstration, Dr. Lessa also tackles the mystery of the "four islands" reported in connection with Mindanao, and discovers the solution by a personal reconnaissance of Davao Gulf.

After further adventures in the Moluccas, Drake sailed across the Indian Ocean and around the Cape of Good Hope, arriving in

England exactly six months after leaving Java. He had a long audience with Queen Elizabeth and presented her with his diary of the voyage, and later he was knighted in the presence of the queen on the deck of the *Golden Hind*. The cargo he brought back from looting Spanish ships and from the Spice Islands repaid his backers beyond their wildest dreams. It is just possible that the diary still exists somewhere in the royal archives and its discovery would provide a treasure of a different kind—and one that would allow this ethnographical reconstruction to be directly tested. I have no fears as to what the result would be, and I am sure that Dr. Lessa would welcome the test of his conclusions as well. He has done an excellent job, as you soon will see for yourself.

FRED EGGAN
*Philippine Studies Program*
*University of Chicago*

# Acknowledgments

THE VAST DOCUMENTATION that characterizes this book demands more than a perfunctory expression of gratitude to the many librarians who have helped to identify and procure pertinent materials for me. Foremost is Charlotte E. Spence, Indo/Pacific Bibliographer of the Research Library of the University of California, Los Angeles. Her assistance was remarkable. Also helpful were three very patient reference librarians, Jean Aroeste, Ruth B. Berry, and Ann T. Hinckley, of the same institution. I cannot name the many members of the staffs of other libraries who showed me kindnesses and guidance, but I would like at least to mention the names of their institutions: The Henry E. Huntington Library, Yale University, Harvard University, The New York Public Library, and The Library of Congress.

Various persons gave me assistance in various ways, some through correspondence, some in conversations, and others while in the Philippines. I wish that I could mention them all but must refrain except for Ruth Frey Axe; Edwin H. Bryan, Jr.; H. de la Costa, S.J.; Robert B. Fox; Mary Virginia Harrison; Evett D. Hester; Frank Lynch, S.J.; Clement W. Meighan; Gerald Nagle, M.M.; Robert H. Power; John Rich, M.M.; and William Henry Scott. In addition to these there were others who are mentioned in appropriate places throughout the book. Assistance with some translations was given by Rita Ventura Loeb, as well as by Susan Martinez Owen and Richard German.

Friends and professional colleagues who read the manuscript were Fred Eggan, Saul H. Riesenberg, the late Andrew Sharp, and the late Stuart and Evonne Glennan. Some of their reactions were joyous, some pained, but all of them constructive.

Assisting me in the production of the cartographic work were Libby J. Hayes and Roger Mac Gowan.

For permission to reproduce maps and drawings I am especially indebted to The Henry E. Huntington Library of San Marino, California (Figures 2, 3, 4, 5, 18, 20, 21, 28, and 29); The Research Library of the University of California, Los Angeles (UCLA) (Figures 9, 13, 14, 15, 19, and 27); and The British Library (Maps 3 and 4, Figures 6 and 25). Others who gave permissions were: The Prints Division of The New York Public Library, The Astor, Lenox and Tilden Foundations (Figures 1, 35); Les Amis des Musées de la Marine and *Neptunia* (Figures 17, 26); The Patrimonio Nacional, Spain, and The Biblioteca del Palacio Real, Madrid (Figure 24); and The Beinecke Rare Book and Manuscript Library, Yale University (Figure 8).

The quotations from Andrew Sharp, *The Discovery of the Pacific Islands*, copyrighted 1960 by the Oxford University Press, are by permission of the Clarendon Press, Oxford. Those from Helen M. Wallis, editor, *Philip Carteret's Voyage round the World* (Hakluyt Society Series II, No. 125, 1965), are by permission of the Hakluyt Society. The passage from Lawrence C. Wroth's, *The Way of a Ship*, is printed by permission of the Anthoensen Press, and that from Richard I. Ruggles' article in Herman R. Friis, editor, *The Pacific Basin*, is printed by permission of the American Geographical Society.

Partial funds for carrying out my work were provided by the Research Committee of the University of California, Los Angeles.

## chapter one

# *The Mystery*

DURING HIS HISTORIC CIRCUMNAVIGATION of the globe almost four centuries ago, Francis Drake set sail across the Pacific from the California coast and did not make a landfall until several weeks later on September 30, 1579. He angrily called the place the "Island of Thieves."

Ever since then the identity of the island that he came upon, before continuing on homeward through the Indian Ocean and around the Cape of Good Hope, has been the subject of much speculation, with most geographers, hydrographers, explorers, and historians declaring in favor of a place in the Carolinian archipelago of Micronesia. (See Map 1.) The only dispute among this particular group of scholars has been in narrowing down the island or island group to one of the scores of islands in the archipelago. Some prefer the Palaus—here considered to be a part of the Carolines, even though they are often given independent geographic status—while others prefer Yap or the atolls of Ngulu, Ulithi, Sorol, or Woleai, which lie within the archipelago proper.

A separate cluster of writers points to the Marianas, a chain of islands outside the Carolinian group and to the north of it, but still within the Micronesian culture area. This claim has a fascinating background and may be looked into first.

### MARIANAS SUSPECTS

The supporters of the Marianas, particularly of Guam, have obviously been influenced by a certain likeness in names rather than

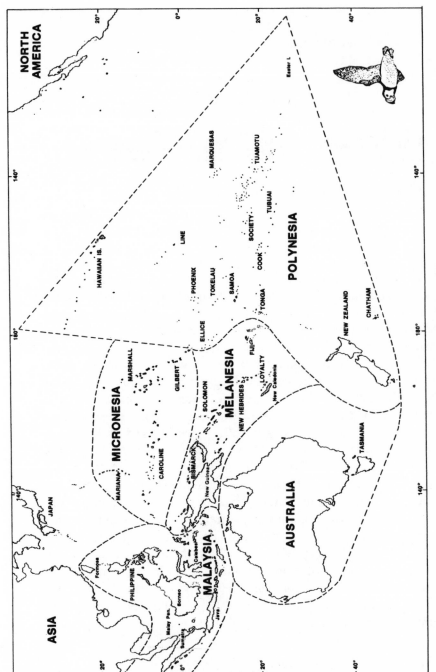

Map 1. Culture Areas of the Pacific

geographical and other considerations. Their assumption is that when Drake finally reached land and engaged the larcenous natives in a brief skirmish, he was under the impression that he had reached the same locale to which Magellan had given the appellation *Islas de los Ladrones*, which of course is translated as the "Islands of Thieves," of which there were two. It does not necessarily follow, however, that Drake's use of the term was due to his understanding that he had come upon Magellan's islands. It is easier to assume that he or his crew coined a similar name merely because they too had been victims of thieving indigenes.

At any rate, the inclination to accept the equivalence of names as a clue to common identity has been the undoing, of all people, of the Naval Intelligence Division of the British Admiralty. This agency tells us in a restricted handbook written during World War II that, "In 1579 Guam was visited by Sir Francis Drake, in the *Golden Hind*" (Great Britain 1943–1945: IV, 319).

Other writers have made the same mistake in identification. Thus, in his book, *A New Universal Collection of Authentic and Entertaining Voyages and Travels* (1768), Edward Cavendish Drake says that Francis Drake "saw the Ladrones" (p. 43). When the explorer Dampier was a seaman aboard a privateer in 1686 he heard Captain Swan urge his crew to sail to Guam because Drake "did run it in less than 50 days" (Dampier 1697:298–300). Ernst Sarfert, a German anthropologist with the Hamburg Südsee-Expedition of 1908–1910, says of Drake that he "reached the Marianas on the 13th of October 1588 [sic]" (Damm 1938:223). Laura Thompson, an American anthropologist whose writings on Guam have been widely read, appears to be unaware that there are alternatives to her ready acceptance of Guam as Drake's island (Thompson 1945:10). Finally, in their otherwise excellent textbook, *A Complete History of Guam* (1964), Carano and Sanchez write unequivocally that one of the early visitors to Guam was Francis Drake (pp. 33, 48), although farther on they add that his Island of Thieves "might or might not have been Guam" (p. 48).

There have been others who have similarly chosen the Marianas, but the above sampling will suffice to demonstrate that not a good deal of deliberation, if any, has gone into their selection.

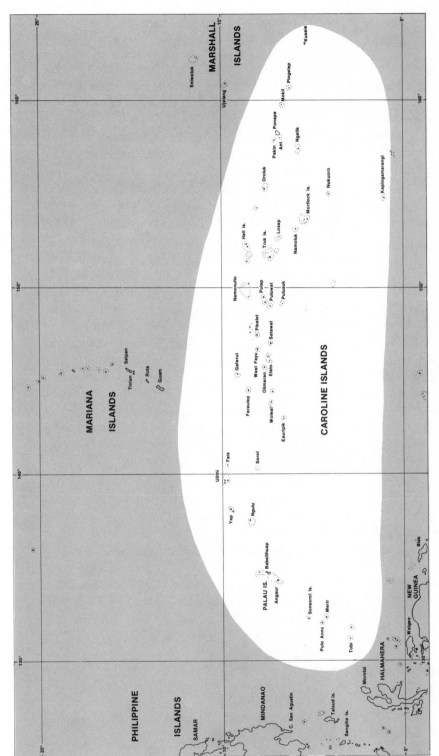

Map 2. The Caroline Islands

## CAROLINIAN SUSPECTS

The advocates of a more southerly locale have sometimes tried to justify their position with one line of reasoning or another, although for the most part they have simply followed without question the authority of some single writer.

Palau (Map 2) has long been a favorite because of the assertion of James Burney, author of the influential work *A Chronological History of the Discoveries in the South Sea or Pacific Ocean*, that, "In 1579 Drake saw the islands, which on account of the disposition and practices of the natives, he named the Islands of Thieves; and which, the circumstances related in his voyage identify with the *Pelew Islands* . . ." (1803–1817:V, 2). Burney had been an officer on the *Discovery*, one of Captain Cook's ships on his third and final voyage into the Pacific, and before that had served with Captain Furneaux on the *Adventure* during Cook's second voyage. Obviously, he was a man with good credentials, although his identification of islands was not infallible. He had never been to Micronesia or the Philippines.

Typical of those willing to follow along passively with Burney's identification of Palau with Drake's island is John Barrow, who writes: "Admiral Burney seems to think, from the description of the natives, the time of the passage to them, and their latitude, that they are the Islands that in our own time have been called the Pellew Islands" (Barrow 1843:152).

The imposing *Dictionary of National Biography*, in its authoritative account of Drake's life and exploits, accepts the Palau selection and thereby exerts still wider influence, especially on persons who are not particularly inclined to go any further than this source in their quest for facts in the life of the great circumnavigator.

Helping to perpetuate the Palau choice even more is Julian S. Corbett, who in his influential *Drake and the Tudor Navy* writes, "John Drake calls the islands Ladrones, and says they lay in 9 degrees, so that Captain Burney is probably correct in identifying them with the Pelew group" (1898:I, 313). Corbett does not tell us that the Palaus are at a latitude approximately two degrees south of the one mentioned.

In company with these influential men is Sir Richard Carnac Temple, who in a volume on Drake for which he wrote a prefatory "Appreciation" of the world-circling expedition makes several references to the Palaus as the Island of Thieves, adding that "to reach the Pelew Islands from San Francisco in a sailing vessel without sight of land was a feat in itself" (Penzer 1926:liii).

Another important writer to endorse the Palau candidacy is John C. Beaglehole, author of the well-known work *The Exploration of the Pacific*, in which he asserts that after leaving the coast of New Albion (California), Drake headed for the Moluccas, "sailing south of the Marshall Islands and through the Pelew group" (1934:74).

The most recent to favor Palau is the distinguished historian, Samuel Eliot Morison (1974:682); but although he could be right, like most others he gives no reason for his choices.

With less influential writers we need not be especially concerned. One of them, E. F. Benson, flatly and indiscreetly informs us: "The group of islands to which they came has been universally identified as the Pelew Islands" (1927:165); but the rest are generally content to make mild statements of varying degrees of conviction. For example, Henry Bourne says Drake "reached what seem to have been the Pelew Islands" (1868:II, 106). His indecision is reflected even more in the words of the Japanese ethnographer Akira Matsumura, who merely says, "it is claimed that the discovery [of Palau] was made in 1579" (1918:6). A. E. W. Mason writes that Drake's island "may have been the Carolines and may have been the islands of Pelew" (1941:180). The historian Boies Penrose states that "an island in the Pellew Group and the southern Philippines were seen" (1952:187). The island in the Philippines is of course not in dispute, for we know that Drake sailed to Mindanao after leaving his Island of Thieves.

The Yap group of high islands, 258 nautical miles northeast of Palau, has a distinguished supporter as Drake's landfall. He is Henry R. Wagner, who bases his choice on a northern latitude of 9 degrees for Drake's island rather than the usually accepted 8 degrees. He thinks that Drake then sailed from Yap to either the southernmost of the Palau group or possibly the coral island of Songosor (Sonsorol) farther to the southwest, where he took on water and wood (1926:500 n.3). Wagner, who is author of *Sir Francis Drake's Voyage around the World*, a splendid study of the circumnavigation, is in this instance bewildered in his views, as we shall see, displaying a lack of requisite familiarity with the southwest Pacific.

It is remarkable that the atoll of Ngulu with its seven little islets should have any "accusers" but it most assuredly does. Its latitude of 8 degrees 18 minutes N is its most obvious qualification and must be the reason why so many important authorities have selected it. One of them is Louis de Freycinet, who at the behest of the French government sailed around the world in 1817–1820 to make scientific observations. He tells us that the islands discovered by Drake are south of Yap and are named Lamaliao Ouron, another name for Ngulu (1827–1839:I[2]:77, 77 fn.1). However, he gives no justification for his choice, which on account of his prestige must have influenced many scholars.

The German geographer Carl E. Meinicke similarly equates the mystery island with Ngulu (1875–1876:II, 361), as does the Spanish geographer Francisco Coello (1885:55). Ngulu is also the choice of the prestigious Oceanic canoe specialist James Hornell (Haddon and Hornell 1936–1938:I, 376). It has likewise been selected by the eminent Hamburg Südsee-Expedition ethnographer Augustin Krämer, who has looked into the matter of identification with more care than most and concludes: "I am inclined to believe that . . . it was the freebooter Francis Drake, not Villalobos, who sighted the Ngulu Islands" (1917:12). But in the next breath he continues: "If, however, the account of de Brosses . . . is correct, that the islands discovered first were situated at latitude 8° and that the voyage from there to the Philippines lasted 27 days, the island in question must be Sorol or, possibly, the islands around Truk." Obviously Krämer, who in any event rejects Palau with some feeling, is not sure of himself, mostly because he has allowed himself to be confused by secondary sources, including the aforementioned de Brosses. Certainly latitude should not be a reason for his wavering between Ngulu and Sorol, for both are at almost the same distance north of the equator, and their respective distances from the Philippines are too similar to enter in as a factor.

Ulithi Atoll, a large atoll complex located at about 10° N latitude at its northernmost island, is the choice of only a few. In his introduction to the British Museum's publication *Sir Francis Drake's Voyage round the World 1577–1580: Two Contemporary Maps*, Frederick P. Sprent, assistant keeper and superintendent of the Map Room of the museum, says of the Island of Thieves that they are "probably one of the Mackenzie [Ulithi] or the Pelew Islands"

(British Museum 1927:5), but he advances no justification for this somewhat casual and very indecisive identification. On the atoll itself, while World War II was still in progress, an audience of thousands of American servicemen, poised there on hundreds of ships destined for action against Japan, heard a broadcast emanating from the local armed forces radio station WVTY to the effect that Francis Drake had been a visitor to Ulithi in 1588 (Vollbrecht 1945:9). The source of this interesting tidbit of information was not revealed.

The small atoll of Sorol is casually suggested as a possibility by the same Ernst Sarfert who we noted earlier had said that Drake had touched at the Marianas. In a bizarre sentence, which may be explained on the grounds that his notes were written up posthumously by another anthropologist, he says: "It is also quite possible that Francis Drake, who reached the Marianas on the 13th of October, 1588, touched our island [Sorol]" (Damm 1938:223). Not only does he have Drake in both the Marianas and Sorol, but like radio station WVTY he has him there in a year when the great English hero was on the *Revenge* off the coast of England, helping to thwart the Spanish Armada.

Sarfert may be the source of the same errors made by the Civil Affairs Handbook, *West Caroline Islands*, issued in 1944 by the U.S. Department of the Navy, which tells us that Sorol was "probably sighted by Drake (1588)" (Department of the Navy 1944:22).[1] Interestingly enough, this same handbook asserts also that Ngulu too was "sighted by Sir Francis Drake (1579)," and although this time the year is not in question the additional sighting is, as we shall see.

One more Carolinian locale, the atoll of Woleai, has been equated with Drake's landfall, the sole writer to do so being Adam Johann von Krusenstern, known also as Ivan F. Kruzenshtern, commander of the first Russian expedition around the world. His arguments are directed against Burney's selection of Palau more than toward support of Woleai, and they are threefold: First, Woleai is farther than is Palau from the Philippines, where we know that Drake eventually landed, and this greater distance is more consistent than the shorter one with the thirteen days that Drake spent at sea after leaving the thieving natives and arriving in the Philippine archipelago. Secondly, if Drake had indeed been to Palau he would have made some remarks regarding the place, which he failed to do. Lastly, the inhabitants of Palau have never shown the least disposition to steal (Krusenstern 1824:II, 319–320). This last remark is strange, for at the time when Krusenstern was writing the Palauans had long since acquired a bad reputation, despite the favorable treatment they accorded Captain Henry Wilson of the East India Company, who spent three months there with his crew in 1793.

## A PHILIPPINES SUSPECT

Frustrated by these many conflicting identifications, Andrew Sharp has come forth with a suggestion that is as ingenious as it is bold. In his invaluable book, *The Discovery of the Pacific Islands* (1960), this provocative New Zealander, who a few years ago startled and dismayed Oceanists with his view that the Polynesians were incapable of navigating their canoes more than three hundred miles with any degree of accuracy, says that the Island of Thieves is probably none other than the island of Mindanao in the Philippine archipelago! He interprets the documentary sources to mean that Drake arrived at Mindanao at a latitude of 8 degrees and coasted that island southward for several days (Sharp 1960:49–50), after which he headed for the Moluccas.

Other than its latitude, which is roughly from 10° N to less than 6° N, a feature that favors the selection of Mindanao is its vast size of 36,537 square miles, as compared with even the largest island or island group of Micronesia, none of which is more than a few hundred square miles in area. The island is high, with five major mountain systems and a peak, Mount Apo, which rises to 9,690 feet in elevation. The eastern coast, or the Pacific Cordillera region, is a rugged mountain zone that extends for more than 250 miles from Bilar Point in Surigao southward to Cape San Agustin in Davao Province. An island like that is hard to avoid bumping up against if one sails westwards at certain tropical latitudes.

Sharp brings to bear on the problem a considerable familiarity with Oceanic geography and navigation, and does not advance his suggestions frivolously. However, his theory cannot properly be evaluated without a thorough understanding of the sources on which he based his ideas. At this point further comments would therefore be premature and will be delayed until a more suitable occasion.

## GOALS AND METHODS

Although it has not diminished his stature as a superb circum-global navigator and towering national hero, controversy has always surrounded Drake, especially as to his motives and ethics. This was true during his lifetime and remains true four centuries after his death. However, I have no intention of either denigrating or glorifying this image. Drake's place in history has long been secured beyond the cavils of critics and the extravagant paeans of patriots. My intention is rather to try to set the record straight for one miniscule episode out of the numerous events in which this daring Englishman participated. It is especially the purpose of my inquiry to examine how far anthropology can throw light on the enigma of his western Pacific landfall. I suppose that my investigation has personal overtones, too, for I have spent some time in one of the island groups in question and have long cherished the ambition, never more than partially realized, to be its historian. I refer to Ulithi Atoll.

A secondary purpose motivates me, and that is to demonstrate the reliability of the ethnohistorical method. My line of inquiry will take advantage of this method, which, essentially, employs written documents in the reconstruction of the cultures of nonliterate peoples. These documents are more or less contemporary with the time in question, although I have stretched this period to some extent on the grounds that some traits of culture change very slowly indeed—a point that I shall discuss in detail in a later chapter. It is fortunate that the Age of Discovery and the ensuing period of European imperialism and colonialism produced some remarkable evidence by nonanthropologists useful for anthropological purposes. Outstanding in this respect, of course, is the name of Antonio Pigafetta, Magellan's young Italian chronicler; but also valuable for the Pacific area are such early Spanish explorers as Loaisa, Saavedra, Villalobos, Legazpi, and Urdaneta. I shall have occasion to mention the names of many others, too, who have enriched the record.

My method of investigation will not be entirely ethnohistorical, for even though it comes late in time there is a useful body of direct ethnological field research. It has to be used with some skill and caution because of the time factor. At my disposal will be numerous reports, two groups of which deserve special mention. The first of these are the extensive publications of the Hamburg Südsee-Expedition headed by Georg Thilenius. The second are the findings of the very large group of American scientists of the Coördinated Investigation of Micronesian Anthropology, headed by George P. Murdock. Added to the reports of these and other professional anthropologists are those of a good sprinkling of competent amateurs.

Desperate for clues I shall of course not overlook the obvious ones of geography and meteorology, as well as the less apparent ones of ecology, botany, and demography.

Before assuming my role as sleuth I am going in the next chapter to make a purposeful digression in which I shall depict the historical setting for Drake's voyage and explain the navigational tools available to ship captains of the Elizabethan age. In this way the hazards of Drake's circumnavigation as well as the doubts about his landfall in the western Pacific can better be appreciated. After that I shall reproduce the documentary sources concerning the incident at the island and extract from them the clues that are at hand for us to work upon. Using these clues I shall immediately proceed to see how they either incriminate or absolve the various places that have been named as the Island of Thieves, after which I plan to offer my own decision regarding this obscure portion of the historic encirclement of the globe.

In passing, I want to say that dates can be very important in my arguments, so I have taken cognizance of the difference between the Julian and Gregorian calendars and made allowance for this when it has seemed important; otherwise, I have let the English Old Style dates stand (see Note 1). There is also the problem of the system used to mark the beginning of a day. Reckoning from midnight is a late innovation. From ancient times, Western astronomers and navigators began their day at noon, although for different reasons, and there was a difference in a day between their method of counting and ours, but this need not concern us. What is relevant is that the civil day, beginning at midnight, produces different dates than does nautical time, beginning at noon. Consequently, historical accounts may occasionally be at variance by one day. I have not tried to be meticulous about making conversions unless they have a crucial bearing on some point to be made. Anyway, the information needed to make conversions is often not supplied in the accounts themselves.

# 𝕭ackground

THE CONTEXT within which Drake's great voyage took place was that of the exploration and exploitation of alien lands by Europeans during the rich developments and commercial expansion of the Renaissance. There was an ingredient of acquisitiveness present in the great maritime ventures, resulting in trading, pirating, and other means of personal and national enrichment. Portugal and Spain were additionally motivated by a burning spirit of evangelism, which acted as a great driving power in the quest to save souls for God.

Behind the mariners were the practical men whose money was necessary to test the speculations of the theorists. Usually they were organized into chartered companies. These could be regulated organizations in which each participant was an independent trader who operated with his own capital but was bound by the general rules of the company. Or they could be joint stock companies in which the organization itself carried on the business, using the joint capital invested by its members, who each shared proportionately in the profits and losses.

If one person had to be singled out to symbolize the motivating force behind what has been called "a burst of maritime exploration unparalleled in history," it would be Prince Henry of Portugal (1394–1460), known to posterity as "Henry the Navigator." He never traveled any farther than Morocco, where he participated in an expedition led by his father against the Moslems. Yet that experience engendered in the young prince, whose mother was English, a vision of greatness for Portugal, so that he dedicated his whole life to the promotion of discovery and the patronage of navigation.

He did not do so haphazardly. On the contrary, he acted with thoroughness, precision, and deliberation. To fulfill his goals he went to live permanently at Sagres near Cape Saint Vincent, where he built a palace and an observatory and surrounded himself with astronomers and cosmographers. He developed a sort of academy devoted to exploration, navigation, and ship design.

Henry was responsible for the effective discovery of the Madeiras and Azores, and the coasting of west Africa as far as the River Gambia. After his death, the impetus he had given to planned and systematic navigation enabled the Portuguese to double the Cape of Good Hope and soon thereafter to reach fabled India by an expedition led by Vasco da Gama. The subsequent voyages of Columbus, who took up residence in Portugal in 1477, owe their stimulus to the tradition and imaginativeness inspired by Henry. In the final analysis, so do the explorations of such men as the Cabots, Cabral, Vespucci, Balboa, Magellan, Verrazano, Cartier, Willoughby and Chancellor, and Frobisher.

The English remained laggards for a long time in the art and science of navigation, envying the Portuguese and Spaniards their success in tapping the rich resources of America, India, China, and the Spice Islands. They were galled by the Treaty of Tordesillas, inspired by Pope Alexander VI, which in 1494 had divided the non-Christian world between the two Iberian sea powers, permitting Portugal to set up Catholic colonies east of a longitude about 45 degrees west of Greenwich and the Spaniards to do the same west of that line. Along with the treaty went inevitable trading monopolies, which the English were anxious to break. But as long as they continued to be retarded in their maritime attainments they could do nothing to assuage their grievances, especially since they had become a Protestant nation and were therefore, in the eyes of many other nations, outside the pale of decency and culture. With Spain and Portugal controlling the known sea lanes to the opulent East, England was left to find its way there by either a northeast or a northwest passage.

This accounts for the formation in 1553 of the Muscovy Company, the first major English joint-stock trading company. It backed the explorations of Richard Chancellor and Stephen

Borough, as well as others, in search of a Northeast Passage to China and India along the north coast of Russia. More important were the efforts of Martin Frobisher, John Davis, and others to find and prove a Northwest Passage to the Orient. Until 1668 one of the objects of the Hudson's Bay Company (not chartered however) was to find this passage.

## SPAIN IN THE PACIFIC

When Drake, who too was interested in the Northwest Passage, came rudely bounding upon the South Sea scene, he was distinctly an interloper, because the Pacific, except for the Portuguese sphere of influence in the distant Moluccas, was a virtual Spanish *mare clausum*. No English ship had ever furrowed its bosom, unless one counts the coastal pirating of John Oxenham in pinnaces he had erected on the west side of the isthmus in 1576 and 1577.

All the planning, all the daring, had been that of the incredible Castilians, who had established numerous settlements and even a university on the western borders of the two American continents. Vasco Nuñez de Balboa had been the first European to see the South Sea from its eastern shores. He had crossed the Isthmus of Darien (Panama) and sighted the vast ocean on September 26, 1513. Descending to the shore, fully armored and holding a sword and shield, as well as a banner, he took possession of all the seas, lands, and coasts to the south in the names of King Ferdinand and his daughter Joanna.

In the meantime, the Portuguese, anxious to break the Venetian monopoly of the spice trade based in Alexandria and to reduce the number of middlemen in the traffic with China, as well as to find the land of Prester John and other "lost" Christian kingdoms, had by 1498 blazed the sea route round Africa to India. By 1511 they had conquered Malacca on the Malay Peninsula, using it as an advance base for exploration and trade. Soon thereafter three Portuguese ships reached various islands in the Banda Sea. Some survivors of this expedition, under the leadership of Francisco Serrão, apparently reached Mindanao in a captured junk and then went on to Ternate, one of the great centers of spice cultivation. Serrão lived on Ternate until he died, making trading trips in local vessels. It has been suggested that he "was the first European to see the open

Pacific, in the sector between the Moluccas and the Philippines, but this is mere conjecture" (Brand 1967*b*:147). But Portugal was not a power in the Pacific, except to the extent that it controlled its westernmost waters in the vicinity of the Moluccas.

Before Drake was yet born, Ferdinand Magellan, a Portuguese navigator sailing under the banner of Spain, had sailed through the treacherous strait now bearing his name and entered the Pacific with three surviving vessels on November 28, 1520. On March 6 of the following year he completed his epic traverse of the sea by reaching the Marianas, which his expedition at first named *Islas de las Velas Latinas* and then renamed *Islas de los Ladrones* because the indigenes had stolen the skiff of the *Trinidad*, in which he sailed as captain-general. On the way he had discovered an island in the Tuamotu archipelago and either Caroline Island or Vostok Island in the mid-Pacific area. A few weeks later he foolishly lost his life in the Philippines. The small *Victoria*, now the last of his original fleet of five ships, managed to return to Spain by continuing westward, but only after further adding to the suffering already endured by the members of the expedition. Not only had Magellan discovered a western passage to the Pacific, he had proved Columbus to be right in his insistence that the world was a sphere.

At a time when Henry VIII still had over two decades remaining on the throne and the Tudor navy was not much of a force to be reckoned with, the Spaniards penetrated the Pacific for a second time. They sent out an expedition from Spain in July 1525, consisting of a fleet of seven ships under the command of García Jofre de Loaisa. Only four of the vessels actually entered the Pacific, three being lost in the dangerous strait. Two vessels went on to complete the westward traverse, doing so independently. Both Loaisa and Sebastián del Cano, who had completed the circumnavigation of the globe in the *Victoria* after Magellan was killed and now was second in command of the new expedition, died before their vessels reached the Philippines.

Hernán Cortés, the conqueror of Mexico, who had already been apprised of Loaisa's voyage, learned from a pinnace which had managed to reach New Spain, that is, Mexico, after being separated from the other ships in a storm, that the expedition had entered into the Pacific. He fitted out an expedition in 1527 that was both to try to learn what had befallen the remnants of Magellan's company and to reinforce Loaisa's vessels. The three ships of the expedition were commanded by Alvaro de Saavedra Céron.

Saavedra reached Mindanao and then the Moluccas in his flagship, but the other two vessels sank in a storm. During his attempted return to Mexico he died, and his successors were unable to continue on in the face of contrary winds, so they sailed back to the Moluccas. Saavedra discovered six islands in the Marshalls, some of the Admiralty Islands off the coast of New Guinea, and various of the Caroline Islands (Sharp 1960:23).

The Spaniards followed up this exploration with a succession of others. In 1537 a ship commanded by Hernando de Grijalva sailed to the Moluccas from Peru. En route he was murdered by mutinous sailors, who continued on through the Gilberts and into the western New Guinea area, where their ship was lost (Sharp 1960:24–26).

Then, in 1542, which is approximately the time when Drake was born, Ruy López de Villalobos sailed from Mexico to the Philippines in a flotilla of six vessels with the fourfold purpose of discovery, exploration, missionization, and colonization. In the months that followed he landed at several of the Marshalls and in 1543 stopped at Fais in the Carolines, where the natives made the sign of the cross and greeted him and his men in Spanish with *"Buenas días, matalotes!"* or "Good day, sailors!" (*Col. doc. inéd. Indias* 1866:V, 119), indicating that the Portuguese had already been there or in the vicinity.[1] Villalobos then sighted either Ulithi or Yap. One of the vessels of his expedition made two unsuccessful attempts to return to America, but in doing so rediscovered some of the islands of the Marianas as well as others to the west of Manus in the Admiralties. None of his ships got any farther than the East Indies, and although the Portuguese begrudgingly assisted his men back to Lisbon, he himself died before then (Sharp 1960:26–32).

The rulers of Spain finally succeeded in 1565 in establishing a permanent colony in the western Pacific. This was at a time when the youthful Drake had sold a coastal bark bequeathed to him by its recently deceased master, and had gone to work for the Hawkins brothers, his kinsmen. Possibly he sailed for them as purser on a voyage to Spain. We are not sure. At any rate, King Philip, intent on settling the Philippines, had sent out an expedition of four ships from Mexico in 1564 under the command of López de Legazpi. Both Legazpi and Andres de Urdaneta, who had been an officer on

Loaisa's flagship and was now sailing on this expedition, have left us ethnographic notes on the Guamanians they encountered en route. After settling in Cebu in the Philippines, the Spaniards sent back one of their ships to New Spain, as Mexico was then called.

But Legazpi's vessel had been preceded by three months by the swift packet *San Lucas*, whose commander, Alonso de Arellano, had detached it from Legazpi's flotilla on the way west and had already reached the Philippines before the other vessels got there. He and his skillful mulatto pilot, Lope Martín, after several months in Mindanao waters without meeting Legazpi, had then returned to Mexico by way of a northerly crossing. His feat is considered to be one of the most remarkable in the annals of the sea. The *San Lucas*, and the vessel that trailed back after it, showed that it was practicable to return to America from the Philippines. For two centuries henceforth the Spanish galleons were to sail westward to the Philippines via Guam at a latitude of about 13° N and return with the westerlies at higher latitudes (Sharp 1960:32–39).

In 1566, a year in which Drake was sailing as second in command under Captain John Lovell in the third slaving expedition to Spanish America, the Spaniards in New Spain were sending out still another vessel, the *San Gerónimo*, to take help to Legazpi. After stopping in the Marshalls it arrived in the Philippines, without, however, its pilot Lope Martín, who had led a mutiny and then in turn had been the victim of a countermutiny (Sharp 1960:40–42). There was nothing noteworthy about this maritime accomplishment, except that it showed that the Spaniards were still busily traversing the great South Sea, without any challengers.

A truly great voyage, however, was one made by two ships sent out from Peru in 1567 under the command of Alvaro de Mendaña de Neira, the goal being to discover and settle the Terra Australis Incognita, a hypothetical continent about which we shall have considerable to say at a later point. Before making their return to America the following year, these Spaniards had discovered many islands in the Pacific: one in the Ellice group; Ontong Java; most of the Solomons; one of the Marshalls; and lonely Wake Island (Sharp 1960:42–48). During this time young Drake was off again for the Spanish Main on a slaving expedition headed by John Hawkins.

Spectacular as they were, the transoceanic voyages did not constitute the entirety of the explorations by the Spaniards, who after

Balboa's pioneer coastings went on to make extensive probings of the Pacific coasts of North and South America. Mention should be made of a third but obscure passage through the strait, after Magellan and Loaisa, in 1540 by one of four ships which had sailed from Spain to occupy and colonize the area around the strait. Captained by Alonso de Camargo, it continued on to Peru (Brand 1967a:126). Further knowledge of the coasts was obtained by the Manila galleons returning annually from the Philippines to Mexico, for the westerlies would take them to the Californias, which they would then coast until they reached Acapulco. However, they did not make detailed explorations until 1595 and 1602–1603. Coastal Peru was of course well scoured after Francisco Pizzaro arrived there in 1532 and brought about the downfall of the mighty Inca empire. He founded Lima three years later. Pedro de Valdivia marched into Chile soon afterwards and established Santiago, La Serena, Concepción, and Valdivia.

The Spaniards could be forgiven, then, if they thought of themselves as the rightful overlords of the Pacific. By 1579 they had explored many of its islands and outlined most of the boundaries of the basin. In many places they had colonies and garrisons. It was they who had been the bold and imaginative planners whose accomplishments made it possible for others to follow. They had greatly advanced nautical science, sacrificed many lives, and expended much wealth.

## DRAKE'S OBJECTIVES

When Drake got his first glimpse of the Pacific, from a tree atop a mountain range, it was 1573. The time was shortly after his famous raid on Nombre de Dios, where after an initial success he had been repulsed. His forces were greatly depleted, but having learned from the Cimarrones—fugitive slaves—that certain Spanish mule drivers were to transport a large amount of gold and silver to Panama, he decided to cross the isthmus. On seeing the great ocean he vowed that some day he would sail upon it. In the words of the chief historian of Elizabethan times,

> he was so inflamed with a desire of glory and wealth that hee burned with an earnest longing to sayle into those parts; and in the same

place, falling vpon his knees, he heartily implored the Divine assistance to enable him, that he might one day arriue in those Seas, and discouer the secrets of them; and to this, he bound himselfe with a religious vow. From that time forward, was his minde night and day troubled, and as it were excited and pricked forward with goads, to performe and acquite himself of this Vow. (Camden 1625:418-419).

These words of William Camden tell us a great deal about the single-mindedness and religiosity of Drake, but they do not serve to explain definitively his ultimate reasons for entering the Pacific and his subsequent behavior after that.

Drake's motives, as with so much else in his life, have long remained unclear. According to most speculation, he must have had one or more of the following objectives in mind: exploitation of the Terra Australis Incognita, discovery of the Strait of Anian, trade with the Moluccas, and the plundering and harassing of the Spaniards. A derivative enigma is why he returned to England by way of the Cape of Good Hope rather than the Strait of Magellan.

The theory of a Terra Australis was of great antiquity and asserted that a vast undiscovered continent extended unevenly from the region of the South Pole into the very tropics. Pliny the Elder, Lucian, and Claudius Ptolemy had referred to a Terra Australis Incognita.

The idea lay dormant for many centuries, mostly because medieval Europeans assumed that it was impossible for human beings to be able to survive the withering heat of the tropics. But in the sixteenth century it began to receive the approval of many geographers of repute. The first printed maps to depict the continent were those of Franciscus Monachus in 1529 and Oronce Finé in 1531, in their efforts to depict Magellan's passage through the strait. Giacomo Gastaldi, an engineer in the service of Venice and one of the leading cartographers of his time, showed the continent in his 1560 map of the world, as did Abraham Ortelius in his often-reprinted 1570 atlas, *Theatrum Orbis Terrarum*. Gerhard Mercator, who pursued the classical theory that the continent had to exist as a structural balance to the northern land masses, depicted the Terra Australis in his own world map of 1569. In Elizabethan England the erudite and influential mathematician and cosmographer John Dee urged that every effort be made to locate it.

Interest in this imaginary continent was particularly aroused when it was assumed that various places sighted by the Spaniards and Portuguese were none other than the tips of peninsulas of the continent, or at least islands lying offshore from it. Most of the coast was thought to lie, however, between 40° and 50° S latitude and to include Tierra del Fuego located south of the Strait of Magellan.

It was, however, cupidity more than curiosity or scientific detachment that impelled men to search out the continent, for it was thought to include not only Marco Polo's fabulously rich places, such as the kingdom of Locach or Beach, with its gold and dyewoods, the land of Malaiur, with its abundance of spices, and the island of Pentan, with its aromatic drugs,[2] but also Ophir. Ophir, it will be recalled, was a region mentioned in the Bible (1 Kings 10:11–12, 22) as a place from which King Solomon's ships brought vast riches, such as gold, silver, precious stones, ivory, sandalwood, apes, and peacocks.

When Alvaro de Mendaña set sail from Callao in Peru in 1567 to explore the Pacific he reached some islands which he believed to be close to the Terra Australis and he optimistically called them the Solomon Islands. Upon his return to Mexico and Peru, word of his discoveries spread to Spain and eventually to England, where the eager interest of merchants was quickly aroused, even though Mendaña had provided no evidence that wealth actually existed in the lands he had discovered. John Dee began to talk about building a "British Empire," and Richard Grenville became the leader of an influential group whose project was to build such an empire in the south. Apparently, the plan was at first approved by the government, which later had a change of heart because of the danger of creating hostilities with the Spaniards. There was too much chance that Grenville might turn to pirating instead of colonizing.

The second of Drake's possible objectives, the Strait of Anian, was an invention of cartographers and geographers who felt the need to reconcile some apparent discrepancies in the accounts of Columbus and Cabot and to provide hope that there was a northwest passage into the Pacific over the top of the world. The earliest explorers of America recorded sailing distances that needed to be interpreted within the framework of belief that they had found the east coast of Asia.

At first it was speculated that Asia must extend far eastward as a continuous land mass or promontory that prevented access to the Pacific from the north. Then, after the width of the north Atlantic had been ascertained more realistically, the idea of an isthmus between America and Asia was proposed, still preventing passage by way of the northwest. Driven mostly by the wish for a navigable route to the Pacific, it was then conjectured that a strait divided the two continents.

First mention of the Strait of Anian, as it came to be called, was made by Gastaldi in a pamphlet published in 1562. His famous map of the world, published in 1560, had shown Asia and North America linked by an extensive land mass but showed no strait. It remained for Bolognino Zaltieri, in a map of North America that was really derived from the world map by Gastaldi, to depict the Strait of Anian in 1566.

Before Drake, attempts had been made by Jacques Cartier and Martin Frobisher, and later by John Davis, Henry Hudson, William Baffin, and a great many others, to locate a northwest passage. At one time it was thought that the strait might be located at a lower latitude on the west coast of North America, and in the search for a passage the British, Spanish, and Americans continued long after to explore the Pacific coast with this in mind. Only after George Vancouver had surveyed the coast in the 1790s were cartographers finally convinced of the folly of their assumptions.[3]

Trade with the Moluccas, the third possible motivation for Drake's voyages, had long been coveted by English merchants, who had an understandable resentment of Portugal's monopoly of the spice market. The daring Portuguese had established their foothold by forging a sea route to the Indies by way of the southern tip of Africa and the Indian Ocean. The Spaniards had attempted to challenge their position by establishing a route through the Pacific, but after the disastrous voyages of Magellan, Loaisa, and Saavedra, they had recognized their failure and quitclaimed and sold their rights to the Moluccas to Portugal, retaining the Philippines.

The importance of the spice market cannot be overlooked. Spices represented a great source of wealth because of the inordinate demand for them in western Europe, where the diet was so monotonous and facilities for the preservation of meat and other foods so poor that people were willing to pay the exorbitant prices asked for spices. It was when the Mongols and Turks had cut off the overland trade routes from the Far East that the search for new routes to the Orient around Africa and across the Atlantic and Pacific was greatly stimulated.

A final possibility as to what Drake had in mind when he persuaded some of the most highly placed persons in England, including probably the queen herself, to subscribe funds to his venture was neither discovery, nor the annexation of new lands, nor trade, but outright piracy.

Piracy was of course common in the sixteenth century, although not as an instrument of national policy. It has been suggested that many Englishmen, including Elizabeth, were restive over Spain's monopoly of trade with its vast, papal-sanctioned empire, and that they shared the feeling that the only way to strike back was through a daring seaman who had already proven his ability to hurt the Spanish king without drawing the government into his depredations, at least not officially.

Many of Drake's contemporaries did indeed think of him, in the words of the Elizabethan navigator Edward Fenton, as a "thief and pirate" (Cove 1963:16). Included among his nonadmirers were John Winter, captain of the *Elizabeth*, and John Cooke, who returned with Winter to England when their vessel was unable to make headway in the Pacific after emerging from the west end of the Strait of Magellan, leaving Drake to continue on alone. Then there were those Englishmen who maintained that the reason Drake had beheaded Thomas Doughty, the gentleman aboard the *Pelican*, was because the latter had discovered that the true intent of the expedition was piracy. They are in general agreement that there had never been any intention other than to raid the Spanish west coast of South America. Some contemporary historians take the same point of view. Ample records exist in the form of depositions made by Drake's Spanish victims to the effect that their assailant was a robber, pure and simple. But their views could be discounted as biased.

Modern historians and geographers have been unable to come to an agreement as to which of the several possible purposes of the expedition may have been the true one. Corbett (1898) played down Drake as a pirate and saw him as essentially an explorer and statesman; Nuttall (1914) looked upon him as a colonizer; and

Wagner (1926) decided that his only objective was to reach the Moluccas. Authorities are not lacking who could be cited in support of any objective, single or multiple.

For one fleeting moment in 1930 it seemed as if the vexing question of Drake's aims had been cleared up by the publication of two articles by Eva Taylor telling of her discovery in the British Museum of two manuscripts bearing on the subject (Taylor 1930*a*, 1930*b*).

The first was a badly scorched three-page draft plan of the voyage, probably drawn up in the spring or summer of 1577, the year Drake left England. It listed the promoters of the expedition, the vessels to be employed, and the nature and extent of the enterprise. Known as Cotton MSS, Otho, E VIII, it said that the expedition was to pass through the Strait of Magellan and visit unknown shores, not under the obedience of any Christian prince, as far as 30° S latitude. Taylor interpreted this to mean the Terra Australis, rather than Chile.

The second manuscript was a report to his father by John Winter, the captain of the *Elizabeth*, dated June 2, 1579, giving his view of the voyage up until the time he gave up trying to find Drake in the South Sea and returned to England. This manuscript, known as Lansdowne MSS, No. 100, indicated that the original plan had been widened so as to permit reconnaissance beyond 30 degrees and a possible voyage into the Moluccas.

Disagreement with Taylor's conclusions regarding the true purpose of the voyage has been widespread, the general feeling being that the two documents do not give a decisive answer to the problem. After all, the Cotton manuscript makes no mention of the Strait of Anian or the Moluccas, which she thinks Drake was supposed to visit after his primary objective, the Terra Australis, had been achieved. Indeed, it says nothing at all of the unknown continent itself. The manuscript was damaged by fire and Taylor has inserted words and phrases which she guesses are approximations to the obliterated passages. Her assumption that the coast to be explored after sailing through the Strait of Magellan was that of the Terra Australis has little merit, whereas that of Chile is much more plausible. There is nothing to indicate that the main purpose of the voyage was to discover the unknown and imaginary continent.

Concerning the Moluccas as a second objective, the Lansdowne manuscript is unreliable in this respect because Winter, who refers to the islands as an agreed-upon rendezvous for Drake and himself, was probably influenced by his desire to justify his action in returning to England. He asserted that he and Drake, before separating, had an understanding that they would meet in the Spice Islands, but that he was prevented from going there by the refusal of his ship's master and crew to sail such a course. It is possible, even probable, that if Winter had indeed planned to go to the Moluccas it was eastward by way of Madagascar, not westward across the Pacific.

Taylor has argued that even though the draft plan makes no mention of either the Moluccas or the Strait of Anian, the plan was changed before Drake left England to include them as secondary objectives. Not everyone would agree, however, that any changes were made while Drake was still in England.

But even those who are of the opinion that changes were made before the fleet sailed from Plymouth see these changes as being of a different character. Williamson, for instance, says that Walsingham, representing the queen, tried to persuade Drake to put into writing a proposition for hostile action against Spain, and, even though he did not succeed in this, he and Drake reached a verbal understanding, so that the secret plan under which the latter set out was that "instead of Terra Australis and its hypothetical treasures, Peru and its proven ones" were to be his objectives (Williamson 1946:172).

The plunder theory is of course an old one that persists to this day. Joseph W. Cove, whose book, *The Silver Circle* (1963), was written with the premise in mind that Drake was really a pirate, says of the draft plan that it is "essentially tentative and deals with suggestions rather than conclusions," and adds that, "It is far more likely that the plan was designed as a cover for the real intention of the voyage, which was to plunder the Pacific coast of Spanish America" (Cove 1963:156).

If Drake's actions are better evidence of his intentions than any draft plans, depositions, letters, relations, and accounts, the advocates of the piracy theory would seem to have the upper hand. If one accepts their point of view, it would explain why Drake's five vessels were armed to the hilt, why Doughty was beheaded, and why no real effort was made to sail toward the locality of the

supposed unknown continent. Yet the matter is not so simply resolved, for Drake did sail as far north as the Oregon coast and then
headed for the Moluccas. How can the piracy theory be fitted in
with these aspects of the voyage?

The English historian Kenneth R. Andrews has supplied a reconstruction and interpretation which does the least violence to the
facts that are available to us, and which are offered here as a
consistent view of Drake's aims and actions.

The promoters of Drake's venture, he says, never intended that
he should circumnavigate the globe, or establish trade with the
Moluccas, or discover the Terra Australis. He was to survey the
coast of South America from the River Plate around to that part of
Chile where there was as yet no Spanish occupation. Knowing that
this was a provocative venture, they made every effort to hide their
intentions from Spain.[4] The promoters most likely took it for
granted that Drake would make the voyage pay by plundering
Spanish shipping. This particular expedition had as its mission the
establishing of contact with the American Indians, with the possible long-term objective of settling and possibly even conquering
Spanish Peru (Andrews 1968:740).

Andrews reminds us that Drake did indeed spend four months on
the east coast of South America, and two more months on the west
coast from 39° S to 28° S. If he then went farther than was provided
for in his letter of instructions, it was because the dangerous
weather conditions in the Strait and the disappointing results of his
reconnoitering compelled him to do so.[5] He now had two choices at
his disposal: the Strait of Anian and the Moluccas. He made some
effort to discover the first, without success, and probably concluded that it lay too far north, anyway, for an easy passage back to
England. He had to settle for the western route, stopping in the
East Indies without the preparation necessary to achieve much for
English commercial interests (Andrews 1968:740–741).

The one emphasis lacking in this otherwise tenable reconstruction is on Drake's freebooting. His promoters must have done
more than "assume" that he would make his voyage pay. There is
good reason to think that Elizabeth, together with the subscribers
listed in the draft plan—the Earls of Lincoln and Leicester, Francis
Walsingham, Christopher Hatton, Sir William and George Winter,
John Hawkins, and Drake himself—were more explicit than this

with respect to the financial gain that was to be had. Drake's purchase of six tons of cloves in the Moluccas was purely incidental, for he had on board the *Golden Hind* a staggering load of silver, as well as gold, jewels, and other booty. His cargo was worth almost £450,000, paying his stockholders 4,700 or perhaps even as much as 10,000 percent on their investment.

## DRAKE'S NAVIGATIONAL AIDS

When Drake made his traverse of the great South Sea after leaving the coast of California, he had at his disposal all the basic aids to navigation except one, which will be considered in due course. In his possession were captured Spanish charts to determine his course, the compass to steer by, and instruments for ascertaining astronomically the latitude of his ship at fixed points of time.

The Spanish maps which made it possible for him to reach the Moluccas were seized on the 20th of April, 1579, when he captured a small vessel off the coast of Nicaragua which was en route to Panama with a cargo of sarsaparilla, lard, honey, and maize. One of its two pilots was Alonso Sanchez Colchero, a man who was very knowledgeable about the Pacific.

Colchero carried navigational charts and sailing directions superior to anything known to Drake. In Wagner's opinion, "Without the navigation chart, and especially the information which he undoubtedly obtained from Colchero, it may well be doubted whether Drake would succeed in getting home again with his cargo" (Wagner 1926:121). A Portuguese map, as well as his Ortelius maps of 1564 and 1570, wrongly showed Drake to be closer in longitude to Ternate than was actually the case. Colchero's charts, on the other hand, even though they were still short of the true longitudinal difference, indicated a difference which more nearly approximated the facts. In addition, they showed that the northwest coast of America extended north to at least forty-three degrees—more than the English supposed.

Wagner has proposed the idea that it was because of what he learned from Colchero, an unwilling collaborator whom Drake once tortured by "hanging" by a rope around his neck, that Drake sailed up the Northwest Coast instead of directly to Ternate. He did this not only to avoid having his booty-laden vessel attacked off Mexico but, according to Wagner, who rejects the Strait of Anian theory, to time his arrival in the Philippines (Wagner 1926:132–133). The Spanish galleons proceeding from Acapulco to Manila sailed almost always before the end of March at the latest. In the middle of April it would have been too late for Drake to set out; he would not be able to avoid the southwest monsoons and the typhoons of the Philippines that begin in July.

It is possible to accept Wagner's suggestion without denying that Drake made a stab at finding the Strait of Anian. It makes sense that the Englishman delayed his run for the Moluccas in order to sail under favorable weather conditions, especially with so valuable a cargo on board his vessel.

As for Drake's next aid, the mariner's compass, it was basically no more than a magnetic needle introduced into ships. It had been used in Europe as early as the latter half of the twelfth century. Probably the Chinese were the first to employ a compass to indicate direction on land, and certainly Europeans knew the power of the magnet to attract iron before the time of Christ. But priority in the invention of the mariner's compass has been given variously to the Arabs, Vikings, Italians, and the Chinese themselves.

The compass went through various developments in Europe, beginning with a crude method of floating the magnetized needle upon water. Ample descriptions of the making and use of the device are available to us, leading Hewson to say that "it is evident that the mariners of the sixteenth century, and doubtless of the century before, were equipped with dry compasses, capped and pivoted, slung in gimbals, and even provided with a crude though misguided method of damping the oscillations" (Hewson 1951:49).

But the compass behaved erratically and lacked the precision it later came to acquire after it was determined in the sixteenth century that the magnetic north and south poles do not coincide with the two geographic poles, the declination varying from place to place. In Drake's time the discrepancy had been ascertained and improvements had been made in the compass itself, although until the seventeenth century it was not known that there also existed a secular variation. The navigator at sea had to know how to determine his variation anywhere in the world, and for this he used the bearing of the sun at noon or an observation of the North Star when it was on the meridian.

Neither of these methods for determining the truth of the compass was without its limitations. Toward the equator the sun was not only at a high altitude when at the meridian, and its direction therefore difficult to tell, but it passed over it too quickly for real accuracy. Moreover, the instruments of the time did not properly inform the observer as to when the sun was at its height. Drake had left England too soon to have been able to take advantage of William Borough's account, published in 1581, of a method of double altitudes which did away with the need for observing the sun at its height.[6] As for the North Star, the higher the latitude the more difficult it was to determine its bearing.

Finally, means for ascertaining latitude were of course available to Drake, having been in use for many centuries.

Knowledge of latitude was basic to that old system of navigation known as "latitudinal sailing." This method required that a navigator, making for a known destination, should drop down to or rise up to the proper latitude and then, as the situation required, sail east or west along that parallel until his destination was reached. Columbus used some latitudinal sailing in his voyages to the Caribbean. Micronesian and Polynesian navigators used the method in their long voyages, although their latitudes were determined empirically by observing stars known to pass directly over their objectives in their east-west courses, rather than in accordance with some system of measurement from the equator. But whether or not this method was used by Renaissance mariners, some knowledge of the latitude of their objectives was necessary in their oceanic voyages.

Drake's principal instrument for ascertaining with accuracy how far to the north or south of the line he might be was the cross-staff, used in conjunction with tables of the sun's declination. Known also as the *baculo de São Tiago*, or staff of Saint James, the cross-staff was first described in some Catalonian writings of the fourteenth century and later was discussed in German publications appearing in 1502 and 1514. Thomas Blundeville outlined its construction and use in his *Exercises* (Figure 2), published in London in 1594—some years, to be sure, after the departure of Drake from Plymouth but nevertheless indicative of the importance with which the instrument was regarded in the sixteenth century.

Deceptive in its simplicity, the cross-staff was nonetheless based

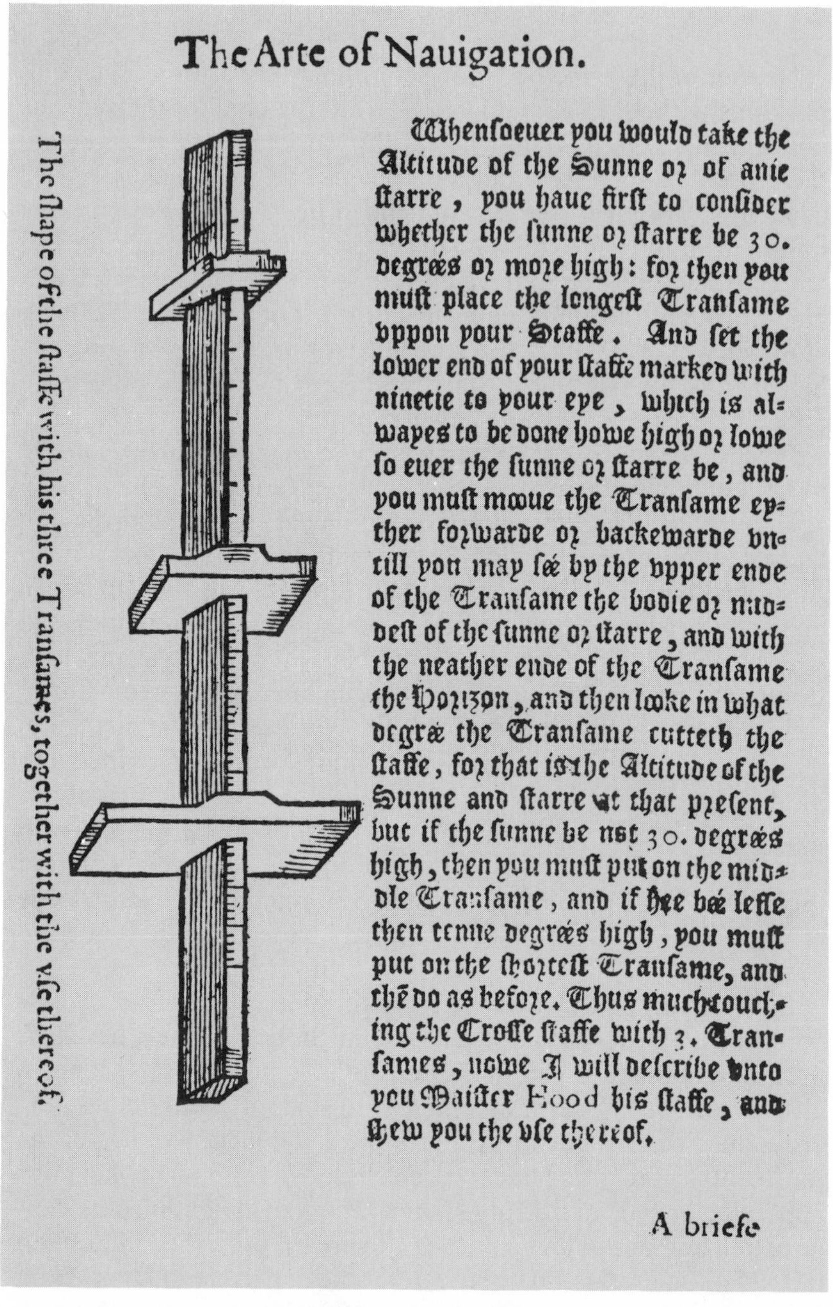

# The Arte of Nauigation.

The shape of the staffe with his three Transames, together with the vse thereof.

Whensoeuer you would take the Altitude of the Sunne or of anie starre, you haue first to consider whether the sunne or starre be 30. degrees or more high: for then you must place the longest Transame vppon your Staffe. And set the lower end of your staffe marked with ninetie to your eye, which is alwayes to be done howe high or lowe so euer the sunne or starre be, and you must mooue the Transame eyther forwarde or backewarde vntill you may see by the vpper ende of the Transame the bodie or middest of the sunne or starre, and with the neather ende of the Transame the Horizon, and then looke in what degree the Transame cutteth the staffe, for that is the Altitude of the Sunne and starre at that present, but if the sunne be not 30. degrees high, then you must put on the middle Transame, and if shee bee lesse then tenne degrees high, you must put on the shortest Transame, and thē do as before. Thus much touching the Crosse staffe with 3. Transames, nowe I will describe vnto you Maister Hood his staffe, and shew you the vse thereof.

A briefe

Figure 2. Cross-Staff. Drake probably used the cross-staff at higher latitudes as it was not useful for solar sights between 20° N and 20° S of the equator. Source: Blundeville 1594:314v. (*Courtesy The Huntington Library, San Marino, California*)

on sound mathematical principles. It consisted of one long staff along which a shorter staff or transom was moved up and down. At local noon a navigator could measure the altitude or angle of the sun above the horizon by moving the transom, which was positioned vertically, up and down until one end rested on the horizon and the other was in the center of the sun. The long staff was scaled so as to indicate 90 degrees of angular measurement and the navigator would read the figure on the scale when the two ends of the transom were in the proper position. Correlations had to be made for the sun's declination for the particular day when the sighting was made (Wroth 1937:26 and plate III).

Aside from the problem of the sun's glare, which some navigators dealt with by using a tinted glass for protection, there was an insurmountable difficulty at low latitudes, where the altitude of the sun at noon aproached or even reached 90 degrees. This was for two reasons: first, the scan of the observer's eye was limited physically to a maximum arc of 60 degrees, and secondly, the spacing between gradations for altitude marked on the long staff came closer together and made the reading susceptible to inaccuracies amounting to degrees of difference from the observed altitude. Between roughly 20° N and 20° S the cross-staff would not be used at all for solar sights (Waters 1958:54–55). At sea the cross-staff was probably used mostly for taking altitudes of Polaris. But, as the Portuguese discovered, the North Star could not be employed to determine latitude if the ship were located south of about 10 degrees latitude (Harding 1952:72).

The astrolabe, borrowed by Renaissance seamen from the ancient Greeks by way of the Arabs, was another instrument used for ascertaining the correct altitude of celestial bodies above the horizontal plane of the observer. It accompanied Drake on his great voyage. Unlike the cross-staff, when used on the moving deck of a ship it could not be operated by a single person. But it had certain advantages, especially because it could be used in the lower latitudes. That is why the Portuguese and Spaniards favored it while the English, more accustomed to sailing at middle latitudes, were inclined to use the cross-staff. It was mandatory between 20° N and 20° S and therefore must have been used by Drake during the greater portion of his Pacific crossing.

The principle of the astrolabe is mathematical and its construction ingenious yet simple. The instrument (Figure 3) consists of a flat metallic disc whose circumference is graduated in degrees from 0 to 360. It has a revolving arm or alidade pivoted at its center. The astrolabe is suspended from the thumb by a ring. The alidade is manipulated until a beam of the sun passes through slits in the vanes at either end of the pointer. The observer reads the figure on the scale to know the angle of the sun and must make the usual corrections for the angle of the sun's declination. This does away with one of the drawbacks of the cross-staff, which requires the observer to keep his eye on both the horizon and the zenith, a feat rendered increasingly difficult as one nears the equator, where the sun tends to be more and more directly overhead. The astrolabe has the further advantage of not requiring the observer to look directly into the sun (Wroth 1937:27 and plate III). This of course was not a problem in sighting Polaris for latitude.

The one crucial device lacking in Drake's repertoire of navigational aids was a means for determining longitude. Had it been available to him there would have been no mystery about the Island of Thieves. Sailors in the open sea could only make crude but risky estimates.

> The story of man's efforts to determine his longitude at sea is one of the most painful in his slow progress towards the mastery of the world in which he lives. His failure to accomplish this feat was a fly in the ointment of scientific complacency for many centuries. To know so much and yet not be able to fix with exactness his position in the open sea was shame and vexation of the spirit, and more, an ever-present cause of destruction of life and goods. Through the long centuries of the mediaeval and renaissance periods, down to the end of the eighteenth century, he continued to determine his east and west position by that process of calculating distances and directions which we know as dead reckoning. (Wroth 1937:71)

Ancient astronomers had a clear concept of longitude and even maintained the theory that its determination rested upon knowing the difference in time between a given meridian and a meridian at another place. But they lacked accurate time recorders. Their recourse was to make use of the eclipses of the sun or the moon in combination with the daily indication of noon by the sun. They compared the local time of an eclipse at one place with the local time of an eclipse at another, and from this the difference of lon-

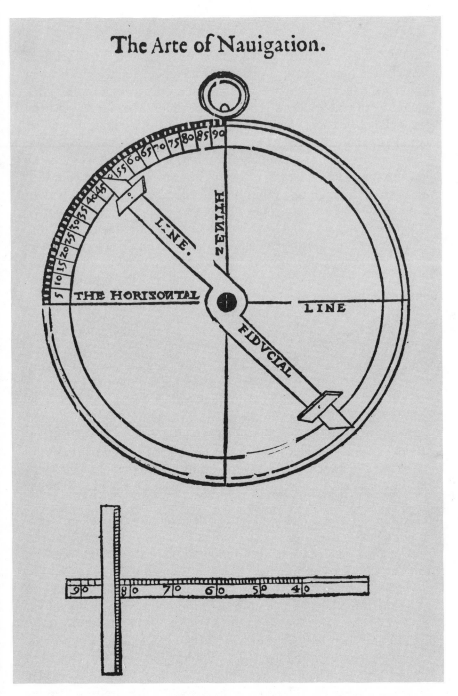

Figure 3. Astrolabe. Drake probably used the astrolabe at lower latitudes, where the cross-staff was not useful for solar sights. Source: Blundeville 1594:318r. (*Courtesy The Huntington Library, San Marino, California*)

gitude could be arrived at. An improvement in this approach was made after tables were prepared in advance, telling when for a given place there would be a lunar or solar eclipse, or an eclipse of a planet by the moon. By discovering the difference in time between the eclipse in each place, some effort at determining longitude could be made.

For many reasons, including the infrequency of eclipses and the inaccuracy of instruments, mariners were never able to make serious use of the method. What they needed was not only a way of accurately determining time where they happened to be but of knowing the exact local time back at a prime meridian.

An approach that aroused much hope was one in which use was made of magnetic declination. The supposition was that this variation was constant—which it was not—and that the agonic line, or line of no magnetic declination, was a meridian—whereas it was curved. For obvious reasons, the method was a failure.

In addition to all these fallacies and errors, navigators had to contend with ignorance of the length of a degree of latitude at the equator, let alone at various parallels as they were located away from that line. Such knowledge was not gained until 1635.

So it was that in practice, dead reckoning took precedence over astronomical efforts. Approximations to longitude were achieved by trying to determine at different intervals how far a vessel had run its course. Speed and time interval were the two known factors for calculating distance. For measuring time a sand or water glass was used; for measuring speed, guesswork based on experience could be fairly useful.

Probably the crudest method for determining the velocity of a moving vessel was to heave a log over the bow of the ship and run with it until one reached the poop, the speed at which one ran forming the basis upon which the ship's speed was reckoned.

On long voyages, however, the most commonly used method was that of the log line and chip. It was employed by Magellan on his famed voyage, but apparently not by Columbus, Vasco da Gama, and their predecessors. At intervals a log called a chip or ship was thrown overboard. It was quadrangular and was weighted at one end with lead to cause it to float upright, and to it was attached the log line. The line, usually about 150 fathoms in length, was allowed to run out while the log remained stationary in the water. The time interval for letting out the line was usually about thirty seconds, and at the end of this time the log line was hauled in and the length which had been released was measured. A variant was to knot the line at intervals of 47 feet 3 inches, and let it out without regard to fixed time. In either method, the length of the line and the time elapsed in paying out the line gave an indication of the speed of the vessel, the velocity being in turn transposed into nautical miles. The navigator would keep a record of the distances and plot their length and direction on a chart, so telling him, in rough fashion, his longitude. Apart from the limitations inherent in the operation itself, corrections had to be made for magnetic variation, as well as for displacement of the vessel caused by current and leeway.

Man had so despaired at finding a better method than this that some thought God simply did not will it, or at least that it was beyond human capability. Of course, the secret was to be found in the chronometer, a method advanced as far back as 1530 by the great Flemish astronomer and cosmographer Gemma Phrisius or Frisius, Gerhard Mercator's teacher. The principle was simply this: the mariner was to keep on board a clock set to indicate always the time when he left port, and thereafter to make daily observations of the sun at noon, the difference in time being translated into degrees away from the point of departure.

There was nothing wrong with the theory, which emanated from the ancient world, but there was with the clocks. They were not accurate enough until the English clockmaker John Harrison proved to the world in 1761 that a watch he had caused to be carried on board H.M.S. *Deptford* bound for Jamaica had permitted its longitude to be reckoned with great accuracy during a period of eighty-one days. Eventually, Harrison collected the reward which the English Parliament had offered for the solution of the vexing problem of longitude (Wroth 1937:79–82; Thrower 1956–1958:375–381; Quill 1966). All this, however, came almost two centuries too late for Drake, who had to rely upon the crude estimates of dead reckoning. We can at least be grateful that he did not have to rely on this method also for ascertaining latitude.

A final observation may be made as to Drake's navigational tools. Mariners had to carry with them books to which they could refer for help, and it has been a matter of speculation as to what

Drake had at his disposal. Nuño da Silva, who spent more than fourteen months with him as a pilot-prisoner, said the English captain carried three books on navigation and gives some general hints as to what they were, but he does not name them. David W. Waters, a retired British naval officer and Admiralty historian, thinks they may have been: first, Nicolas de Nicolai's translation of Pedro de Medina's manual *L'Art de Naviguer*, 1554; second, either Eden's translation of Cortes' work *The Arte of Navigation*, 1561, or Bourne's *Regiment for the Sea*, 1574; and third, either Maximilian of Transylvania's *De Moluccis Insulis*, 1523, or Pigafetta's *Le Voyage et Navigation faict par les Espanolz és isles de Mollucques*, 1525 (Waters 1958:536). There are, however, other possibilities (Boulind 1968:359, 361).

## *THE* GOLDEN HIND

Of the five ships, all heavily armed, which were in Drake's flotilla when he left Plymouth, only the *Golden Hind* remained to cross the Pacific. The small pinnace *Bark Benedict* was exchanged for a captured Portuguese ship that was later abandoned; the flyboat *Swan* was deliberately broken up for its firewood and iron; the *Marigold* disappeared off southern Chile; and the *Elizabeth* turned back to England.

Originally called the *Pelican*, the vessel was renamed while at the entrance to the Strait of Magellan in order to honor Christopher Hatton, one of the main subscribers to the expedition, whose crest was a golden hind.

Not a good deal is known about the *Golden Hind*. There is no detailed authentic picture of it. All we have is a tiny ship engraved on a gold band around a cup made of coconut shell that was presented to the queen by Drake. Pictures on maps and elsewhere are rough approximations only (Figure 4). Even though the ship was kept as a national monument in a dry berth at the Royal Navy Yard at Deptford until about 1662, when she rotted to pieces, there is very little reference to her in the literature. Most of what we do know about the most renowned ship in English history comes not from English sources, which are sparse, but from men taken captive by Drake in the course of his marauding: Nuño da Silva, San Juan de Anton, Cornieles Lanberd, Alonso Sanchez Colchero, and

Figure 4. The *Golden Hind*. The details of Drake's flagship are not known, the vessel having deteriorated and no authentic picture having been made. This engraving appears as an insert on a map labeled "Civitas Carthagena" appearing in a contemporary book. Source: Bigges 1588: following p. 18. (*Courtesy The Huntington Library, San Marino, California*)

Francisco de Zárate, as well as others who had had some contact with Drake at various places where he landed. This poverty of sources causes one writer to lament: "As a rule naval occurrences of the past appear as before a black curtain; we see and hear the actors but the ships are left to our imagination and to this rule Sir Francis Drake's voyage in the *Golden Hind* is no exception" (Robinson 1949:56).

In a more dogged effort than others have made to describe the ship with greater accuracy, Gregory Robinson has reached some acceptable conclusions, none of which, however, depart in any great measure from those that had previously been stated or conjectured. The keel of the ship, he figures, was probably a little over fifty-nine feet, and her extreme breadth was nineteen feet. She had an actual draft of thirteen feet, which is why Drake, confronted with so much booty on board, had to rid himself of guns and cargo in the Moluccas before completing his voyage home. The sheer of the vessel was slight, probably due to her French design.[7] Her tonnage cannot be estimated with much assurance, the guesses ranging from English figures of 100, 120, and 150, to Spanish figures of 200 to 400.[8] She was double-sheathed against worms but not leaded. It is generally agreed that she carried eighteen pieces of artillery, some made of bronze and some of cast iron. Apparently she carried a roundhouse and it was probably there that Drake lived, spending a good deal of time shut up in it with his very young cousin—painting! About her rig there is greater certainty. In addition to her mainsail she had a mizzen sheeted to an outlicker. She carried a spritsail and had fore and main topgallant sails (Robinson 1949).

This "floating arsenal," as she has been called, had along a large number of pikes, partisans, pistols, harquebuses, steel shields, coats of mail, and crossbows, as well as devices for setting fire to a ship or her sails (Wagner 1926:29–30, 370).

The victualling of Drake's ships can only be surmised, for there are no specific records of what was taken aboard in England. Perhaps the closest approximation that can be made comes from the draft plan discovered by Professor Taylor, in which it was proposed that the food supply should include biscuit, meal, beef, pork, fish, butter, cheese, rice, oatmeal, vinegar, honey, sweet oil, salt, beer, and wine (Taylor 1930*b*:141). There is no assurance that these were the actual supplies taken along. Still, they conform to the findings of Dorothy Burwash for English merchant shipping between 1460 and 1540. Of that period she writes: "Though no Hakluyt has chronicled their hardships, the dry records of our period make it clear that the seaman suffered as much from unappetizing food and cramped quarters as did their Elizabethan successors" (Burwash 1947:72). She goes on to speak of a diet of salt meat, salt and smoked fish (herring and cod), bacon, cheese, oatmeal, peas, honey, butter, salt, pepper, ship's bread or hardtack, bread baked on board from meal, and beer and wine (Burwash 1947:72–74). On the basis of the known list of foods put on board two of the vessels of Edward Fenton's ill-starred voyage (Wagner 1926:33), commissioned in 1582 by the earl of Leicester to make a commercial expedition to the Moluccas, Burwash's list is matched in all its details, except that vinegar, mustard, sweet oil, spices, and raisins could be added.

Drake is known to have appropriated food and wine from Spanish and Portuguese ships which he captured in both the Atlantic and Pacific. For that reason one must read with caution a statement made in a deposition by Cornieles Lanberd, a merchant native to Flanders, to the effect that when he was a prisoner on board the *Golden Hind* he saw "a great deal of flour, meat, fish, Spanish wine, conserves and vegetables, besides a quantity of Biscuit" (Wagner 1926:370). Lanberd had been captured by Drake off the coast of Nicaragua in March 1579, after the capture of the *Cacafuego*,[9] so that some of the vessel's food supplies may have been acquired after leaving Plymouth. However, in all justice it should be observed that nothing noted by Lanberd need have been stolen and could have been part of the original victuals.

When on land Drake and his men replenished their supplies with whatever was available locally, and it is worthy of note that while they were in the Strait of Magellan they killed 2,000 penguins, described as very fat and without fishy flavor. The smallest weighed ten or twelve pounds. Many seals, too, were killed (Wagner 1926:55, 61, 75, 340).

Although the records are silent on the subject, a diet of ship foods, deficient in ascorbic acid, must surely have troubled many members of the expedition and caused the death of some. The only hint of scurvy is to be found in a statement by Winter to the effect that after entering into the South Sea, "Most of our men fell sick of the sickness which Magellan speaketh of . . ." (Taylor 1930*b*:149). The seamen of the time were not yet the beneficiaries of such preventive and remedial measures as the use of certain vegetables, sour lemons and oranges, and especially lime juice—antiscorbutics which were soon to be discovered independently by both the English and the Spaniards. Drake's men must have been cruelly tortured by weakness, anemia, spongy gums, ruptures of the skin and mucous membranes, and the brawny hardening of the muscles of the calves and legs that goes with the other changes in the body.

In addition to the food supplies to be taken aboard the vessels, the draft plan of 1579 lists several "necessaries": wood, coal, candles, wax, lanterns, platters, tankards, dishes, bowls, buckets, and so forth, as well as helves, mattocks, hatchets, and crows of iron, which were probably part of the equipment to be carried should it be necessary to throw up temporary fortifications. Included in the carpenter's stores were canvas, cordage, pitch, tar, rosin, twine, needles, fishing nets, hooks, and other gear. Apparel was to include woolen and linen cloth, shoes, hats, caps, and so on. There were to be presents for "the lords of the countries" to be visited (Taylor 1930*b*:141–142).

## DRAKE'S MEN

No one knows for certain how many men were aboard Drake's five ships when they sailed from England on a late autumn sea. They have been variously estimated at from 140 to 164.

Before reaching the Strait of Magellan, Drake had decided to consolidate his flotilla by doing away with the flyboat *Swan*, which was broken up for firewood and the iron in her, and the canter *Christopher*, which was abandoned by having her float out to sea.[10] The men on these two small vessels had been transferred to the remaining three. A report by John Winter tells of enough "sea fowls" being killed, while the *Golden Hind*, *Elizabeth*, and *Marigold* were in the Strait, to serve 140 men seven weeks (Taylor 1930*b*:149), so presumably there were at least that number of men in the expedition before the second of these three ships turned back to England and the last-named sank with all its men.

It is known that accompanying the expedition were many soldiers, as well as musicians, a shoemaker, an apothecary, a tailor, a chaplain, and several boys. On the *Pelican* itself when it started out it is said that there were on board twelve young gentlemen, ostensibly there to learn navigation but probably accompanying the expedition either for adventure or some financial stake in the undertaking. Of these, at least three were no longer alive when Drake began his traverse of the Pacific: Doughty had been executed, another gentleman had died at sea, and a third was killed at St. Julian by Indians.

As Drake made his way up the South American coast in the only ship remaining to him, his men numbered many less than originally. According to Nuño da Silva, the Portuguese pilot who had been made a prisoner by Drake off Cape Verde in Africa, when the ship left Guatulco, a port in Guatemala, she carried victuals for eighty-eight men, of whom three were boys. When it set sail from California in July her complement had been reduced to about seventy, and when she cleared the East Indies on March 26, 1580, it was down to fifty-nine men. There were only fifty-six men left out of the original crew when Drake brought the *Golden Hind* home into Plymouth harbor on September 26, 1580.

The character of the men who composed the English crews during the great age of discovery has been depicted by Robert R. Cawley, whom I take the liberty of paraphrasing and quoting extensively. The seaman in the time of Elizabeth, he says, "had a fine combativeness about him, a combativeness shared by everyone on board, from admiral to shipboy." He had a zest for fighting, a chip-on-the-shoulder attitude which partially explains his fondness for piracy. He was world-famed as a scalawag and a thief, and exulted in the reputation. (Cawley 1927:977)

Although the joy of a good fight may have lured many a young Englishman to take to the sea, there were many other motives, "among them curiosity to behold wonders which every new corner of the world was revealing." Some of the tales he heard from voyagers were however too outlandish for his credibility. (p. 978)

The same skepticism which made him doubt the weird stories of the sea pervaded his religion, for though his masters tried to engraft religion upon him, his religion had an external quality about it. He had a "partial disbelief in the Almighty's direct power over the elements." His whole conception of the deity seems tinged with a bold streak of patriotism, for English religious intolerance is seen in the way in which God's power increases proportionately as he is contrasted with the gods of other nations.[11] In the final analysis, the ordinary mariner put his faith largely in his own astute sagacity. (pp. 978–979)

He had, however, a substitute for his lack of religion, possessing "a code of superstitions in which he believed implicitly." As if the sufferings of thirst, hunger, and storms were not enough, the sailor was tortured by the terrors created by his own belief in mysterious signs and portents, all the way from the ship's cat to the light of St. Elmo which appeared on the sails.[12] (pp. 979–980)

He had to have indomitable courage, of course, to meet the trials of the sea, as well as those of land. The perils of voyaging created "a kind of sailors' fraternity" which reduced the Englishman's sneering attitude toward foreign nations and made him feel some compassion toward fellow sufferers on the sea. French, Dutch, and even Spanish accounts might damn the English for being brigands and thieves, but seldom for being cruel. (pp. 980–981)

As for the pastimes of the sailor, they have to be inferred from what the ordinances of ships forbade him to do: blaspheme God or swear, communicate ribaldry or filthy tales, play dice, cards, or other devilish games, or brawl or fight. He drank much beer and wine, carried on board ship. (p. 981)

Finally, says Cawley, the English seaman "had to serve something more concrete than country, or even a Sovereign who was the symbol of it," so he served his leader. To him, Drake was the quintessence of a reckless buccaneer, as Gilbert was an undaunted explorer, and Raleigh the patriotic courtier who cherished a dream of gold. (p. 982)

Not all Drake's men were English. Some were Scots and others Biscayans, Frenchmen, Flemings, and Danes. The records do not seem to reveal how they were recruited but undoubtedly the sea appealed to all of them as a sphere of action and adventure, with high promise of a handsome fortune for those who survived.

Extraordinary talents were needed to command the crew of an expedition of such long duration and great risk as that of Drake, and the admiral-general had the requisites. An impartial historian has conceded that, "in days when mutinies were common, his influence over his men was very remarkable" (Harte 1936:353).

His crew, of course, never threatened mutiny against him, as had those of Columbus, Magellan, Grijalva, Pericon, and Mendaña. They sided with him in the clash with Doughty as if he were one of them. The difference in the social position of the two men aggravated the friction. "For Doughty, a soldier, a courtier and a scholar, would look down upon Drake as a mere sailor and upstart" (Harte 1936:350).

When Drake set out on his memorable voyage his men did not know his true destination, having signed on in the belief that they were to sail to Alexandria. The practice of keeping destinations a secret had been newly introduced into England, being copied apparently from the Turks, the purpose of course being to thwart any possible treachery (Dyer 1924:134). There is nothing, however, to lead one to suppose that Drake's seamen resented the deception, despite the greater distances and dangers it entailed. On the contrary they most likely welcomed the opportunity afforded by the true plan to serve their own interests. In Elizabethan times an ordinary seaman in the queen's ships was paid ten shillings a month, so that it was not surprising that a sailorman preferred to sail in the "ships of reprisal" or "merchant ships," where there was prospect of gain by plundering a Spanish treasure ship or looting a town on the Spanish Main (Dyer 1924:142). For sailors like this, Drake in his piratical role must have been far more acceptable than he would have in any mercantile one.

Drake, in short, was respected by his men. Those who have condemned him by the standards of the eighteenth-century enlightenment, the Victorian and Edwardian eras, the Geneva Convention, and the founding articles of UNESCO (cf. Boulind 1968:370–371) ought to measure him in terms of his own times (Porten 1970:258).

## chapter three

# Documentary Sources

THE ONLY DOCUMENTARY EVIDENCES available for un-raveling the puzzle of the trans-Pacific leg of the circumnavigation do not come from Drake himself, since his records were lost. What happened to them remains a question mark, as well as a great misfortune, for his logs were generally illustrated with excellent paintings of the coasts along which he sailed. His log or diary of the circumnavigation, as well as a letter concerning the voyage, are said to have been presented by him to Queen Elizabeth. It has been suggested that she kept them to prevent their publication, and so deny foreign nations the possibility of benefiting from them.

Because of this unhappy state of affairs it will be necessary to utilize whatever is in fact available, however indirect it may be.

It occurred to me in the course of my probings that cartography might be a useful source of information. I would like to address myself to it first because it can be dealt with briefly; after that I will consider other sources in greater depth.

## CONTEMPORARY MAPS

Maps made during Drake's lifetime are of no assistance in de-termining the identity of the disputed island. Almost the first car-tographic notice of his voyage makes no mention of Drake's name and fails to show his route. It consists of a brief inscription on a map by Michael Lok, printed from a woodcut, appearing in Richard Hakluyt's *Divers voyages*, published in 1582. But this map was originally drawn to represent Martin Frobisher's subarctic discoveries in 1576, 1577, and 1578, and may actually have been made before the publication of Hakluyt's book. The reference to Drake is altogether incidental and indirect, consisting only of the inscription, "Anglorum 1580," to show that the English were among those to visit the Moluccas. These words seem to be a later addition to the original map.

What seems to be the earliest map purporting to show Drake's route is one that was apparently published in Antwerp about 1581, being drawn by an unknown cartographer of no great professional skill (Map 3). The British Museum, which owns the only unbound copy—the only others are included in copies of a later French work—has reproduced this map (British Museum 1927). Drake's route is shown, but not that of Cavendish. This is important in dating the engraving because it was customary to depict both circumnavigations together after Cavendish had completed his voyage in 1588. Drake is shown sailing directly from "Nova Albio" (California) to "Moluccae" in a curving line. No attempt is made to depict a stop at any intervening islands, which anyway are not labeled.[1]

A world map engraved by the famous Dutch cartographer Jodocus Hondius, and projected in hemispheres, was published about 1590, probably in Amsterdam (Map 4). The British Museum has a copy and reproduced it, together with the one mentioned above, to commemorate the 350th anniversary of the departure of the *Pelican* from Plymouth (British Museum 1927). It depicts not only Drake's track but that of Cavendish as well. We know that Hondius lived in London from about 1583 to 1593, associated with prominent seamen, and possibly visited the celebrated vessel at Deptford, where it was on exhibit. Yet his map is of no assistance in unraveling the mystery of the Island of Thieves. It shows Drake sailing directly to the Moluccas from Nova Albion, without going near Mindanao, where it is said that he stopped for water and wood.

The so-called Silver Map, a medallion cast or struck in silver sometime after 1584[2] to commemorate Drake's feat in circling the globe, traces the great voyage but sheds no light on the Island of Thieves, which is not depicted. It is a beautifully executed representation of the world and reflects a fine command of the cartographic art by an unknown craftsman. The route from the coast of

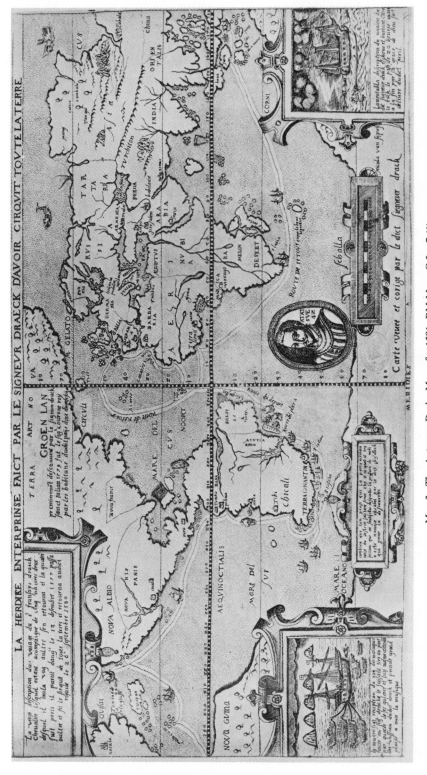

Map 3. The Antwerp Drake Map of c.1581. BM Maps C.2.a.7.(1).
*(Courtesy The British Library)*

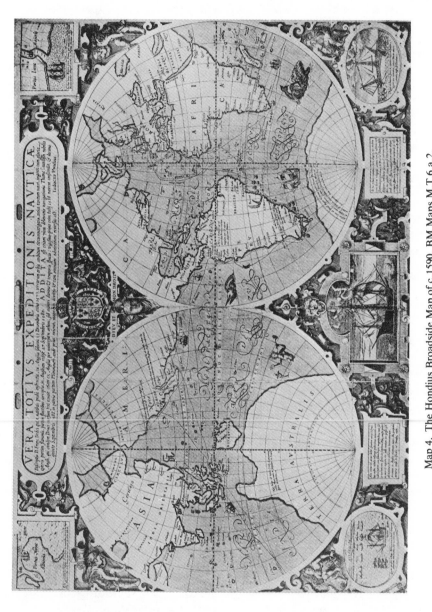

Map 4. The Hondius Broadside Map of c.1590. BM Maps M.T.6.a.2.
(*Courtesy The British Library*)

California shows the *Golden Hind* going straight southeast to the waters between Mindanao, which is labeled, and the Gilolo Islands (Halmahera), also labeled. It furthermore shows Drake skirting northwest of the "Ins. Latronum" or Islands of Thieves, which Miller Christy, the author of *The Silver Map of the World*, says are "perhaps the Pelew Islands" (Christy 1900:12, fn.18).

But Christy's identification is more than dubious, for the route does not show Drake to be at all within sighting distance of the Palau Islands. Moreover, the cartographer shows the Ins. Latronum at about 16 degrees north of the equator, which would appear to mean that he probably had Magellan's Ladrones in mind, they being located at about 13 degrees at Guam. The Palaus are actually about six degrees farther south than the Marianas.

The Silver Map, then, contributes nothing to the problem of identification. Like other maps it does not show Drake sailing southwest toward the equator and then making a turn to the north, as we know that he did from certain depositions made by his cousin John Drake. For all its exquisite workmanship, it is a medallion and contains several errors, including a date of 1579 instead of 1578 for Drake's emergence into the Pacific, and a date of 1580 for his "discovery" of Nova Albion or California, which he actually sighted in 1579.

In 1592, four years before Drake died, the English cartographer Emery Molyneux constructed a terrestrial globe on which he too traced the voyages of both Drake and Cavendish, with equally unenlightening results.

If contemporary maps are of no use in solving our problem, the next avenue to be explored is that of the literature that was produced after Drake had returned home and been knighted by the queen for his great feat. However, as will soon be evident, there is much less here than one might expect.

## LACK OF CONTEMPORARY LITERATURE

The conspicuous lack of contemporary literature on Drake's voyage must be seen in a wider context which inhibited also the reporting of other maritime accomplishments, including for example Thomas Cavendish's successful duplication of Drake's circumnavigation, a voyage which produced no books in England.

The circumstances of the times have been interpreted by John Parker in his *Books to Build an Empire*, in which he advances first of all a political consideration. In the first half of Elizabeth's reign, he reminds us, the queen was unable openly to espouse imperialistic projects because of fear of retaliation by Spain, which at that time was the strongest nation of the continent. At home, there was the danger of rebellion by those who remained loyal to the Roman church and thought of Elizabeth as the illegitimate offspring of a heretic king and therefore not a legitimate queen. Spain would have made the most of this ill-feeling, so that until that nation could be successfully confronted Elizabeth was forced to hide her encouragement of the imperialistic spirit (Parker 1965:94–95).[3]

Added to this was the lethargy of the London merchant community, whose interest was in the export of cloth to the Continent rather than overseas markets. Those joint-stock companies which did venture abroad were still small in size and could keep their shareholders informed of their undertakings without recourse to the printing press (Parker 1965:95).

Finally, says Parker, there was the state of affairs prevailing in English education. Geography and current history were taught hardly at all in the schools, and those nobles and gentlemen who did read history looked back in time rather than on the prevailing scene. An interest in literature on exploration and the outer world simply did not find receptivity in earlier Elizabethan England. The country was still nationalistic rather than imperialistic and lacked the drive needed to want to go abroad. This apathy was in large measure promoted by a failure to identify, either emotionally or practically, with expansionism (Parker 1965:95–97).

## ACCOUNTS OF THE CIRCUMNAVIGATION

It was perhaps the geographer Richard Hakluyt who did most to arouse England to an interest in travel and exploration, and for this we must be grateful, for he was responsible for the first printed account of Drake's voyage.

Hakluyt had a passionate interest in the history of discovery and he combined it with patriotic fervor to produce in 1589 an outstanding anthology, *The principall navigations, voiages and discoveries of the English nation*, later expanded into a three-volume work with a somewhat similar title, published in 1598–1600[4] and continued in greatly expanded form since the last century by the Hakluyt Society. His book, which did not immediately arouse publishers into printing similar collections of travels, included an account of Drake's global voyage.

This account, whose full title is "The Famous voyage of Sir
Francis Drake into the South Sea, and there hence about the whole
globe of the earth, begun in the yeere of our Lord, 1577," or the
"Famous Voyage" for short, consisted of six unnumbered folio
leaves inserted between pages 643 and 644 of the first edition of
Hakluyt's book (Figure 5). Obviously, the decision to print it came
late, and the insertion was probably made after 1594 or 1595.

There are some, notably Sir Julian Corbett, who attribute authorship of the "Famous Voyage" to Francis Pretty, yet there is no
evidence that this gentleman-at-arms wrote the account or even
sailed with Drake. The misapprehension appears to have resulted
from the fact that Pretty accompanied Cavendish on the latter's
own circumnavigation, which followed shortly after that of Drake.
He wrote an account of Cavendish's expedition which was published by Hakluyt, and this may be the source of the later confusion.

It is altogether possible that the "Famous Voyage" was not only
published by Hakluyt but even written by him, using three or more
sources (Wagner 1926:238). These sources are two manuscripts in
the British Museum and probably a manuscript by Francis
Fletcher, about whom I shall soon have more to say. The portion
dealing with the Island of Thieves cannot itself be assigned to any
known source, not even Fletcher. In any event it forms only a small
portion of the whole report.

The second account of Drake's voyage is far more substantial
than the above, and although it has been called by Wagner "the
most untrustworthy of all" (1926:286), this criticism was not meant
to apply so much to that portion of the voyage dealing with the
mystery island as to other portions.

This report was published in 1628 as *The World Encompassed*
under the alleged authorship of Sir Francis Drake, nephew of the
great sea hero (Figure 6). Actually, it was a compilation by an
unspecified person[5] from various sources, particularly a manuscript by Francis Fletcher, the chaplain. Other sources, dealing with

person: and such as pleased their fancie, (which were the yongest) they inclosing them about offred their sacrifices vnto them with lamentable weeping, scratching, and tearing the flesh from their faces with their nailes, whereof issued abundance of bloode. But wee vsed signes to them of disliking this, and staied their hands from force, and directed them vpwards to the liuing God, whome onely they ought to worshippe. They shewed vnto vs their wounds, and craued helpe of them at our hands, whereupon wee gaue them lotions, plaisters, and ointments agreeing to the state of their griefes, beseeching God to cure their diseases. Euery thirde day they brought their sacrifices vnto vs, vntill they vnderstoode our meaning, that we had no pleasure in them: yet they could not be long absent from vs, but daily frequented our companie to the houre of our departure, which departure seemed so greeuous vnto them, that their ioy was turned into sorrow. They intreated vs, that being absent we would remember them, and by stelth prouided a sacrifice, which we misliked.

Our necessarie busines being ended, our Generall with his companie trauailed vp into the Countrey to their villages, where wee found heardes of Deere by 1000. in a companie, being most large, and fat of bodie. Great heards of Deere.

We found the whole Conntrey to be a warren of a strange kinde of Connies, their bodies in bignes as be the Barbarie Connies, their heads as the heads of ours, the feete of a Want, and the taile of a Rat being of great length: vnder her chinne on either side a bagge, into the which she gathereth her meate, when she hath filled her bellie abroad. The people eate their bodies, and make great account of their skinnes, for their Kings coate was made of them. Abundance of strange conies

Our Generall called this Countrey, Noua Albion, and that for two causes: the one in respect of the white bankes and cliffes, which lie towards the sea: and the other, because it might haue some affinitie with our Countrey in name, which sometime was so called. Noua Albion.

There is no part of earth here to be taken vp, wherein there is not a reasonable quantitie of gold or siluer. Gold and siluer in the earth of Noua Albion.

At our departure hence our General set vp a monument of our being there, as also of her Maiesties right and title to the same, namely a plate, nailed vpon a faire great poste, whereupon was ingrauen her Maiesties name, the day and yeere of our arriuall there, with the free giuing vp of the prouince and people into her Maiesties hands, together with her highnes picture and armes, in a peece of sixe pence of currant English money vnder the plate, where vnder was also written the name of our Generall.

It seemeth that the Spaniards hitherto had neuer bene in this part of the Countrey, neither did euer discouer the lande by many degrees, to the Southwards of this place.

After we had set saile from hence, we continued without sight of land till the 13. day of October following, which day in the morning we fell with certaine Ilands 8. degrees to the North-ward of the line, from which Ilands came a great number of Canoas, hauing in some of them 4. in some 6. and in some also 14. men, bringing with them coquos, and other fruites. Their Canoas were hollowe within, and cut with great arte, and cunning, being very smooth within and without, and bearing a glasse as if it were a horne daintily burnished, hauing a prowe, and a sterne of one sorte, peelding inward circle wise, being of a great heigth, and full of certaine white shels for a brauerie, and on each side of them lie out two peeces of timber about a yard and a halfe long, more or lesse, according to the smalnes, or bignes of the boate. October. Certaine Ilands in 8. degrees. Strange Canoas.

This people haue the nether part of their eares cut into a round circle, hanging downe very lowe vpon their cheekes, whereon they hang things of a reasonable weight. The nailes of their hands are an ynche long, their teeth are as blacke as pitch, and they renew them often, by eating of an herbe with a kinde of powder, which they alwaies carrie about them in a cane for the same purpose.

We leauing this Iland the night after we fell with it, the 18. of October, we light vpon diuers others, some whereof made a great shewe of Inhabitants. Ilands.

We continued our course by the Ilands of Tagulada, Zelon, and Zewarra, being subiect to the Portingals, the first whereof hath growing in it great store of Sinnamon.

The 14. of Nouember we fell with the Ilands of Molucca, which day at night (hauing directed our course to runne with Tydore) in coasting along the Iland of Mutyr, belonging to the King of Ternate, his Deputie or Viceking seeing vs at sea, came with his Canoa to vs without all feare, and came aboord, and after some conference with our Generall, willed him in any wise to runne in with Ternate, and not with Tydore, assuring him that the King would be glad of his comming, and would be ready to doe what he would require, for which purpose he himselfe would that night be with the King, and tell him the newes, with whome if he once dealt, he should finde Nouember. The Ile of Ternate.

Figure 5. Page from the "Famous Voyage." The earliest account of the Island of Thieves appears here. Source: Hakluyt 1589. (*Courtesy The Huntington Library, San Marino, California*)

# THE WORLD
## Encompaſſed

By
## Sir FRANCIS DRAKE,

Being his next voyage to that to *Nombre
de Dios* formerly imprinted;

Carefully collected out of the notes of Maſter
FRANCIS FLETCHER *Preacher in this imployment, and diuers others his followers in
the ſame*:

Offered now at laſt to publique view, both for the honour of
the actor, but eſpecially for the ſtirring vp of *heroick ſpirits,
to benefit their Countrie, and eternize their names
by like noble attempts.*

LONDON,
Printed for NICHOLAS BOVRNE
and are to be fold at his ſhop at the
*Royall Exchange.* 1628.

---

Figure 6. Title Page of *The World Encompassed*. The first edition appeared in 1628 and was "collected" by Drake's nephew from Fletcher's notes and other sources. Source: Drake 1628. (*Courtesy The British Library*)

parts of the voyage that do not concern us, consisted of published partial accounts by Edward Cliffe, Nuño da Silva, and Lopez Vaz. Thrown in gratuitously by persons unknown are faulty statements of fact as well as discourses on religion, morals, customs, and the weather, which from internal evidence seem to be products of the seventeenth century (Wagner 1926:287).

It is not possible to say who wrote the section dealing with the Island of Thieves. It may have come from a portion of Fletcher's manuscript known to be lost. The portion preserved to us in the British Museum as Sloan MSS, No. 61, is irrelevant to our inquiry.

However, taking both the "Famous Voyage" and *The World Encompassed* as accounts of the whole voyage, and assuming them to be derived from the same principal source, probably Fletcher, I shall take the liberty of referring to them as utterances by the chaplain, so that when I say "Fletcher says," I really mean "Fletcher et al. say." This is done only as a convenience and carries no final implications as to authorship of the accounts.

Brushing aside all other sources that are either secondary or irrelevant for the problem in question, we come finally to two depositions made by Drake's young cousin, John Drake, while he was a prisoner of the Spaniards in South America after having been captured in connection with a later expedition under Edward Fenton. The youthful John—not to be confused with Francis Drake's brother, also named John but killed in the Caribbean in 1572—had no notes to refresh his memory when under interrogation by the Spaniards, so he gives no dates. These two depositions were printed in 1911 by Lady Eliott-Drake in both the original Spanish and in translation, and in 1914 were also translated in part by Zelia Nuttall in her valuable *New Light on Drake*. They have none of the details concerning the Island of Thieves provided by either the "Famous Voyage" or *The World Encompassed* but they do contain important statements not recorded in either of these documents.

To sum up, the only sources relative to the solution of the mystery surrounding Drake's island are: the "Famous Voyage," often attributed to Pretty but probably taken from a lost manuscript by Fletcher; *The World Encompassed*, "authored" by the younger Sir Francis but probably derived chiefly from Fletcher; and two depositions made by John Drake while a prisoner of the Spaniards.

## *THE TEXT OF* THE WORLD ENCOMPASSED

What does our chief source, *The World Encompassed*, have to say? It is important to reproduce its exact words, for we will have to read and interpret them with utmost care if we are to derive a decision from them.

The ship left the California coast at the close of July 1579, and Drake "bent his course directly to runne with the Ilands of the Moluccas." The account, which I have extracted from the original edition,[6] continues:

> And so hauing nothing in our view but aire and sea, without sight of any land for the space of full 68. dayes together, wee continued our course through the maine Ocean, till September 30. following, on which day we fell in kenne of certaine Ilands, lying about eight degrees to the Northward of the line.
>
> From these Ilands presently vpon the discouery of vs, came a great number of canowes, hauing in each of them in some foure, in some sixe, in some fourteene or fifteene men, bringing with them Coquos, fish, Potatoes, and certaine fruites to small purpose.
>
> Their canowes were made after the fashion, that the canowes of all the rest of the Ilands of Moluccas for the most part are: That is of one tree, hollowed within with great art and cunning, being made so smooth both within and without, that they bore a glosse, as if it were a harnesse most finely burnished: A prowe and sterne they had of one fashion, yeelding inward in manner of a semicircle, of a great height, and hanged full of certaine white and glistering shels for brauery: On each side of their canows, lay out two peeces of timber about a yard and a halfe long, more or lesse, according to the capacitie of their boate. At the ends whereof was fastned crossewise a great cane, the vse whereof was to keepe their canowes from ouerthrowing, and that they might be equally borne vp on each side.
>
> The people themselues haue the neather parts of their eares cut round or circlewise, hanging downe very low vpon their cheekes, wherein they hang things of a reasonable weight: the nailes on the fingers of some of them, were at least an inch long, and their teeth as blacke as pitch; the colour whereof they vse to renew by often eating of an herbe, with a kind of powder, which in a cane they carrie about them to the same purpose. The first sort and company of those canowes beeing come to our ship (which then by reason of a scant wind made little way) very subtilly and against their natures, began in peace to traffique with vs, giuing us one thing for another very orderly, intending (as we perceiued) hereby to worke a greater mischiefe to vs: Intreating vs by signes most earnestly to draw neerer towards the shore, that they might (if possible) make the easier prey

both of the ship and vs. But these passing away, and others continually resorting, wee were quickly able to guesse at them what they were: For if they receiued anything once into their hands, they would neither giue recompence nor restitution of it, but thought what euer they could finger to bee their owne: Expecting alwayes with browes of brasse to receiue more, but would part with nothing: Yea being reiected for their bad dealing, as those with whom we would haue no more to do, vsing vs so euilly, they could not be satisfied till they had giuen the attempt to reuenge themselues, because we would not giue them whatsoeuer they would haue for nothing: And hauing stones good store in their canowes, let flie a maine of them against vs. It was farre from our Generals meaning to requite their malice by like iniure. Yet that they might knowe that he had the power to doe them harme (if he had listed) he caused a great peece to be shot off not to hurt them but to affright them. Which wrought the desired effect amongst them, for at the noise thereof they euery one leaped out of his canow into the water, and diuing vnder the keele of their boates, staied them from going any way till our ship was gone a good way from them. Then they all lightly recouered into their canowes, and got them with speed toward the shoare.

Notwithstanding other new companies (but all of the same mind) continually made resort vnto vs. And seeing that there was no good to be got by violence, they put on a shew of seeming honestie, and offering in shew to deale with vs by way of exchange; vnder that pretence they cunningly fell a filching of what they could, and one of them puld a dagger and kniues from one of our mens girdles, and being required to restore it againe, he rather vsed what meanes he could to catch at more. Neither could we at all be to ridde of this vngracious company, till we made some of them feele some smart as well as terror: and so we left that place by all passengers to bee knowne hereafter by the name of the *Island of Theeues*.

Till the third of October wee could not get cleare of these consorts, but from thence we continued our course without sight of land till the 16. of the same moneth, when we fell with foure Ilands standing in 7. deg. 5. min. to the Northward of the line. We coasted them till the 21. day, and then anchored and watered vpon the biggest of them called Mindanao. The 22. of October as we past betweene two Ilands, about sixe or eight leagues South of Mindanao, there came from them two canows to haue talked with vs, and we would willingly haue talked with them, but there arose so much wind that put vs from them to the Southwards. (Drake 1628:82–84)

In such quaint Elizabethan language, spelling, and punctuation, then, we have the principal account of the happenings that ensued after the first sighting of land from the time of departure from New Albion. For the present I shall make no effort to interpret or evaluate it but will instead press on immediately to the next source of information available to us.


## THE TEXT OF THE "FAMOUS VOYAGE"

As I have already said, the earliest published version of the above happenings as it appears in the "Famous Voyage" is probably no more than a collapsed and paraphrased rendition of the same Fletcher manuscript from which *The World Encompassed* drew its account of the Island of Thieves. Nevertheless, I am reproducing it below because I shall have occasion later to make reference to those portions of it that either corroborate *The World Encompassed* or depart from it.[7] The pertinent portion of the "Famous Voyage" is as follows:

> After we had set saile from hence, we continued without sight of land till the 13. day of October following, which day in the morning we fell with certaine Islands 8. degrees to the Northward of the line, from which Islands came a great number of Canoas, hauing in some of them 4. in some 6. and in some also 14. men, bringing with them coquos, and other fruites. Their Canoas were hollowe within, and cut with great arte, and cunning, being very smooth within and without, and bearing a glasse as if it were a horne daintily burnished, hauing a prowe, and a sterne of one sort, yeelding inward circle wise, being of great heigth, and full of certaine white shels for a brauerie, and on each side of them lie out two peeces of timber about a yard and a halfe long, more or lesse, according to the smalness, or bignes of the boate.
>
> This people haue the nether part of their eares cut into a round circle, hanging downe very lowe vpon their cheekes, whereupon they hang things of a reasonable weight. The nailes of their hands are an ynche long, their teeth as blacke as pitch, and they renew them often, by eating of an herbe with a kind of powder, which they alwaies carrie about them in a cane for the same purpose.
>
> We leauing this Island the night after we fell with it, the 18. of October, we light vpon divers others, some whereof made a great shewe of Inhabitants.
>
> We continued our course by the Islands of Tagulada, Zelon, and Zewarra, being subject to the Portingals, the first whereof hath growing in it great store of Sinnamon. (Hakluyt 1589:643 [i])

Here again I shall refrain from making interpretations or other comments, preferring to bring together all the raw material before doing so in the belief that this is the most efficient way of proceeding.

## JOHN DRAKE'S VERSIONS

As for the two depositions by John Drake, the relevant portions are brief but contain some valuable points.

The first deposition was made in 1584 through an interpreter at Santa Fé in what is now Argentina and contains the following pertinent passages:

> From there they went to the islands of Los Ladrones. On account of the cold they went no higher than forty-eight degrees. From New England they steered to the S.W. to the island of Los Ladrones, which is in nine degrees. In these islands there are Indians, very warlike, of whom they killed twenty, as a hundred of their canoes came out. They go about naked. From the islands of Los Ladrones they went, in nine days, to an island the name of which he does not know: it lies in seven degrees, and they steered to it towards the south and the south-west. They remained a day at this island, taking in wood and water. From there they went to the Moluccas, steering to the south-west, and taking twenty days on the voyage. (Fuller-Eliott-Drake 1911:II, 357)

Some new bits of information are given in this deposition that do not appear in Fletcher's account: the latitude was nine degrees instead of eight; there were about a hundred canoes; the men were naked; and twenty natives were killed. Moreover, John says that it took nine days to go from Los Ladrones to the next island, whereas Fletcher says it took thirteen.

John Drake's second deposition was made under examination of the Tribunal of the Inquisition at Lima, Peru, in 1587. The relevant portion is as follows:

> Thus they sailed with only one ship in the direction of the Moluccas, but on account of the currents which opposed them they altered their course towards China before reaching one and a half degrees of latitude. They proceeded to the Island of Los Ladrones, which is in nine degrees. There many Indians came to them with fish, and gave it to them in exchange for beads (cuentas) and other trifles. The Indians embarked in canoes which were very well made, with short

oars with which they rowed very well; they were naked and carried darts and stones. They took from each other the beads and things which were given to them in payment: the strongest remained in possession while the quarrelling went on the whole time.

They sailed to a large island called Bosney, where they took in water and wood, and then made for the Moluccas. (Fuller-Eliott-Drake 1911:II, 393)

Note should be made that Drake first went south as far as one-and-one-half degrees north of the equator, implying that when he reached the Island of Thieves he must have been sailing west northwest. The position of the island at 9 degrees instead of 8 is reaffirmed. No mention is made of a conflict. An unidentified island named "Bosney" is spoken of for the first time.

## ☙ chapter four ❧

# *The Clues*

THE PRECEDING DOCUMENTS must be sifted through carefully in constructing any argument purporting to solve the mystery of the Island of Thieves. The clues are not only geographical but demographic and ethnological as well. One wishes that they were more numerous and conclusive than they are, but on the other hand if they were too decisive there would be no mystery to unravel and no need for this investigation.

## *THE GEOGRAPHIC CLUE*

The outstanding geographic fact contained in the record is Fletcher's statement that the islands in question were "about eight degrees to the Northward of the line." Any islands not approximating this criterion must be eliminated as suspects, although we must keep in mind the possibility that John Drake's estimate of nine degrees has some validity.

It is also possible that there were errors in the use of the cross-staff or astrolabe. Certainly, Wagner has shown that the latitudes given in *The World Encompassed* were not infallible, but, as he admits, these could be the result of a faulty secondhand record rather than mistakes in Drake's measurement of the angle of the sun above the horizon at noon. The discrepancy of one degree between the latitudes given by Fletcher and John Drake cannot be attributed to astronomical error.

There are other geographic considerations bearing on the solution. They concern distances between places, the course steered, and other physical factors, but these are more conveniently considered at more appropriate points.

## THE DEMOGRAPHIC CLUE

Demographically, the island or islands would have had to be populated by no fewer than about 2,200. This figure is of considerable importance. I arrived at it by taking John Drake's statement that the *Golden Hind* was greeted by a hundred canoes, and Fletcher's statement that there were from four to fifteen men in each. Assuming that the average boatload was made up of eight men, all of whom were over the age of fourteen and under the age of seventy, then 800 able-bodied men came out to meet the ship.

Without going into the details, I then estimated by the use of modern population tables that 1,400 women and children, as well as aged persons, remained on land. These, added to the men in the canoes, give the total of 2,200 that I have decided upon.

The age bracket I selected for the native reception party, and the exclusion of women from it, are based both on accounts in the literature and my own experience in the west Caroline Islands. Under the tranquil conditions of contemporary times, women, children, and the aged do not ordinarily come out to meet ships, and if treachery had indeed been contemplated against the English there would have been all the more reason not to have them under foot. As for the use of modern population pyramids, I tried to exercise discretion based on my extensive study of Carolinian population figures and the results of two detailed censuses I once conducted, eleven years apart, on a Micronesian atoll.[1]

Admittedly, this is all very crude but probably good enough for our purposes.

## ETHNOLOGICAL NEEDS

Ethnologically, there are several qualifications that must be met by any place identified as the Island of Thieves, some of which are more important than others.

Without question, canoes furnish the most diagnostically valuable clues. Anthropologists tracing the migrations of native peoples, particularly in Oceania, have made extensive use of canoe features, and no better examples of this can be given than the reconstructions of such men as Dixon and Haddon and Hornell. A perusal of their writings, as well as others of similar kind, convincingly demonstrates the complexity and diversity of Pacific Island canoes.

Among the more important of the features to be considered are the following: The canoe-type—whether it is a dugout or is built up; whether it has one, two, or no outriggers; whether it has a double hull and consequently no outrigger at all. The parts of the hull—the details of the bow and stern; of fore and end pieces; of prow affixes and stern affixes; of bulkheads, frames, ribs, cleats, struts, and stanchions; of weather and lee platforms; and so on. The outrigger apparatus—the number of outriggers and outrigger booms; the shape and material of the float; the type of outrigger attachment; and so forth. The mast—whether it is a pole mast, sheer mast, or tripod mast. The sail—whether it is a square sail or a fore-and-aft spritsail or lateen sail; and so on. Many more details than this can be taken into consideration in identifying the provenance of a canoe, among them being paddles, oars, bailers, and such kinds of rigging as stays, shrouds, halyards, sheets, guys, and vangs (Haddon and Hornell 1936–1938:III, 5–12). But by now anyone should be convinced, if ever there was any doubt, that with such diagnostic variations the locale from which a boat originates can be determined with authority.

Of course, the details left by Francis Fletcher and John Drake are comparatively meager. They do not approach the potential implied by the above listings. Nevertheless, they will be exploited to the utmost in tracking down the identity of the larcenists who so exasperated Drake that he was impelled to fire upon them and give their land an uncomplimentary name.

The canoes described by Fletcher had to be double outriggers, or possibly canoes having double outlayers. The booms of Oceanic outriggers vary in length, depending on the size of the hull, but the "yard and a halfe . . . more or lesse" is about right for smaller outriggers, although on the short side if they were equipped with sails.

According to Fletcher, the two projecting pieces of timber on each side were "fastned crossewise" with a length of "great cane," their purpose being "to keepe their canowes from ouerthrowing, and that they might be equally borne vp on each side." This description seems beyond question to be that of two booms on each side of the canoe, with a bamboo float fastened to each set of booms.

Another possibility must be considered, however, and that is that the canoes had double outlayers instead of double outriggers. An outlayer has been defined as "a pole or a simple framework balancing apparatus, and may be single or double" (Haddon 1920:77). It differs from an outrigger in that it does not rest on water. Outlayers, compared with outriggers, are uncommon devices. I shall return to the matter of outlayers at a later point, but for the moment suffice it to say that there is nothing in Fletcher's description that would rule out the possibility that this is what the canoes were equipped with.

In the face of the explicit description left us by *The World Encompassed* it is puzzling that James Hornell, a distinguished authority on Oceanic canoes, has asserted that what Drake and his men saw were single outriggers balanced on their leeward side by a projecting platform (Haddon and Hornell 1936–1938:I, 376). The kind of platform that he had in mind is complex and could scarcely be described simply as two projecting pieces of timber fastened across with a great cane or bamboo.

The canoes encountered by the *Golden Hind* seem to have had no sails, for none are mentioned in the records. If sails had been used they most likely would have drawn mention. We know from numerous accounts in the literature that when native crafts had sails they used them in surrounding European vessels. Early explorers and traders sometimes mention with some awe how canoes would outdistance them with ease and even encircle their cumbersome ships when they had way. They also mention sails being lowered when a ship wished to come alongside for visiting or trading.

In his second deposition, John Drake does say that the natives "rowed very well with oars." No significance should be attached to John's use of the word "oars" instead of "paddles." Until 1624 there is no evidence that a paddle meant any more than a small spadelike implement with a long handle, used for clearing a ploughshare of earth. It then came to mean a particular kind of oar, used without a rowlock, that is dropped more or less vertically into

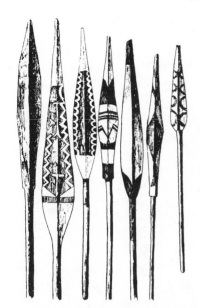

Figure 7. Paddles. In most of the South Seas, paddles rather than oars are used. These specimens are from Palau. Source: Krämer 1926:182.

the water, and pulled and pushed backward so as to propel a canoe forward.[2] In using an oar, the rower has his back to the direction in which he moves his boat; in using a paddle, the paddler faces forward. Paddles are used throughout Oceania (Figure 7) and the New World, whereas in Europe propulsion through the water is predominantly by oars. The significant thing is not the semantic distinction between the two but the fact that John found that he recollected oars but says nothing of sails.

The canoes seen by the men of Drake's storm-beaten ship must have been basically dugouts, being "of one tree, hollowed within with great art and cunning." They could, however, have been modifications of simple dugouts, with a washstrake on either side of the hull and an endpiece at both the head and stern—the so-called five-part canoes. They could not have been of the built-up variety, in which each side is built up of two or more strakes (side planking) and the dugout underbody is reduced in size or even eliminated in favor of paired planks. The words, "one tree," argue against that possibility. Thus, "sewn" hulls do not qualify.

It is important to know that the canoes were very smooth, for "they bore a glosse, as if it were a harnesse most finely burnished." It is noteworthy that no mention is made of paint.

Even more important is that the boats were similar at both ends, each end extending in an inwardly curving semicircle of great height. These ends, incidentally, would make it impossible for the canoes to be entirely of one piece. For an end to be of great height it would have to be shaped from a block of wood separate from the hull, so there must have been a fore endpiece and an after endpiece. However, if the canoes could be propelled or sailed forward in either direction, what was "fore" and what "aft" may have been

Figure 8. Moderately Lengthened Earlobes. The man is Pigene, a native of Ulithi. Source: Lütke 1835–1836:atlas, pl. 25. (*Courtesy The Beinecke Rare Book and Manuscript Library, Yale Unitversity*)

*dess. et Lith. par Choris*

*Lith. de Langlume*

*Kadou,*

*habitant des iles Carolines.*

Figure 9. Extremely Lengthened Earlobes. The man is Kadu, an informant on the Kotzebue expedition. Source: Choris 1822:pl. 17. (*Courtesy Special Collections, UCLA Library*)

entirely relative, reversing themselves as the canoe was turned around.

From each end of the canoes there were suspended "certaine white and glistering shels for brauery" or ornamentation. Even the shells must be considered in trying to decide the provenance of the boats.

As for other ethnological clues, they may be skimmed over more quickly.

According to John Drake, the men were naked. *The World Encompassed* and the "Famous Voyage" make no reference to dress or lack of it.

Fletcher says they had long ears that were "cut round or circlewise, hanging downe very low vpon their cheekes, wherein they hang things of a reasonable weight" (Figures 8 and 9). Drake makes no comment.

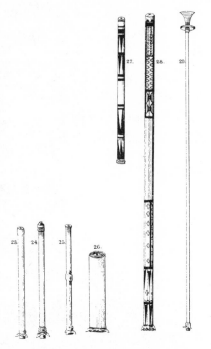

Figure 10. Lime Containers. Bamboo tubes have long been used throughout the South Pacific to contain lime for sprinkling on the Areca palm nut. These specimens are from Palau. Source: Kubary 1892:pl. 23.

They, or at least some of them, had long fingernails, says Fletcher. If this attracted John's attention, he makes no mention of them.

Their teeth, according to Fletcher, were "blacke as pitch." This statement has greater diagnostic value than appears on the surface. John does not mention teeth in his two depositions.

Obviously the natives were betel-nut chewers, for according to Fletcher they often ate "of an herbe, with a kind of powder, which in a cane they carrie about them" (Figure 10). We know of course that betel-nut chewers place the nut of the *Areca catechu* palm and some powdered lime on a betel pepper leaf, which they mold into a ball and masticate as a stimulant. Young John fails to mention the betel.

Fletcher says that at one point the natives "let flie a maine" of stones against the English. For the time being we shall assume that

Figure 11. A Stone Sling. The sling was once common in much of the South Seas. This coconut-fiber specimen is from Yap. Source: Müller-Wismar 1917–1918:I, fig. 289.

this means they made use of slings (Figure 11). John complements Fletcher by noting that the natives carried stones.

John says that the natives carried darts (Figure 12). Fletcher is silent on the subject.

The tactic used by the natives was to show outward honesty in order to draw the ship near shore, all the while coveting materials on the vessel or actually stealing them. Fletcher gives us this information, whereas John fails to discuss it.

So much for the criteria—geographical, demographic, and ethnological—that I have been able to assemble.

## CULTIGENS

The perspicacious reader may have noted that I have not included among these precious clues the references made by Fletcher to "Coquos, fish, Potatoes, and certaine fruits," and by John Drake to "fish." For "certaine fruites" and fish the answer is obvious: unidentified fruits could be anything at all, and fish are ubiquitous in the seas of the world. Coconuts must similarly be excluded as having no forensic value, the coconut palm being a very important plant food found on virtually all Pacific Islands. It need not concern us that botanists and anthropologists have debated whether its origins are to be found in tropical America or the Old World. What is important is that it can only be diffused over long distances by man, and that in pre-Columbian times it had been brought by aboriginal seafarers to all the islands where they settled, even tiny islands and atolls whose soil could grow only a limited number of cultigens.

The sweet potato, *Ipomoea batatas*, aside from the once-raging controversy in ethnobotanical circles concerning its origins, presents some problems that must be mentioned before dismissing it along with the coconut. By now it is generally accepted that it originated in America in pre-Columbian times and was a valued and widespread cultigen which had penetrated into the Pacific,

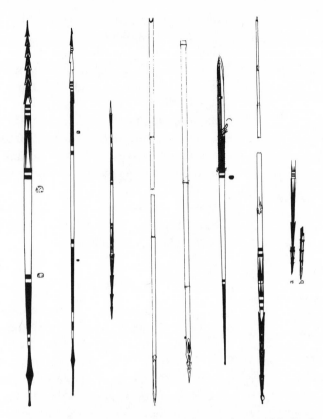

Figure 12. Spears. The spear was the chief weapon in most of the South Seas. These specimens are from Yap. Source: Müller-Wismar 1917–1918:I, figs. 280–287.

although not everywhere. An excellent examination of the literature on this problem by Conklin (1963) leads him to the conclusion that the presence of the sweet potato in Micronesia and Malaysia at the time of first European contact is to be "seriously questioned." He is particularly insistent on another point, which has occurred to me, too, and that is that the various words for "potato" have been confusedly applied not only to the sweet potato itself, but to a whole range of herbaceous root crops, including yams (*Dioscorea*) and some other tuberous food plants. I accept his questioning of the meaning assigned by some to Pigafetta's sixteenth-century use of the word *batate* in connection with Guam and Palawan in the Philippines when he was there with the Magellan expedition. Conklin is convinced, and I think rightly so, that it refers to cultivated yams, which are of course members of the Dioscoreaceae, a family different from that of the morning glory family to which the sweet potato belongs and of course unrelated to the so-called yam of the food markets of the United States, where the word is mistakenly applied to a variety of sweet potato.

It is my assumption that the "potatoes" seen by Drake were either long-established Old World tubers such as true yams or even postcontact sweet potatoes introduced by Spaniards from the Pacific coast of Mexico. In any event, by the time he came upon the scene, "potatoes," whatever their nature, had already diffused to all those parts of the Pacific in which we are interested and cannot be regarded as useful clues.

I would have been delighted if anthropometric clues were at my disposal, but none whatsoever are provided. Even if they had been, however, they might have proven too generalized, as with the sweet potato and coconut, for me to use with any degree of success. Another line of evidence, however scant, might have been that of simple linguistic expressions. These would have to have been more than simple dialectical terms to discriminate one atoll group in Micronesia from another, for the ones in question have a common language.

Looking back over what I do have, these seem to be the resources—chiefly ethnological—which must be used to test the suspects. They may be few and not always decisive, yet they should be enough to lead to a final verdict.

## CULTURAL STABILITY

One has the right to ask if the ethnological details left behind by Francis Fletcher and John Drake can be equated with modern anthropological accounts. Can we trust that the old descriptions have validity for cultures that have been studied in recent times? After all, three or more centuries is a long time, and during that period the native cultures could have changed so drastically as to render comparison unreliable.

The answer to this question is that anthropologists, who once had to convert people to the idea that native ways of life are not immutable, nevertheless recognize that they are remarkably stable when contrasted with complex urban civilizations. They know that no culture is ever as static as the old classical evolutionists assumed, but at the same time they concede that it can retain its basic features and specific details with remarkable tenacity if the people in question are at a relatively simple level of technology and political structure and are not greatly influenced by an impinging complex way of life.

The notion of stability is implicit in the principle of ethnological analogy used by archaeologists in interpreting the meaning of artifacts which they encounter in the course of their work. According to this principle, firsthand accounts of primitive societies can be used for the interpretation of archaeological data, and have even been used in the reconstruction of prehistoric religions going as far back as the early Palaeolithic (James 1957). One archaeologist identified 62 out of 273 classes of thirteenth-century Kayenta artifacts by using analogies with modern Hopi culture (Anderson 1969:137). These are only scattered examples.

But archaeologists generally stop short of equating ethnographic analogy with genetic continuity. Only occasionally do they commit themselves to the possibility that an artifact has remained in continuous use from the prehistoric past into the historic present. Nevertheless, they do so when the archaeological record merges without break into the historical record, as is true, for instance, of the Pueblo Indian kiva. The kiva is a semisubterranean ceremonial structure for males, having distinctive forms and functions. Its features are a firepit, partition wall, bench, ventilator, and smoke-hole hatchway. It goes all the way back to A.D. 900, at least. All modern pueblos are provided with kivas (Martin, Quimby, and Collier 1947:113, 125, 159).

Culture stability can also be verified with confidence through the use of baselines provided by ethnohistorical materials. These consist of early written observations, usually left by explorers, travelers, missionaries, traders, and administrators, and enable us to confirm that a practice or artifact noted among a preliterate people many years ago is still part of the same cultural tradition seen at a later point in time.

A classic example, made familiar to the layman through the writings of Thor Heyerdahl, is that of Peruvian balsa rafts. Descriptions and drawings have been left by numerous men. Those who are impressed by names and dates can thrill to the following list, which is only partial: Juan de Sáamanos in 1526, Gonzalo Fernando de Oviedo in 1535, Augustin de Zárate in 1555, Bartolomé de las Casas in about 1559, Girolamo Benzoni in 1565, Inca Garcilasso in 1609, Joris van Spilbergen in 1619, Bernabé Cobo in 1653, G. Juan and A. de Ulloa in 1748, Alexander von Humboldt in 1810, W. B. Stevenson in 1825, Benjamin Morrell in 1832, and François E. Paris in 1841–1843 (Heyerdahl 1952:516–543). Through the writings of these men a continuous record has been provided which substantiates that the Peruvian balsa raft, with its variants, was preserved intact for more than three centuries.

The South Pacific is laden with good examples, but I have selected only one (cf. Lessa 1961:15–19, 82–88). In 1722 Father Cantova questioned some natives from Woleai and Faraulep who had been stranded on Guam. Among many other things, he recorded a major portion of the Olofat trickster cycle, the most important of all Carolinian myths. It differed in no substantial way from a version I myself collected in 1948. It resembled a version collected on Woleai in 1804 by Luis de Torres and published from his notes by Adelbert von Chamisso in 1821 and by Louis de Freycinet in 1829. Early in the present century, versions were collected from various islands by Ludwig Kohl-Larsen, Max Girschner, and several members of the great Hamburg Südsee-Expedition of 1908–1910.

A modest instance of persistence which does not have as early documentation as has the above is nevertheless of some interest because it has survived Christianization and strong acculturative forces. It is the so-called clothes-burning mortuary ceremony of the Luiseño Indians of southern California, and was first described about 1814 by Father Geronimo Boscana, a missionary. The ceremony is basically a reenactment of the death of the mythical ancestor, Wiyot, and is conducted according to a rule of reciprocity by a religious chief representing the appropriate Luiseño "party." I witnessed a full performance in 1952, but there have been many others since then. Careful comparison shows that the ritualistic elements are basically unchanged (White 1953).

The Gwambe of Mozambique illustrate how an entire culture can remain essentially unchanged over a long period of time. In 1559 and 1560 they were described by two Portuguese priests, Gonçalo da Silveira and Andre Fernandes. It was possible to compare Gwambe culture as it existed around 1900 with the mid-sixteenth-century baseline through the use of elderly European and African

informants interviewed a few years ago, as well as through the use
of the literature of those who had contacts with the Gwambe and
their neighbors late in the nineteenth century (Fuller 1955). It
would consume more space than is desirable to list all the cultural
traits that remained constant over a period of over three-and-one-
half centuries of time. They included essentially the whole of the
economy and material culture, social structure, and social
mechanisms. "Dress, whether in 1559, 1800, 1822, or 1900, varied
little" (Fuller 1955:98). Similarly steadfast were "religious rites and
secular affairs in which drinking, music, and dancing were important" (Fuller 1955:110). A few more instances, randomly selected,
of the persistence of Gwambe traits, include: the technique of
manufacture of bark cloth, the marimba as the chief musical instrument, the *lobola* or dowry for obtaining a wife, generation and
primogeniture as the basis of a man's social and political position,
emphasis on the patrilineal and patriarchal family, worship of the
*mozimo* or ancestral spirits, and trial by ordeal. Even at a third
point in their history, about 1950, "the description of the culture as
given by the Portuguese priests would be recognized by the
Gwambe as applying to themselves today except for minor details"
(Fuller 1955:251).

An outstanding application of the anthropological check method
in the solution of a problem of identification is one made by three
specialists in the American Indian (Kroeber 1925:275–278; Heizer
and Elmendorf 1942; Heizer 1947). It happens that it too is linked
with Drake, but this time in an attempt to solve the problem of
locating his anchorage in California, over which there has been
much disagreement. Using ethnographic and linguistic materials
contained in *The World Encompassed* and other early sources,
Robert F. Heizer concludes in a monograph written expressly on
the subject that Drake could not have seen the Yurok Indians, and
while the culture described by Fletcher and others could apply to
either the Pomo or the Coast Miwok, the linguistic evidence favors
the latter (Heizer 1947:278–279). Although allowing here and there
for minor changes over a span of three-and-one-half centuries, the
anthropologists investigating Drake's anchorage have assumed the
kind of cultural stability for which I have been pleading.

# The Carolinian Suspects

ARE THE CLUES scattered here and there in the testimony of Francis Fletcher and John Drake enough to identify the "thieves" who boarded the *Golden Hind*?

Certain South Sea islanders have good alibis and are beyond suspicion. For instance, the Melanesian culture area lies wholly south of the equator, whereas the scene of the pilfering was north of it.

Polynesia, too, except for a few barren islands and the Hawaiian archipelago, is in the southern hemisphere.[1] The southernmost point in Hawaii, however, is at a parallel of 18°40′ N and therefore too high in latitude. Besides, the Hawaiian islands were not discovered until 1778, when the incomparable Captain Cook was on his third and final voyage of exploration in the Pacific. This was mostly because the winds that were used to make a round trip to the Orient by sea went far to the north or south of the group. The track of the Spanish galleons did not come close to it.

As for the islands of Micronesia, geographic considerations eliminate most but not all of them. The Marianas are not under suspicion because Guam, the southernmost island of the chain, lies at 13°15′ N at its lowest tip. The Marshall and Gilbert groups are, among other things, too far east. This leaves the Carolines, specifically Palau, Yap, Ngulu, Ulithi, Sorol, and Woleai, all mentioned in the opening chapter. To them will be applied geographic, demographic, and ethnological tests.

## THE QUESTION OF LOCATION

Of all the islands in the Carolinian archipelago the one farthest
north is Ulithi Atoll, sometimes referred to in the literature as
Mogmog or the Mackenzie Islands. At its northernmost end it is
located at a parallel of 10°05′ N. Aside from the fact that it is not
hopelessly situated in terms of latitude, the reason why some have
suspected it is because they have assumed that Drake first skirted
the Marianas and then headed southwest, in which event Ulithi
would have been in his path. Yet from John Drake's second deposition we are told that the *Golden Hind* had already sailed close to the
equator before veering northward to reach 9 degrees. Francis
Drake was probably completely unaware of Ulithi, whose discovery is surrounded with uncertainty. Historical records bearing on
the atoll indicate that it could have been discovered from about
1525 to 1527 by the Portuguese Diogo da Rocha, sailing from the
Moluccas, and was possibly visited in 1537 or 1538 by another
Portuguese, Francisco de Castro, sent also from the Moluccas on a
proselytizing mission (Sharp 1960:14–15). Ruy Lopez de Villalobos, sailing from Mexico, may have sighted it in 1543 (Sharp
1960:28–29). Despite the strong likelihood that at least one of these
men saw Ulithi, we do not get a firm report until Bernard de Egui
anchored there in 1712 (Krämer 1917:75).

Yap has been under some suspicion, but someone who is meticulous might argue that it is too far north, with its southern end at
9°26′. While this latitude is too high for Fletcher it certainly is not
too high for Drake's young cousin. Anyway, it is better located
than Ulithi, so that it must be kept under surveillance for the time
being. Historical records relative to its discovery indicate that it,
too, may have been sighted from about 1525 to 1527 by the same
Rocha (Sharp 1960:14–15). It may also have been seen in 1543 by
Villalobos (Sharp 1960:27–28). However, the first firm report of
discovery does not come until the Nassau Fleet, under the command of Gheen Hugo Schapenham, sighted it in 1625 (Sharp
1960:79). Needless to say, this was after Drake's voyage.

The significance of the Villalobos and Nassau Fleet voyages is
that their efforts to reach the Philippines and the Moluccas brought
them into the vicinity of Ulithi and Yap. In like manner, Drake's
projected route could have carried him to the same area.

The four remaining islands under scrutiny have acceptable latitudes—Palau (at Babelthuap), 7°30'; Ngulu, 8°36'; Sorol, 8°07'; Woleai, 7°22'—although it could be argued that the first and last are too low for John Drake. But he was testifying from memory.

Whether these islands meet more than the geographical test remains to be seen. For the moment it should be observed that all but Palau are atolls. Palau is mostly a group of high islands. Neither Fletcher nor John Drake come to our aid by telling us whether the Island of Thieves was high or low.

Some information concerning the discovery of each of those islands with suitable latitudes may be of use in helping to make a judgment about them. The first firm report of the discovery of Palau was not made until 1710, when Francisco Padilla found it after having been sent to find the islands which were known from earlier explorations to exist to the east of the Philippines (Sharp 1960:94). But Padilla was not on the usual trans-Pacific sea lanes; he had sailed from Manila. It is possible that the Portuguese discovered Palau almost two centuries before Padilla. Even if this were so, they were on a special mission out of the Moluccas and not on the usual east-west or west-east tracks. The point is that Palau is off the beaten path of the Moluccan-bound mariner, otherwise it would have been discovered much earlier than it was.

Ngulu and Sorol were discovered very early, by Arellano of the *San Lucas* in 1565 (Sharp 1960:36). His route, however, was irregular in that it took him through the Marshalls, after which he discovered the Carolinian islands of either Oroluk or Minto Reef, Truk, and Pulap, as well as Ngulu and Sorol (Sharp 1960:36). But Villalobos had taken much the same route before him. Ngulu and Sorol may be considered to be reasonably close to the usual east-west transit of most voyagers, even though to the south of it. Drake could have followed a route that would have taken him to either atoll.

Woleai is a different matter. One has to go out of his way to encounter it. It was not discovered until 1797, when James Wilson of the missionary ship *Duff* stopped there (Sharp 1960:180). Captain Wilson's route was atypical, to say the least. His route took him from Tonga to the Marquesas, Mangareva, the Tuamotus, back to Tonga, then to Fiji, and from there to various islands of the western Carolines, of which he discovered not only Woleai but also

Satawal, Lamotrek, Elato, and Ifaluk. The lateness of his discoveries, as well as their large number, would argue that Woleai could hardly be considered to be on the Moluccas run.

## THE DEMOGRAPHIC TEST

Turning now to the next criterion, which is that of demography, certain places fail utterly to meet the specifications and on that account alone could be eliminated from further consideration. Nevertheless, they will be retained until they have been thoroughly examined. All of them are atolls.

Such islands suffer from severe ecological limitations. Their low limestone islets provide a limited range of resources, being at the very margin of nonfertility, with virtually no minerals and no humus. The problem of fresh groundwater is acute, for not only is it in scant supply but often brackish in quality. However, in contrast marine life is highly developed both on the reefs and in the lagoon, providing the inhabitants with much of their sustenance. Were it not for the sea, it would not have been possible for certain islands of this kind to have supported the relatively dense populations known to have flourished under aboriginal conditions.

One of the lesser populated atolls under investigation is Ngulu, which had thirty-five inhabitants in 1843 (Cheyne 1852:141). It had about one hundred in 1870, about fifty in 1909, and sixty-four in 1930 (Eilers 1936:214). It cannot be objected that these figures reflect depopulation of the severe sort known to have been prevalent in many Pacific islands after contact with Europeans. Under optimal conditions the number of persons who could be supported on Ngulu could never reach the necessary requisite.

Moreover, it is altogether possible that Ngulu was settled only in recent years and that no one lived there at the time of Drake. There is an oral tradition which suggests this. It tells of a Ulithian who was rewarded with a Yapese bride for his services to the chief of a village on Yap. He kept expressing a burning desire to go fishing for *likh*, so that after much pleading he was given a canoe and allowed to sail with his wife and some Yapese. He found Ngulu. The landfall, as the story goes, was not altogether fortuitous, for the man had heard of the existence of the place and had planned secretly to find it. Upon his return to Yap the chief gave him permission to settle there with his wife, and they begat children, who in turn begat other children, until a colony was established (Lessa 1961:45–47). It is true that oral tradition is notoriously unreliable for historical reconstruction, unless the time span is moderate. If this tale of discovery recounts an adventure that took place no more, let us say, than two centuries prior to the present time, it may be said to have some credibility, especially since it is not embellished by incredible or supernatural motifs.

Regardless of the story, which does not preclude the possibility that it deals with a resettlement, the accounts of European voyagers would seem to suggest that at least in certain periods of time the atoll was devoid of people. For instance, Arellano, the discoverer of Ngulu, does not mention seeing either canoes or signs of habitation when he sailed past the atoll in 1565 (*Col. doc. inéd. ultramar* 1885–1932:III, 27). The great French explorer Dumont d'Urville arrived in 1828 on the *Astrolabe* and doubled the atoll in a northerly direction, saying he cruised the two islands to the north for less than an hour and was unable to discover a trace of population, and that he surveyed the four southern islands, too, but he makes no comment about signs of habitation there, present or absent (Dumont d'Urville 1830–1834:V, 393, 394). None of this is conclusive evidence that Ngulu was uninhabited in 1565 and 1828, but it suggests that such was possible, or at least that there were too few inhabitants to make it worth commenting on. Certainly, the atoll was inhabited at some times, even if only by a few natives, for Kadu, the Woleaian who accompanied the explorer Kotzebue on his 1815–1818 expedition, says that there were "not above thirty people on Ngulu" early in the last century (Kotzebue 1821:III, 133). In the second edition of his book of sailing directions, James Horsburgh briefly notes that "the inhabitants come off their canoes at times, to ships passing near, bringing with them coconuts, smoked fish, and pieces of cloth of their own manufacture" (Horsburgh 1817:II, 440). On March 12, 1834, according to reliable records, some natives of Ngulu attacked the Boston schooner *Dash*, killing three men and wounding the captain, who managed to escape with the remainder of the crew (Ward 1966–1967:V, 152–158). Whether or not the atoll was occupied continuously or sporadically, it surely never had a population of any great magnitude.

Another way of looking at the matter of Ngulu's demographic

qualifications is through secondhand reports made by early missionaries. In 1696 Father Clain interviewed some Carolinians who had been cast on the island of Samar in the Philippines and obtained from them the names of thirty-two islands with which they were familiar. One of them was "Lamuliur," another name for Ngulu. They named three islands, of the thirty-two, which they said were "inhabited only by birds," the others being populated by a "numberless multitude of men" (Clain 1700:403). Ngulu was not one of the places specifically mentioned as being without people, so there is the likelihood that it had a population of some sort. As for the "numberless multitude of men," it must be remembered that the natives of the atolls who were shipwrecked on Samar came from an area where only a few thousand people would seem to them to be an enormous population.[2]

Father Cantova, a Jesuit missionary who interviewed some Carolinians stranded on Guam in 1721, found out from them that "Six or eight leagues distant [from Yap] are three other small islands, Ngolii, Laddo, and Petangras, which form a triangle" (Cantova 1728:217).[3] He reports no more than that, so we do not know if Ngulu was inhabited at the time. The inference, however, is that if the castaways on both Guam and Samar remembered to include this atoll in their listings, it must have had some significance. It could have been occupied, even if only sporadically.

Whatever else may be said about Ngulu, there is nothing to encourage the belief that it ever sheltered the two thousand or more souls needed to qualify as Drake's island.

The small atoll of Sorol is just as unqualified as Ngulu. When Arellano discovered it in 1565 he was greeted by a mere two canoes, a "fleet" hardly worthy of an Island of Thieves. It is reported to have had a population of 20 inhabitants in 1862 (Gulick 1862:363). It had 20 in 1900, 72 in 1903, 156 in 1909, and 75 in 1914 (Damm 1938:229). Occasionally, no one has lived there, as in the early part of the last century (Kotzebue 1821:III, 136) and again in 1933 (Damm 1938:229).

Ulithi Atoll has always been reported to have had more people than either Ngulu or Sorol, yet it too must be eliminated by the demographic test. The earliest head count was taken there in 1731 by the same Father Cantova who had interviewed the castaways on Guam a few years before. Their accounts had filled him with a burning desire to visit their homeland and convert as many pagan souls as possible to the religion of Christ. Soon after establishing his little mission he managed to take a crude census, although shortly afterwards he and all his men, except for a Filipino boy, were massacred by the angry natives. According to the census there were 592 people living on the atoll (Carrasco 1881:263–279). Even though most evangelists of the time were prone to exaggerate the numbers of their potential flocks, he had already begun his baptisms of the young and was probably well aware of the numbers yet to be administered the sacrament. The maximum population on record is 797, tallied by the German government in 1903 (Senfft 1904). I have taken two censuses, the first showing 421 inhabitants in 1949 (Lessa 1955) and the second showing an increase to 514 in 1960 (Lessa and Myers 1962).[4]

Woleai, slightly dubious because of its low latitude, has consistently had a larger population than any of the three preceding atolls. The question is, How much bigger? Enough to qualify? Some startling figures from more than one ethnohistorical source cause one to wonder.

We can begin with Captain James Wilson, the discoverer of the atoll. He estimated that in 1797 there were 3,150 heads on Woleai, a number that would more than fill the requirements. However, neither he nor any other persons on the London Missionary Society ship *Duff* went ashore. His estimate was arrived at when his crew counted the canoes that came out to the ship and found there were 150, each manned by seven persons on the average, making 1,050 in all. He explains his method for arriving at the total population as follows:

> if we add half as many left on shore, and double that number for the women and children, the population of this group alone will amount to three thousand one hundred and fifty souls, which according to the appearance of the islands, must often be pinched for food. (Wilson et al. 1799:302)

The total is so large for an atoll that I would prefer to find both the count and the methodology in error, but to do so would require me to renounce Fletcher's estimates and my own method of calculation, however independently it may have been conceived. True, there were some women in the canoes, but not enough to make a difference, unless some remained at a distance and could not be identified as to their sex. The encounter was a peaceful one, enabling the tally to be made without pressure.

As if this jolt were not enough, corroboration of a sort comes from Louis de Freycinet, sailing on the frigate *Uranie* on orders from the French government. He says that early in the last century there were three thousand people on Woleai (Freycinet 1827–1839:II[l], 102). He did not visit the atoll in his circumnavigation of the globe but obtained his information on Guam from a native pilot from Satawal Atoll, which is not far from Woleai.

A hint that both Wilson and Freycinet may have been wrong comes from a statement by Krusenstern to the effect that in 1787 Woleai had only one thousand inhabitants (Krusenstern 1819:93). His source was Admiral Josef Espinosa, who got his information from a native of Lamotrek, closer still to Woleai than Satawal. This native had been wrecked on Guam with twelve others on May 26, 1787. One thousand inhabitants would be too few for Drake's island.

The figure rises again with Andrew Cheyne, an unscrupulous trader and adventurer who published a useful book of sailing directions and other information. According to him there were 1,500 souls on Woleai when he was there in 1844 (Cheyne 1852:137–138). This represents a reduction of Wilson's figure by more than half but is still surprisingly high. It is not enough, however, for the Island of Thieves.

The population estimates for Woleai keep declining as the years go by. It is hard to know if this is due to greater caution in making conjectures or reflects depopulation due to European influence. At any rate, the medical missionary Luther H. Gulick gives a total of only "perhaps 600" people on Woleai around 1862 (Gulick 1862:174). This is less than one-fifth of Wilson's estimate, made only two-thirds of a century before. Gulick does not give the specific source of his figure but he seems to have consulted all available records in his survey of all the Micronesian islands.

Around 1905 Woleai was holding fairly steady with 661 inhabitants, if we can accept a German government count (Senfft 1905:54). In 1935 it had 570, according to a Japanese report (Department of the Navy 1944:34). According to a rough American calculation it had 488 in 1958 (Trust Territory 1959:5). All this was during a period of admitted depopulation. But the decline from 1797, if Wilson's estimate is reliable, is remarkable.

A wholly fresh approach to the problem of the shortcomings of atolls is not through past population estimates but the capacity of such islands to support the large population demanded by the Fletcher account. For Ngulu Atoll to support the minimum of 2,200 souls, as Table 1 indicates, it would have to have a population density of 12,941.2 persons per square mile, and Sorol Atoll a density of 6,111.1. This of course is absurd, as the people would have little more than standing room.

Table 1. Hypothetical and Actual Population Densities of the Carolinian Suspects

| Island Group | Land Area (sq. miles) | Population Density per Square Mile | |
|---|---|---|---|
| | | Hypothetical (1579) | Actual (1951) |
| Ngulu Atoll | .17 | 12,941.2 | 288.2 |
| Sorol Atoll | .36 | 6,111.1 | 27.8 |
| Woleai Atoll | 1.75 | 1,257.1 | 230.3 |
| Ulithi Atoll | 1.80 | 1,222.2 | 262.8 |
| Yap Islands | 38.67 | 57.0 | 71.7 |
| Palau Islands | 189.00 | 11.6 | 34.8 |

SOURCES: The figures for the land area and the 1951 actual population density are taken from the Department of the Navy, *Report on the Administration of the Trust Territory of the Pacific Islands, for the Period July 1, 1950, to June 30, 1951* (p. 80). The hypothetical densities have been calculated by me on the assumption that there were 2,200 inhabitants on the Island of Thieves.

The two other atolls would have very high densities, too, but nowhere near as much as these. Ulithi, with a larger dry-land surface than either Ngulu or Sorol, would have to have a density of 1,222.2, which is not completely out of the question but is far-fetched if actual censuses over a span of more than two centuries are kept in mind. Woleai would need a density of 1,257.1 persons per square mile, which is high enough, yet if in 1797 there indeed were 3,150 people there, the density would have to have been 1,800.0 persons per square mile, a crowding that strains one's credulity. On account of this, Wilson's estimate seems all the more questionable.

As for the compact island group of Yap it has a land surface of 38.67 square miles and in 1951, close to the nadir of population, had a density of 71.7 persons per square mile (Department of the Navy

1951:80). Yap can support a large population because it is west of the andesite line and therefore continental in nature. In 1899 it had 7,808 inhabitants (Hanaihara 1939:41), with possibly far more than that at the peak of overpopulation before the coming of the first European explorers into the area. But it could not have had anywhere near the peak of 51,000 speculatively estimated by Schneider, who assumed that both the abandoned and occupied dwelling sites he saw in 1947–1948 were once occupied simultaneously (Hunt, Kidder, and Schneider 1954:22). As Table 1 shows, even under the severe depopulation being endured in 1951, Yap had an actual population density beyond that required by the hypothetical figure. In short, it had enough men to man the canoes belonging to the "vngracious company."

The Palau cluster, which has remained in the running on account of its favorable latitude, has an area of 189.0 square miles of dry land (Department of the Navy 1951:80), some of it being of volcanic origin and therefore vastly richer than the coralline soils of the atolls. Even during the period from 1880 to 1920, when the ravages of newly introduced diseases had reduced the population to its lowest point, all of the larger islands of the group continued to support great numbers of people. For the year 1783, a retrospective figure of forty thousand to fifty thousand people was proposed by Semper (1873:350–352), with subsequent declines to about one-tenth that number. As Table 1 indicates, the Fletcher-Drake sources would require a hypothetical population density of only 11.6 people per square mile, whereas the actual density has consistently surpassed that ratio. However, it is necessary to bear in mind that the islands of Palau extend in a narrow chain stretching seventy-seven miles in length and it would be unreasonable to suppose that all of their inhabitants knew of the arrival of the *Golden Hind*. Nonetheless, Palau without question must be considered on the basis of population to qualify more readily than any other Carolinian island under consideration.

All this leads to the inevitable question as to what population density is possible on an atoll. Augustin Krämer states loosely that one thousand people can subsist on the products of one square kilometer of atoll land under very favorable conditions (1937:201). But there is no simple formula for estimating population support capacities; indeed, there is no formula at all. As Wiens reminds us in his fine work, *Atoll Environment and Ecology*, there have been no satisfactory analyses of the problem of population pressure on the food and other resources of human livelihood on coral atolls. The facts simply are not available to construct a suitable formula for the satisfaction of minimum subsistence standards for man.

In evaluating population pressure on an atoll, says Wiens, it is necessary to take into account not only the per capita areas of land but the amount of rainfall as well, for wetness has a direct bearing on food productivity. And even though the land provides needed human food from vegetable sources and from such animals as are supported by terrestrial plant foods, the per capita areas of reef and lagoon are not to be overlooked. Such places are the habitat of fish, mollusks, and crustaceans. Moreover, just as the productivity of land varies with differences in rainfall, as well as soil and ground-water conditions, so the productivity of the reef, lagoon, and fringing sea varies with certain local conditions. The atoll reef area is the most important source of marine food, being as much as twenty-four times as productive of fish as a unit area of lagoon. Unfortunately, the qualitative data to verify qualitative comparison estimates are lacking, according to Wiens, and the population-support capacity is further complicated by the inclusion in land estimates of islands that are either barren or have vegetation that is not food-producing (Wiens 1962:458–462).

The real shortcoming of Carolinian atolls is not, however, merely a question of population density. These small islands simply do not have the land area, regardless of density, to support large populations. This is not true of the Marshalls and Gilberts, which have large atoll populations far exceeding those of the Carolines, but only because the land areas are large.[5]

## ETHNOGRAPHIC TESTS

The ethnographic evidence has been surprisingly neglected by everyone, excepting Krämer and also Hornell, who has expressed some curiosity about the identification of Drake's island. Yet it is as crucial as latitude and demography in arriving at the truth. The information has always been available to modern scholars, yet for some inexplicable reason it has generally been overlooked or misinterpreted, to say nothing of being occasionally corrupted.

Among the lesser traits of culture there are some that have limited diagnostic value for the reason that they are too prevalent throughout the island world of the Pacific; yet they constitute interesting facets of our search and at least merit some attention. These traits are: betel-nut chewing, lengthened ear lobes, long fingernails, blackened teeth, slings, darts, and perfidious tactics.

## WHO CHEWED A CERTAIN HERB

The natives of the Island of Thieves must have done enough chewing to have left an impression on Fletcher, whose description of what he saw leaves no doubt whatsoever that the people were addicted to the betel nut.

Three ingredients go into the making of an envelope of the concoction. First is the betel nut itself, its appearance being like that of a large acorn. It is the reddish seed of the areca palm (*Areca catechu*), and must be broken down into fragments or slices. The plant whose leaves supply the wrapper for the nut is the betel pepper (*Piper betle*) and is allied to the kava used by Fijians and Polynesians. The leaves impart an agreeable zest to the nut. The nut kernel is mixed with air-slaked lime, carried characteristically in a bamboo container. When these three ingredients are chewed they redden the saliva, which is produced in superabundance and often oozes untidily from the mouth. The veteran chewer shamelessly sprays his surroundings with his crimson expectorations. The effect of habitual chewing is to discolor the teeth a dark brown. Betel contains a harmless narcotic stimulant.

Many of the preceding facts are related more colorfully in the language of Captain Henry Wilson, who in 1783 was shipwrecked on Palau in the *Antelope*, a packet belonging to the East India Company.

> Each Chief had in his hand a basket of *beetle-nut*, and a bamboo finely polished and inlaid at each end, in which they carry their *Chinam*; this is coral burnt to a lime, which they shake out through one end of the bamboo where they carry it, on the leaf of the *beetle-nut*, before they chew it, to render it more useful, or palatable. It was observed that all their teeth were black, and that the *Beetle-nut* and *Chinam*, of which they always had a quid in their mouths, rendered their saliva red, which, together with their black teeth, gave their mouths a very disgusting appearance. (Keate 1793:27)

Wilson's account proves that the chewing of the betel is not a recent introduction on Palau. Horace Holden, an American seaman wrecked on Palau forty-nine years later, also mentions the chewing of the nut, which he calls *abooak* (Holden 1836:32).

Yap's ethnohistorical documentation does not extend very far back in time, so for this place it is necessary to rely on more recent evidences of betel-nut chewing. The English trader Captain Cheyne complained that when he was on Yap in 1843 a number of chiefs and natives looked on, "chewing betel-nut, but rendering no assistance," while a bêche de mer curing house was being built (Cheyne 1852:152). Alfred Tetens, a German sea captain and trader with much experience in Micronesia, says in his memoirs that King Karakok of Yap, when he was not smoking cigarettes or sipping beverages, was always "chewing betel nuts coated with lime" (Tetens 1958:11). Other nineteenth-century observers could be cited to substantiate these findings.

The chewing of betel among the Carolinian suspects is limited virtually to Palau and Yap, for only on these islands is it possible to grow the proper plant ingredients: the betel-nut palm with its red fruit and the betel pepper with its pungent leaves. Atolls cannot grow them with consistently successful results.[6]

The unlikelihood that the inhabitants of the low islands were regular masticators of the nut is borne out by the literature. An anthropologist with the Hamburg Südsee-Expedition of 1908–1910 who worked on Woleai makes no mention of betel (Krämer 1937). Neither does Arno Senfft, a district officer for the German government who was there ahead of him. In fact, he says, "the only stimulant used is tobacco" (1905:55). Had the Woleaians been chewers when the *Duff* stopped at their atoll it surely would have been mentioned by Captain Wilson, who is silent on the subject.

For Sorol, researchers with the Hamburg expedition say specifically that "the custom of betel chewing is unknown" (Damm 1938:230). No one has contradicted them.

There is no evidence that Ulithians have ever been chewers, except in a desultory way. Canoes and ships coming from Yap, I have observed, usually carry aboard some nuts and leaves for some men of the atoll. But communication between the two places has apparently never been common enough to insure a steady supply.[7] Anthropologist Paul Hambruch, who spent two weeks on Ulithi in 1909, confirms my own judgment when he says: "Betel has been brought from Yap, but it is not important" (Damm 1938:318).[8]

The residents of Ngulu may have been slightly more habituated to betel-nut chewing than those of Ulithi because of their closer proximity to Yap, with which it is strongly allied. Members of the Südsee-Expedition give no hint that the practice was present when they were on Ngulu early in the present century, although they do include native terms for betel pepper and betel lime in a word list for the atoll (Eilers 1936:242). Yet Kadu, a Woleaian who was picked up in 1817 in the Marshalls by the Kotzebue expedition, included Ngulu in those places where, he said, the custom of chewing the betel prevailed. The other islands were Palau, Yap, and the Marianas. Ngulu cannot be discounted as much as the other atolls, then, although by no stretch of the imagination could its people be considered addicted.

## WHO WENT NAKED

One wishes that the nudity of the men of the Island of Thieves were as conclusively asserted as their chewing of the betel. John Drake mentions it twice, but briefly. On the other hand, *The World Encompassed* and the "Famous Voyage" are silent on the subject, which is strange when one considers that a certain delicacy prevailed in such matters in the heavily constumed Europe of those days. One would expect some commentary.

If one looks at Palau, there is no equivocation concerning the sheer nudity of the men, and perhaps of the women, too. Josef Somera, pilot of the first ship known definitely to have visited the island group, is the apparent author of a map (Map 5) of the western Carolines, drawn in 1710, which is embellished in the upper left-hand corner with a crude drawing of three natives labeled: "FF. Picture of the Indians and people of Panloc completely nude" (Krämer 1917:71).

Two other firsthand observers have commented similarly on the Palauans' lack of clothing. One of these is the same Captain Wilson who described for us the use of betel nut in Palau when he was there. The other is Horace Holden, whose credentials are suggested by the title of his book, *A Narrative of the Shipwreck,*

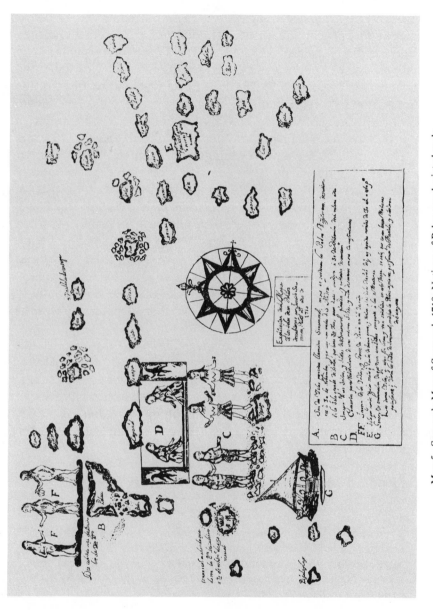

Map 5. Somera's Map of Sonsorol, 1710. Natives of Palau are depicted nude.
Source: Krämer 1917:71.

*Captivity and Sufferings of Horace Holden and Benj. H. Nute; Who Were Cast Away in the American Ship* Mentor, *on the Pelew Islands in the Year 1832*, etc. Holden twice says that the men "were entirely naked" (1836:32, 47). Wilson had said that the natives were "perfectly naked, having no kind of covering whatsoever" (Keate 1793:26), and further on had reaffirmed this description by saying that "the men were entirely naked" (Keate 1793:318). Indeed, when Abba Thule, the "king," went to pay a courtesy call on Wilson he "was perfectly naked" (Keate 1793:55).

The Carolinians who were stranded on Guam in 1721 told Father Cantova that on Palau "the men and women there are entirely nude" (Cantova 1728:218). This testimony, added to that of Somera, Wilson, and Holden, is too conclusive to allow for doubt, but two other witnesses should be allowed to testify. William Wilson says that when the missionary ship *Duff* arrived at Babelthuap in the Palau group, the men were quite naked "without seeming conscious of shame" (Wilson et al. 1799:308). Finally, Kadu supplies the statement that "only at Pelli the men are entirely naked" (Kotzebue 1821:III, 191). Would that all testimony were as convincing as this.

In contrast to Palau, the remainder of the west Caroline islands have never been said to lack clothing. The dress of the natives, especially the men, is remarkably uniform in the basic garments. Old records indicate that accessory clothes were once more ample than in modern times; but the usual clothing consisted essentially of a wraparound skirt for women (except on Yap) and a woven plant-fiber loincloth for men (Figure 13).

Perhaps the earliest notice in these matters is provided for an unidentified island, most likely Ulithi, where Diogo da Rocha stopped for four months in 1525–1526.

> Their dress consisted of woven material, which was very soft and flexible, and which served them as our shirts do us. On top of it they wore another long garment more coarsely woven, without any shape whatsoever, like a loose piece of cloth, that covered them from the waist down. (Barros 1563:260 r-v)

This statement is not very enlightening as to the exact nature of the garments, and the fault may be that of Barros, the sixteenth-century Portuguese historian who is our source. But the important

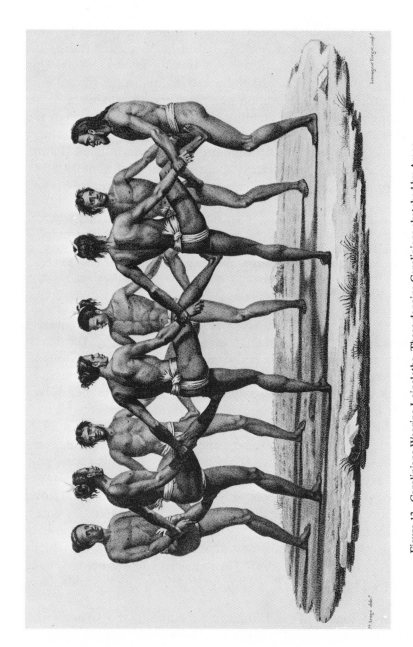

Figure 13. Carolinians Wearing Loincloths. These dancing Carolinians sketched by Arago, an artist with the Freycinet expedition, are incompletely naked. Note their elongated ear-lobes. Source: Freycinet 1827–1839:atlas, pl. 56. (*Courtesy Special Collections, UCLA Library*)

thing is that by no stretch of the imagination could one call these people, living on the so-called Islands of Sequeira, naked. However, it is altogether possible but not at all damaging that Barros has given us a description belonging to an entirely different locale. This is not implausible, for although he had access to the official Portuguese records of exploration he is not always reliable.

Other descriptions, fortunately, are more trustworthy. They are consistent with observations made by anthropologists and others who have seen western Carolinians at first hand. Thus, Father Clain, describing the garments worn by the "half nude" Carolinians from the Fais area who were stranded on Samar in 1696, says,

> The men have no clothing other than a sort of waistband which covers their loins and thighs, and which is wound several times around their bodies. On their shoulders they have more than an ell and a half of coarse cloth with which they make themselves a sort of hood that they tie by the fore-part and hang down carelessly in back. (Clain 1700:404)

The "waistband" seems much more like the conventional garment than does the "long garment" mentioned above by Barros. It is noteworthy that both he and Clain mention an upper garment, which seems to have had only a sporadic continuance into modern times. It was probably used by sea travelers to protect themselves against long exposure.

Of the Ulithians who came out to meet his vessel in 1712, Bernardo de Egui, captain and chief pilot of the patache *Santo Domingo de Guzman*, says, "They are almost nude and wear only a few leaves for decency" (Krämer 1917:98). If it was indeed leaves that they wore, they were possibly made from the unopened frond of the coconut palm, as on distant Ponape in the eastern Carolines. But they may not have really been leaves. At any rate, the men must also have worn the traditional loincloth known in modern times, for elsewhere he says, "They gave us some loincloths made of *abacá* [banana fiber]" (Krämer 1917:90). These would have been woven on a loom.

Anthropologists of the Hamburg expedition, who visited virtually all the Carolines early in the present century, are so consistent in describing the male garment that it is hardly worth citing them. Variations are mostly in patterns and the way in which the ends of the loincloths are arranged.

In view of all this it comes as a jolt to read that when Woleai was discovered in 1797 by Captain James Wilson of the *Duff*, he found that "The greater number of the men were naked also . . ." (Wilson et al. 1799:303). The culture of Woleai is remarkably akin to that of Ulithi, Ngulu, and Sorol, and all the other west Carolinian atolls, so that it would be incongruous for the people to have an atypical clothing practice.

Closer reading of Wilson's words, however, as well as those which form the context in which they occur, casts a different interpretation on what would seem to be the only instance of nudity in the western Carolines, exclusive of Palau. The commentator had just written in praise of the women—who had come out in canoes to greet the ship—for the "decency and modesty of their behavior," despite their being "almost naked" (Wilson et al. 1799:302). The men could have been naked only in the sense that the women were nude—as they were—but only "almost." To dispel any doubt about this interpretation, the sentence about the men continues: "some had a sash mat wrapped around their middle; others added an ornamental belt round their body, near the navel" (p. 303). The evangelists on the ship were obviously sensitive to nudity and if it had been complete they undoubtedly would have expressed some revulsion at any exposure of the men's genitals.

The only conclusion that can be drawn is that Palau alone fits the description of the nudity attributed to the men of Drake's island. Elsewhere in the western Carolines, even though a great amount of flesh might be exposed to view, the genitals at least were covered. In all the archipelago the situation on Palau seems to have been paralleled only in Ponape and Ant, where the men encountered in 1529 by Saavedra were observed to be stark naked (*Col. doc. inéd. Indias* 1864–1884:V, 91).[9] But these places are far to the east and outside the scope of our inquiry.

## *WHO CUT THE EARS CIRCLEWISE*

As for the stretched ear lobes seen by the men of the *Golden Hind*, they are characteristic of the Carolines, including Palau, even though there may be some personal choice in the matter. Writing about Freycinet's Carolinians, who were seen both in some of their native atolls as well as in the Marianas where they were immigrants, Arago says that "the lobes of their ears [were] pierced with so large an opening that they descended almost to the shoulders" (Freycinet 1827–1839:II [1], 93). Arno Senfft, a German official, describes how the mutilation was performed on Yap early in the present century.

> When children are between ten and twelve years old, their ears are pierced by certain men, the wound is smeared with hot oil and a little bamboo rod (*morr*) put in the hole; every second day the opening is enlarged and later it is filled with the leaves of the *rietj* plant, a Dracaena. The hole is used for attaching ear ornaments of mussel shells, flowers, leaves, feathers, and so on. The opening is made larger in girls' ears than in boys'. (Senfft 1903:52)

Writing afterwards on the appearance of the typical Yapese youth, Willard Price says, "The hole in the lobe of his ear usually accommodated a package of cigarettes . . ." (Price 1936:75).

There is reliable evidence that the custom of distension is old on Ulithi, for Father Cantova has left a note about the practice as he observed it in the atoll in 1731, when he was there to set up a mission station (Carrasco 1881:267). He had already observed such lobes among some Carolinians from the same general area who had been marooned on Guam (Cantova 1728:198, 239).

For Ngulu there is no early mention of lobe distension, nevertheless there is documentation of its presence early in the present century: "To decorate their ears the natives wear rings made of coconut beads or coconut kernel (*ila*) . . ." (Eilers 1936:223). With their origins in Yapese and Ulithian culture, there can be no doubt that the natives of Ngulu followed the practice of ear mutilation from the beginning.

Early documentation is similarly lacking for Sorol, yet when the German anthropologist Ernst Sarfert was there in 1909 he found that the natives were decorating their ears by hanging shell and coconut rings from a small tortoise-shell ring inserted in the pierced ear lobes, and that young people liked to put leaves and blossoms in the holes (Damm 1938:235).

During this same period of time the natives of Woleai were seen decorating their ears in essentially the same way as was being practiced on Sorol, but Krämer, the source of this information, adds that the lobes were "not lengthened very much" (Krämer 1937:223). This seems strange, for Otto Senfft, who was on Woleai only a few years before, says that "the lobes of the ears are gradually distended until they can be drawn across the outer ear like a ribbon" (Senfft 1905:55). A picture of Kadu, the native of Woleai who accompanied Kotzebue on part of his expedition around the world, shows his left earlobe in profile, and it hangs below his jaw (Kotzebue 821: III, frontis.).

The lobes of the natives of Palau were long enough in the eighteenth century to have attracted the attention of the survivors of the *Antelope*, who noticed that the men had their left lobes bored (the women, the right) and that beads were inserted in them (Keate 1793:319). Arriving fourteen years later, the people on the *Duff* observed that the Palauans had a custom of "slitting the ear, through which some of them put vegetable ornaments at least an inch thick" (Wilson et al. 1799:307). Stretched lobes were noted among some Palauans brought to Hong Kong in the 1870s (Clapham 1877:92). In view of these observations, it is surprising to find a statement by an anthropologist of the Südsee-Expedition saying that, "The natives of Palau rarely distend the lobes of their ears and only to a slight degree, while the central Carolinians, especially the people of Yap, enlarge them considerably" (Krämer 1917:11).

The natives of Palau may not have been particularly given to elongating their lobes between 1908 and 1910 but they nevertheless did so in earlier times. This enables them to qualify in this respect, at least, as the "thieves." Also qualifying, however, are the indigenes of Yap, Ngulu, Ulithi, Sorol, and Woleai.

## WHO WORE LONG FINGERNAILS

The long fingernails seen by Drake and his men seem to have left an impression, as well they might, for they were completely alien to Elizabethan seamen who had seen no other aboriginals than those of the New World. However, the literature on the Carolines is almost as silent as a mummy on the subject. There is no reference to fingernails in those publications of the Südsee-Expedition dealing with Palau, Yap, Ngulu, Ulithi, Sorol, and Woleai. Other publications dealing with these islands are apparently as mute. Thus, Gaimard fails to mention fingernails in his anthroposcopic study of various west central Carolinians, including Woleaians (Freycinet 1827–1839:II [1], 93–96).

However, there is an occasional reference to long nails occurring elsewhere in the Carolines. On Truk, fingernails up to five centimeters long are found once in a while among chiefs and are called *ku tam* (Krämer 1932:97). Truk is not one of the places under consideration as Drake's island, but its culture is so characteristic of most of the atolls of the central and western Carolines, including Ngulu, Ulithi, Sorol, and Woleai, as to suggest that the practice cannot be ruled out for those places, and possibly Yap, too. Lütke, who was in the Mortlocks in 1828, is of some assistance when he writes: "Several *tamols* (chiefs), like Chinese dandies, let their fingernails grow" (Lütke 1835–1836:II, 69). An anthropologist who worked in the Nomoi or Mortlock Islands, echoes his words, saying that a few chiefs "let the nails of their forefingers grow long like the Chinese" (Krämer 1935:10).

There is an occasional hint in the literature that some Carolinians used elongated fingernails as a weapon in fighting. Indeed, in a tale which I collected on Ulithi a dreadnaught kills ten ogres, one by one, by slashing off their heads with his long thumbnail (Lessa 1961:58–59). Fiction may possibly follow fact, allowing of course for exaggeration in the efficacy of this mode of attack. Another possible explanation for allowing the nails to grow long is that they assist a *bwe* diviner in slicing young coconut leaflets into strips in preparation for the divinatory ritual. This usage has in fact been confirmed in the literature (Lessa 1969:357).

On account of these suggestions, it is not possible to dismiss the occurrence of long fingernails out of hand. We must concede that the trait may have had currency in all our islands, except for Palau, where Krämer says the people did not have long nails (1917:11). Unfortunately, the ethnohistorical literature, which is often so useful in other respects, does not come to our aid in resolving the problem more conclusively.

## WHO BLACKENED THEIR TEETH

I have some preliminary comments to make regarding the teeth "blacke as pitch," described in these words by *The World Encompassed*. I suggest that Fletcher's explanation that the discoloration came from chewing the betel nut is not the right one. Habitual mastication produces a dirty dark-brown color rather than a really black one. I am not an authority in such matters and base my conviction on the betel-stained teeth I have seen among such inveterate chewers as the Balinese and the Yapese. One would suppose that the literature would be of some assistance in this respect, but all I have been able to find are statements about discoloration, or about "blackness" in the sense of dirtiness.[10] What I think that Fletcher saw was a purposeful blackening produced by the use of herbs applied to the teeth for that purpose. I have seen artificially blackened teeth in the Carolines and would never confuse them with betel-stained teeth. Accordingly, I shall treat black teeth as a separate trait from nut-stained teeth.

The Germans, with their customary thoroughness, have given us a good account of the blackening process as they encountered it on Yap at the turn of the century.

> In this place it is fitting to mention also the Jap people's curious custom of staining their teeth black. In the early stages of puberty the girls begin to change their beautiful, snow-white teeth into black horrors. In the whole expanse of the island there is only one place, the village of Gatschalau in the district of Nimigil, where the earth necessary for this operation is found, in a swamp. The earth is well-pulverized, put in the cooked leaves of the *kell* tree and pounded up with them, and now placed on the teeth in the evening by means of a little wooden stick. The paste remains on all night and is spat out in the morning. By repeating this process several times a month, in time it becomes possible to obtain brilliant black teeth. In the early years it is still easy to regain the original white by scraping, later this becomes ever more difficult and finally the teeth retain their black color to the end. The earth bears the name of *rungedu*. In addition the Jap people use the blossoms of various trees which, when rubbed in, serve to blacken the teeth. (Germany, Reichstag 1903:5524)

Contrary to the revulsion felt by the man who penned these words, those who practice blackening see much aesthetic merit in it, as the following example illustrates. It comes from Yap.

> Being a young man of fashion, his teeth were a gleaming ebony. This effect had been achieved not merely by the stains of betel-chewing but by a special blackening process, using a paste of groundsel and other herbs applied to the teeth every day for five days.
> "Too bad," said Tol. "Makes very sick. But it gives good black, yes?" And he displayed his teeth from ear to ear. (Price 1936:27)

A Japanese ethnographer who visited Yap in 1915 asserts that the blackening of teeth there was "almost limited to women only" (Matsumura 1918:96), but he must have observed inadequately.

Captain Wilson of the East India Company found, much earlier than the above observations had been made for Yap, that Palauan men and women blackened their teeth by mixing various herbs with a little *chinam* (burned lime) into a paste, which was applied every morning while the patients lay with their heads on the floor. The process was very painful and took five days to complete (Keate 1793:319–320). Holden, the American who was cast away on Palau in 1832, speaks of the teeth of the people as being entirely black, but he mistakenly attributes it to the chewing of betel and not the special concoction mentioned by Wilson (Holden 1836:32).

It is puzzling that the eminent German ethnologist Augustin Krämer, in arguing against Palau as the island where Drake tarried, lists as one of his reasons the following: "The natives of Palau do have black teeth from chewing betel, but they do not blacken them on purpose, as is the custom among the people of Yap and the Chamorros" (1917:11). It is one thing to be ignorant of the facts, and another to fly in the face of them. Krämer not only knew of Wilson's observations on the deliberate blackening of teeth on Palau but includes an extensive quotation from the nineteenth-century Russian anthropologist Mikluko-Maclay to the effect that the blackening of the teeth was known as *molau* or *melau* and was a painful operation which was endured because white teeth were regarded as ugly. Krämer also notes a comment by the Polish anthropologist Kubary to the effect that only those people who had had their teeth blackened dared to eat the locust shrimp, the others fearing that their teeth might turn striped like the animal.[11] To cap it all, Krämer even gives us the recipe—from his own field notes!—for preparing the paste (1926:32–33). So much for Palau.

As for the atolls, the people did not have the necessary ingredients to blacken their teeth, so they would have had to wait until a visit to Yap. As a consequence, in my opinion, relatively few men had the operation. An additional line of reasoning causes me to think that blackening was really a means of masking the still uglier discoloration caused by chewing the betel, and if this were so, then the residents of the atolls had little need for making their teeth black.[12] So does Gaimard's statement that the teeth of Freycinet's

Pulusuk-Puluwat-Pulap Carolinians—all likewise atoll dwellers—were a dazzling white (Freycinet 1827–1839:II [1], 93). I am therefore inclined to disqualify the people of Ngulu, Ulithi, Sorol, and Woleai as Drake's thieves, at least on this score. The silence of ethnohistorical and other sources on the subject encourages me to do so.

### WHO THREW STONES

The stone sling, a clue whose presence on Drake's island has been inferred, used to be widespread throughout much of Oceania, especially Polynesia and Micronesia. It was never the principal weapon, being subsidiary to spears and clubs, but it had a respected place in the warrior's armamentarium. For obvious reasons, it has been said, early missionaries to the islands found their converts especially appreciative of the biblical story of David and Goliath.

Members of the Hamburg expedition of 1908–1910 testify to the more modern occurrence of the sling in the Carolines, but among the exceptions are Ngulu, Sorol, and Woleai. The absence of the weapon on these atolls is to be explained, no doubt, as the result of the pacification that followed in the wake of European control. In the old days the sling must have had some place in the culture. Indeed, it is known to have been present in Woleai, at least, when the *Duff* was there in 1797 (Wilson et al. 1799:304), and was still to be found in the atoll a few years later, according to information given to Chamisso by Kadu, his Woleaian informant (Kotzebue 1821:III, 214). Captain Cheyne also mentions it (Cheyne 1852:138).

Although there are no early accounts to show that the sling was to be found in Ulithi and Yap in the old days, it must have had some existence then, for it was reported present when members of the Hamburg expedition collected specimens for their museum. Indeed, Captain Cheyne saw "slings and stones" in Yap in 1843 (Cheyne 1852:146). If the people of Yap had them, the natives of nearby Ulithi must have had them too, albeit their stones would have had to have been coralline.

Palau's response to the criterion of the sling is surprising. Captain Wilson makes no mention of the weapon, even though he was there for three months while building a vessel to replace the one that had been shipwrecked. Inasmuch as he devotes some attention to Palauan weapons, especially the spear and the dart thrower, his omission of the sling may be significant. A German anthropologist of the Hamburg expedition says that he found the weapon only on the little island of Ngajangel in the Palau group (Krämer 1926:130). Jan S. Kubary of the Museum Godeffroy had said much the same thing before that, writing that the sling was "quite like that of the Caroline Islands" and "was formerly used by the inhabitants of the Kayangl group," but was not adopted by the Palau islanders proper (Kubary 1892:156). Kayangel or Ngajangel (spelled both ways and more) is an atoll about fifteen miles north of the main Palauan group and is often treated separately from it. It is not characteristically Palauan. Therefore, the criterion of the sling is not truly met by the Palau Islands.

## WHO CARRIED DARTS

The presence of the dart in the Carolines is well attested to, even though the word "dart" implies a hurling weapon, whereas the literature more often speaks loosely of "spears," which of course may be either hurled or thrust. It is not always possible to know which of the two is meant in any given instance, but it is very likely that all localities made use of both types. Sometimes there is no equivocation, as when mention is made of dart throwers. At any rate, the clue is not a vital one and is mentioned only in one of John Drake's two depositions. We must pursue it only because of the need to track down anything at all that might have a bearing on the problem of the Island of Thieves.

We may begin with Palau, where the evidence of darts is good. As we shall see later on, the indigenes who stole from Padilla's *Santísima Trinidad* were armed with spears. Detailed information on throwing spears is given by Kubary, who also provides drawings (Kubary 1892:155–156; pl. XXII). Earlier than that, it was noted by Captain Wilson that in 1783 the arms of the men of the king of Peleliu "consisted of bamboo darts from five to eight feet long, pointed with the wood of the betel-nut tree and bearded," these being used for close quarters; but for distance they had short ones which they threw with a bamboo dart thrower (Keate 1793:88–89). It was observed by Mathias Wilson, brother of the captain of the *Antelope*, that in the battle between antagonistic kings on Palau, in which some of the stranded English took part, "spears were mutually directed with much animosity" (Keate 1793:139), and in a later battle the English and their Peleliu allies "were often greatly annoyed by the enemy, who rushed down on us with a shower of spears" (Keate 1793:168). Elsewhere, Captain Wilson comments that spears were the chief weapon in Palau and says that darts were hurled with the aid of slings or dart throwers (Keate 1793:314). Finally, mention of spears is made three times in Holden's account of his being shipwrecked on Palau (Holden 1836:32, 37, 45), but it is not clear if they could be hurled.

There is no denying that the natives of Yap were possessed of darts. Among the weapons seen on Yap in 1817 were bamboo "javelins, long wooden pikes, and slings" (Choris 1822:19). Darts hurled with the aid of a bamboo dart thrower also have been reported for these islands, and so have two-pointed lances "thrown straight, and merely by the hand" (Kotzebue 1821:III, 213). A later observer writes that "the most formidable of all the Caroline spears were those of Yap, fashioned out of the wood of the *Bû* or areca palm" (Christian 1899:137), but, if he is right in saying that they were often nearly twelve feet in length, they must have been a thrusting rather than a throwing weapon. However, spears appearing in some of the photographs of his book seem short enough to be hurled. In 1909–1910 a member of the Thilenius expedition found a considerable variety of spears on Yap, and these are abundantly illustrated in the report of his research (Müller-Wismar 1917–1918:I, 189–191, table 59).

For Ngulu the evidence is not wholly conclusive. A member of the Thilenius expedition found no spears early in the century, which is not surprising in view of the fact that the Germans were in control at that time, but the natives were said to have known fishing and fighting spears in former times (Eilers 1936:232).

Natives of Ulithi, when questioned by members of the Thilenius expedition in 1909, at first denied that they had any spears, but when Hellwig discovered several of them, still others were brought to light, and the fact was stressed that these were old pieces that had been manufactured on the islands (Thilenius and Hellwig 1927:230; see also Damm 1938:339). As these spears were used also for fishing they could have been hurled.

Sorol provides for us an interesting example of the need to take negative evidence of a trait with some caution where the circumstances of culture contact have intervened in a manner to weaken or eliminate the trait. Thus, a member of the Thilenius expedition writes: "There are no weapons. Spears were used only for fishing. . . . Slings, bows and arrows are unknown. . . . Apparently the natives never engaged in wars, for the natives have no recollection of battles" (Damm 1938:265). Yet Arellano tells us that men armed with spears as well as clubs came out to meet the *San Lucas* at Sorol in 1565 (*Col. doc. inéd. ultramar* 1885–1932:III, 26, 27).

Evidence has been given early in the last century of the presence of spears on Woleai (Kotzebue 1821:II, 421), but it should be noted that they are not reported by Captain Wilson of the *Duff* nor by Krämer of the Thilenius expedition.

### WHO FEIGNED HONESTY

Did the "thieves" of Drake's island have a distinctive style of procedure, a *modus operandi*, that might betray their identity? The question has some merit and cannot be dismissed categorically.

The behavior of Drake's indigenes was doubtlessly motivated by larcenous exuberance and impelled by basic human aggressiveness, executed in accordance with a simple plan of duplicity. The situation was not new. It had confronted many an exhausted and malnourished European crew that had been at sea for weeks or months and was more anxious to mend itself than to engage in needless skirmishing.

As far back as 1521 Magellan had lost his skiff in the Marianas, and in 1565 Arellano had experienced so much trouble with natives who tried to trap the *San Lucas* that he thought surely he must be in the same archipelago, "the pilot assuring me that these were the islands where the small boats were stolen from Magellan, because as they were daring and warlike there was no other place where they could have been taken" (*Col. doc. inéd. ultramar* 1885–1932:III, 22). In reality, the islands where Arellano had his troubles were those of Pulap Atoll, located at a latitude of 7°38′ N in the Carolines. The pilot's judgment of course had been influenced by the same kind of reasoning which later caused others to equate Drake's island with Magellan's. His mistake was understandable.

Two days before the unpleasantness at Pulap, Arellano had had an unnerving experience in the treacherous waters of Truk, a complex atoll made up of a cluster of high volcanic islands set in a vast lagoon completely surrounded by an atoll reef with many coral islets. Here the people of the island of Toloas tried to entice the *San Lucas* into an enclosed harbor, claiming at the same time to be protecting the Spaniards against an oncoming fleet of "more than a thousand" canoes from other islands whose men were heavily armed with spears, clubs, and slings. In the words of the captain,

> They approached screaming so that it seemed as if the earth would drown, thinking that those who had arrived first already had us in their hands. This seemed bad to me and besides there was no place to get out, so we decided to leave through the reef, as we saw that the Indians were demoniacal and that they came with bad intentions. (*Col. doc. inéd. ultramar* 1885–1932:III, 14)

The Toloas "Indians" who were already on board tried to control the movements of the vessel, and two canoes succeeded in reaching it. Its occupants tried to seize the small boat which the Spaniards had on board.

> Those who had entered first were not looking, rather they were stealing. They stole some things of iron and leapt into the water with them . . . one of them furiously grabbed an iron spoon and started to throw himself in the water. Another started beating him with it, so he and the others leaped into the water. (*Col. doc. inéd. ultramar* 1885–1932:III, 14)

More Indians boarded the little ship as it tried to make its way to safety through the rocks and reefs. After a troubled night, day broke and the Spaniards reluctantly fired their culverin at some pursuing canoes. Arellano could ill afford to spare even a single nail, as he had expected to rely for supplies as well as food on the other vessels of Legazpi's fleet, from which he was now separated. "We were so unprepared and subject to the mercy of God that if a nail was needed, it had to be taken out of another part. . . ." (*Col. doc. inéd. ultramar* 1885–1932:III, 19)[13]

After his adventures at Truk and Pulap, which are of course in the central Carolines and therefore not among our suspects, Arellano reached tiny Sorol. Even there two canoes, under sail and with men armed with spears and clubs, came out to meet the *San Lucas*. This time the Spaniards apparently were in a vengeful mood and decided to inflict some preventive damage on the natives with their culverin and harquebuses, "although not as much as they deserved considering the bad intentions they had" (*Col. doc. inéd. ultramar* 1885–1932:III, 27). Reading Arellano's account of his minor encounter at Sorol, suspected by some to be the Island of Thieves, it is hard to believe that Drake could have come here fourteen years later and been harassed by men in a hundred canoes.

To cite an even earlier example from the Carolines than that of Arellano, Saavedra had a relatively mild but typical confrontation with some natives of Ponape after he discovered that high island far to the east in 1529. Sailing in the *Florida* he was met, says Nápoles, by four or five "Indians" in a proa who

> came so close to us that they talked to us, and by signs it seemed to us that they said we should take in our sails, and one of them threw a heavy stone at us which hit the side of the ship at the stern and split the board on which the hit was made. The captain ordered an *escopeta* to be loaded, and that they should be shot at; the shot missed them, and so they went to their island and we to our voyage. (*Col. doc. inéd. Indias* 1864–1884:V, 91)

This indecisive meeting had the potential for a far greater aggression, as the population of Ponape must have numbered many thousands in those days. That the natives were capable of greater fight than this seems to be borne out by a native tradition to the effect that the people had once fought some foreigners who were clad in iron and had along a man in a black garment with a crucifix. Many Ponapeans lost their lives in the skirmish because the foreigners had "solid skins" (armor), but they eventually subdued them by spiking them in the eyes through their visors (Hambruch 1932:4). There is no way of proving this tradition to be based on fact, although it seems to be credible. However, Ponape is not one of the islands under suspicion. Even so, Saavedra's experience may say something about aggression but not much about wily tactics for luring Europeans into unsuspecting traps.

The frantic effort to obtain European artifacts is well illustrated by a later but better example from the Carolines. The *Santísima*

*Trinidad*, a Spanish patache commanded by Francisco de Padilla and piloted by Josef Somera, arrived at Sonsorol in the extreme western Carolines late in 1710. The vessel was soon boarded by some natives, one of whom made off with a saber, even though relations were apparently very friendly (Somera 1715:80). But this is not the example in question.

Arriving shortly thereafter at Babelthuap in the Palau Islands, the ship was met by several canoes whose occupants tried to convey by gestures and words that they were a peaceful people. Some of them swam from the canoes to the ship, where they stole everything they could lay hands upon. Writes Somera in his "Diary,"

> One who had swum up rushed to the channels and grasped one of the chains, trying to break it with his hands, and as he was unable to do so despite all his efforts, he bit into it with his teeth so as to exert more force and carry it off. They did the same with the rings, pintles, and bands of the rudder, and as they were unable to tear off anything and carry it away, the Brother gave them a piece of broken dish, a string of glass beads, and a little sugar. . . . (Krämer 1917:50)

The islanders in the canoes were "all armed with spears and with arrows," and therefore were made to leave; but as they withdrew they shot arrows at the ship, so Padilla discouraged them further with a discharge of musketry.

Late sources such as this are more detailed and plentiful than those of the sixteenth century, and even though comparatively recent they cannot be ruled out as invalid merely because they belong to a time much later than that of Drake. Captain Cheyne furnishes examples from Ulithi and Yap which occurred in the last century (Cheyne 1852:140, 154–163). To be sure, he had an unsavory and somewhat paranoic character, and was brutally slain by the enraged natives of Palau for rape, but his accounts nevertheless have some validity. I myself collected a purportedly true story of the cutting off of a Philippine vessel in Ulithi during the last century, my informants being explicit about details and names, and on reflection I am led to believe that this episode was the same one reported secondhand and in less detail by Cheyne for 1836. However, no deceit or enticement seems to have been involved, the massacre of all but two of the crew having taken place because the captain of the vessel tried to kill some Ulithians after someone had stolen his shirt.

Turning to Ngulu, several newspapers in Salem and Boston reported in 1834 that an American schooner, the *Dash*, got on a reef earlier that year and was attacked by natives as it attempted to heave off. Three men were killed and the captain wounded, but the survivors made their escape in boats and succeeded in reaching Palau (Ward 1966–1967:V, 152–156). It is strange, however, that when the captain eventually reached Boston at the end of the year (the earlier reports had come from persons who had heard in Manila of the incident) and was interviewed by one of the same newspapers mentioned above, the article published by the paper made no mention of the so-called massacre. It states that as the vessel passed within a mile of Ngulu, "a number of canoes come off, and offered some trinkets for sale; they appeared friendly but were not permitted to come on board" (Ward 1966–1967:V, 157). That same evening the schooner struck the coral reef and "a number of canoes come off to them from the island they had passed the day previous, which was about 10 miles distant; the canoe men appeared friendly, and on making them some small presents they went away, anchoring their canoes on the outer part of the reef" (Ward 1966–1967:V, 157). The newspaper article, which is skimpy, says nothing about an attack. Yet, earlier accounts are explicit about the encounter, which most likely did take place.

When all these instances from the Carolines are brought together they present a composite picture of the enticement of Europeans by seemingly friendly islanders into situations wherein the Europeans were subsequently harassed by theft or worse.

However, not all contacts were unfriendly, even for the same island. When Diogo da Rocha and his men stayed for almost four months in the Islands of Sequeira (Ulithi?) to repair a rudder and await favorable winds, they apparently experienced no trouble; indeed, they remarked on the peacefulness and friendliness of the natives, whom they were sorry to leave and promised to revisit (Barros 1563:260r, v). This was in 1525 and 1526. Similarly, the people on the missionary ship *Duff*, who discovered Woleai but stayed only a brief time, liked what they saw of the natives, despite being dismayed by the scantiness of their dress. On Palau, where Padilla had some trouble and the islands subsequently gained notoriety for the hostility of their inhabitants, the survivors of the *Antelope* made fast friends with the natives, and when they sailed they were allowed to take with them Lee Boo, the second son of the "king," the Abba Thulle (Keate 1793). Circumstances often dictated the reaction of the indigenes to the arrival of Europeans, and there is no clear-cut correlation between hostility and prior lack of contact with Westerners.

The format of aggression goes beyond Micronesia. Instances from Melanesia and Polynesia are often very similar, except that a special touch was added here and there in the latter area, where the natives occasionally used pretty young girls, sometimes even stripped entirely naked, as decoys. But cupidity combined with duplicity does not yield a useful clue. There are too many islands of thieves throughout the whole Pacific. The only ones that can be ruled out are the places that had too few canoes and men to be a threat to a ship.[14]

## WHO FASHIONED CERTAIN CANOES

Last but most important of all in the identification of Drake's landfall are the native boats that he saw coming out to meet him. The so-called proas of the Carolines are outriggers with lateen sails and have prows and sterns which are identical in construction and reverse their roles when tacking. When under way, the outrigger is on the windward side and the sail on the lee side. These, rather than paddling canoes, are the characteristic vessels of these islands. There is no assurance that the canoes seen by Drake were sailing canoes, but for the present I will proceed as if they were.

Early descriptions of Carolinian canoes are almost nonexistent. There is only a brief statement by Arellano that soon after discovering Truk in 1565 he entered the reef surrounding the islands and "a big canoe with a lateen sail came towards us" (*Col. doc. inéd. ultramar* 1885–1932:III, 12).

A fuller description comes from the pen of Father Cantova, who writes about the large deep-sea canoes of the Carolinians who were dispersed while en route to Woleai and landed instead on Guam.

> The islanders' boat is of remarkable construction. It has a fine mat of palm leaves for all its sails; the prow and the stern are similar in appearance, and both terminate in a point raised in the shape of a

dolphin's tail. Four small compartments for the convenience of the passengers are observable—one at the prow, the second at the stern, and two others at each side of the mast where the sail is attached, jutting out beyond the gunnels and having the shape of two wings. These compartments have a roof made of palm leaves, similar to the top of a carriage, designed to protect against the rain and the heat of the sun. Within the hold of the boat are various compartments where the cargo and foodstuffs are stored. What is astonishing in this vessel is that not a nail is to be seen and that the planks are so well joined to each other by a kind of twine that they use, that the water cannot creep in. (Cantova 1728:194–195)

The good Father was so engrossed by the several compartments, which are not found in smaller proas staying close to land, that he completely forgot to mention the outrigger, whose existence is nevertheless implied. The taillike endpieces which he describes should be borne in mind for future reference, as should the use of planks in the construction of the hull.

From a different area of the Carolines comes an account based on observations made in 1783 by the men of the already mentioned East India Company merchantman, the packet *Antelope*. The locale was Palau, an island group of much importance. The canoes seen there by Captain Wilson were described as follows:

They were, like most other canoes, made from the trunk of a tree dubbed out; but our people, who had often seen vessels of this sort in many other countries, thought those of *Pelew* surpassed in neatness and beauty any they had ever met with elsewhere; the tree out of which they formed grew to a very considerable height, and resembled much the *English* Ash.—They were painted red, both within and without, and inlaid with shells in different forms.—When they went out in state, the heads and sterns were adorned with a variety of shells strung on a cord, and hung in festoons.—The smallest vessel that they built could hold four or five people, the largest were able to contain from twenty-five to thirty.—They carried an outrigger, but only on one side; and used latine sails made of matting.—As they were not calculated to resist a very rough sea, they rarely went without the coral reef, and seldom, within it, had any violent sea to encounter, whenever it blew hard the natives always kept close under shore. (Keate 1793:315–316)

Specific mention is made of a single outrigger, of paint, and of shells, and possibly of a dugout hull. These are significant traits.

Truly detailed descriptions, often replete with measurements and draftsman's sketches, do not come until the last century and are found in the writings of Duperrey, Freycinet, Dumont d'Urville, Lütke, Paris, and Kubary. These are supplemented in the present century by the work of Krämer, Müller-Wismar, Sarfert, and Hambruch, among others. Mostly they describe the flying proa of *popo* design (Figure 14), used throughout the central and western Carolines. There are other sailing canoes, but they are localized and specialized, such as for warfare, racing, fishing for flying fish, and coastal and lagoon transport of cargo. They do not figure in the usual accounts of Carolinian canoes; in fact, they are seldom mentioned except in specialized publications.

The flying proa, to put it bluntly, could not have been the type of canoe described in the documentary records. The main reason for my saying this is that the double outrigger is unknown in the Carolines or anywhere else in Micronesia. Yet it was clearly the double outrigger that is described in *The World Encompassed*.

A highly dubious claim for the existence of the double outrigger in Micronesia was once made by Roland B. Dixon (1928:76–81) on the basis of a suggestion by Wilhelm Müller-Wismar that certain cross bars on the larger Palauan canoes are vestiges of the boom braces of double outriggers as known on the Indonesian canoes of Mindanao, Sulu, and Sangir (Müller-Wismar 1912:245). Neither Dixon nor Müller-Wismar, however, maintained that the double outrigger existed during historical times. They suggested that it underwent its change within traditional times. Certainly, ethnohistorical documents for the Carolines make no reliable reference to a double outrigger.[15] There can be no doubt that at the time of da Rocha, de Castro, Saavedra, Villalobos, and Arellano—earliest of the visitors to the Carolines—the natives of these islands were sailing the single-outriggered proa of today, even though dugouts with one outrigger but without sails were often employed close to land and were propelled exclusively by paddles.

James Hornell, having in mind the latitude given in the account of Drake's landfall, has backed the identification of Ngulu as Drake's island, and in doing so has thrown the matter into confusion by his foolish insistence that what Drake saw was not only a platform extending over the single outrigger but also, on the other side, a counterpoise platform to maintain balance (Haddon and

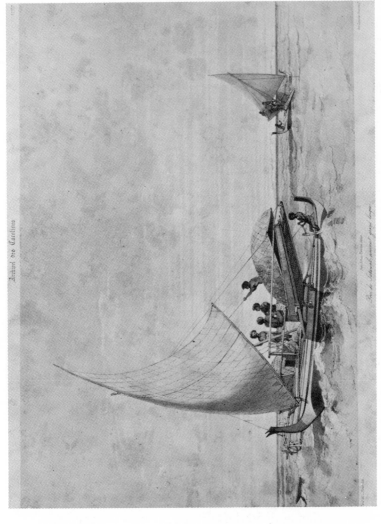

Figure 14. Carolinian Proas. The ubiquitous *popo* as depicted by Admiral Paris has not changed perceptibly for centuries. Still in use, it is lateen-sailed, twin-ended, and single-outriggered. These Satawal canoes are exactly like those of Yap, Ulithi, and the rest of the west-central Carolines. Source: Paris 1843:II, pl. 107 (*Courtesy Special Collections, UCLA Library*)

Hornell 1936–1938:I, 376). He does not even entertain the possibility that Drake saw two outriggers, or perhaps two outlayers.

Since Hornell is probably the foremost authority on Oceanic sailing vessels and has outlined his case in more detail than any other writer, it is necessary to investigate his amazing claim for Ngulu more thoroughly.

Actually, the whole of his argument is not long, and I present it in its entirety. He begins by stating, "The earliest detailed reference to the canoes of the Carolines is a fleeting vision left by Sir Francis Drake, who sighted the Ngulu Islands, westernmost of the archipelago, on October 13, 1579" (Haddon and Hornell 1936–1938:I, 376). Then he quotes a brief description of the canoes without identifying its ultimate source, which is obviously Elizabethan. He continues, saying,

> That these islands belonged to the Carolines and not to Palau is attested by the statement that "two pieces of timber lay out on each side," whereby is clearly indicated the presence of the windward and lee platforms characteristic of the Caroline type of sailing canoe as opposed to that of the Palau Islands which has no lee platform or indeed any prominent lee projection of any kind. Other features equally distinctive of the Caroline Islands proa are also described in a few vivid and picturesque phrases which define them as clearly as if pages had been devoted to the task. (Haddon and Hornell 1936–1938:I, 376)

That is all.

Obviously, Hornell has not delved very far into the matter, and it turns out that his source material is the "Famous Voyage," as published in a popular little book on the earliest voyages around the world (Alexander 1916). Contrary to what Hornell says, the "Famous Voyage" does not contain a single word more than those contained in the quotation he cites. The description of the canoes is confined to one long sentence, less even than Fletcher's account in *The World Encompassed*. Perhaps Hornell had read the latter and retained some of its passages in his head. If he did so, he failed to share them with his readers.

As it is, Hornell's use of the "Famous Voyage" is injudicious and his interpretation wrong. How he could conjure up a windward and a lee platform out of the source statement that "on each side of them lie out two peeces of timber about a yard and a halfe long, more or lesse, according to the smalness, or bignes of the boate" is incredible.[16] If he had read *The World Encompassed*, which seems to have drawn more fully on the same documentary material as the "Famous Voyage," he would have seen mention additionally of a great cane fastened crosswise to the two pieces of timber, to keep the canoe from overthrowing. Even this, however, would not support the allegation that the canoe had two platforms. Hornell would have us imagine that the man who was the chronicler of Drake's voyage was, like Cantova, so impressed by the platforms that he did not think of mentioning the unique outriggers, which the Elizabethans could not possibly have seen before. It is true that the lee platform of Micronesian canoes does a certain amount of balancing, but that is not its chief purpose, which is to provide space for cargo and passengers. There are some Carolinian proas of the *popo* type in local use that do not even have such a platform, achieving balance by other means. The prime purpose of two outriggers, on the other hand, is indeed "to keepe their canowes from ouerthrowing, and that they might be equally borne vp on each side" (Drake 1628:82).

If Hornell was thinking of two outlayers, which may, as we have already done, be defined as a pole or a single balancing apparatus, and may be single or double, then he ought to have said so; but in any event these have never been reported for any part of Micronesia.

Further damaging to any claim that Drake saw Carolinian canoes are the floats of the outriggers. There can be no doubt that the canes or bamboos alluded to by Fletcher were floats. But in the Carolines, including Palau, floats are made of breadfruit wood or some other soft wood, not bamboo. They are shaped like a canoe hull, except that they are solid, and are sharp and pointed at each end, with a median ridge at the upper surface. They could not possibly be carved into this shape if bamboo were the material used. If, on the other hand, the bamboo parts belonged to outlayers, these same islands would have to be eliminated because their canoes do not employ this balancing device.

Incidentally, with reference to the two pieces of timber that lay out on each side, most Carolinian canoes have two booms rather than three or more; but this is not enough to qualify them as the

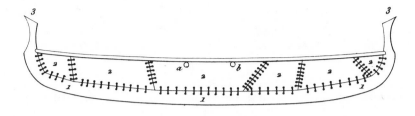

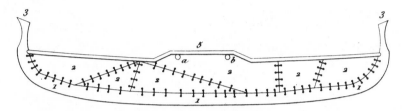

Figure 15. Sewn Canoe. Most west-central Carolinian canoes are incomplete dugouts, parts of the hull being "sewn" together. Source: Freycinet 1827–1839:atlas, pl. 52 (figs. 8, 9). (*Courtesy Special Collections, UCLA Library*)

canoes Drake saw. For the Oceanic area, two booms are not distinctive enough.

What about the other features of the canoes? If we were to interpret literally Fletcher's statement that they were made of one tree, then the canoes were dugouts. But except for Palau, west Carolinian canoes are characteristically built up of planking upon a dugout base. This would eliminate Ngulu, Yap, Ulithi, Sorol, and Woleai, whose proa hulls are made up not only of three main pieces—the hull proper and two endpieces—but others sewn irregularly to the side (Figure 15). On atolls, where there is no large timber, the number of parts sewn together may be large, unless the canoe is built on the high island of Yap and transported back. But even on Yap seven pieces are typical for the *popo*.

All Palauan canoes, on the other hand, are carved out of a single tree trunk, preferably the magnificent *Serianthes grandiflora*, whether they were used for racing, trading, specialized fishing, or war (Haddon and Hornell 1936–1938:I, 422). In pointing this out, Hornell was not arguing in favor of Palau, which, as the reader will already have surmised, he places outside the Carolines. Hornell's main argument against Palau as Drake's island is that its canoes

*Chapter Five*

lacked the counterpoise platform on the lee side of the canoe
(Figure 16), but this was a straw man of his own making. Nevertheless, only Palau had true dugouts, unless we want to include the
little boats used in the Carolines when fishing in the lagoons. They
carry only about two to four people, so they cannot be included in
our analysis, although it is possible that such inshore or lagoon
canoes might have mingled with larger ones in greeting European
visitors.

The "glosse" of the canoes seen by Drake is another reason for
eliminating all Carolinian canoes, excepting the Palauan, which
had a "varnish" and a high polish, as has been attested to by many
commentators beginning with Captain Wilson (Keate 1793:316n.;
Kubary 1895:278, 278n.; Krämer 1926:112, 113, 185, 190). In the
rest of the west Carolines, the *popo* was painted in varying patterns
of red, black, and white, and other canoes had at least red and

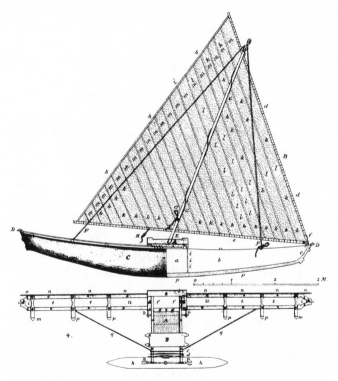

Figure 16. Palau Racing Canoe. The *kaep* was a single-outriggered,
twin-ended, sail dugout canoe. Source: Kubary 1895:pl. 52.

perhaps one or both of the other of these colors. These Carolinian canoes were made smooth on the exterior of the hull but were never truly glossy, as were the canoes mentioned in the "Famous Voyage" and *The World Encompassed*.

Also lacking diagnostic value are the head and stern "of one fashion." These are found in almost all Carolinian canoes, to be sure, on account of the reversibility of their ends, but they are likewise found in many of the canoes of the rest of the southwest Pacific.

The "yeelding inward in manner of a semicircle, of a great height" does not fit the most common of the canoes of the western Carolines, the *popo*, whose endpieces are high but rise straight up and then curve slightly outward in a forked shape resembling wings or a dolphin's tail. Other types of Carolinian canoes similarly fail to curve inward, especially in the Palaus, where the ends of the canoes are neither high nor curved.[17]

The "glistering shels" of the canoes seen by Drake are absent from the Carolinian *popo* but are found in the *tsukpin* of Yap, an uncommon sacred sailing canoe used to catch flying fish. However, the ends of the *tsukpin* curve outward, not inward, although the total profile is slightly crescentic (Figure 17). Palauan canoes partially qualify because their former racing canoes usually had cowrie shells suspended from various parts of the outrigger, as well as from the outer projecting thwarts. Their war canoes, too, were adorned with shells, not only at the head and stern but also on the outrigger and the thwart bars, whenever they went out in state or on a military expedition (Haddon and Hornell 1936–1938:I, 432—433, fig. 311).

Having said all this, I find it necessary to suggest once again that in terms of the evidence, Drake may have seen no sailing canoes at all, only paddling ones. Admittedly, this is very unlikely as sailing craft were present in any locale where he could possibly have been, so that all we can say is that paddling canoes may have predominated. In the western part of the Carolines paddling canoes are small and varied, and used in the lagoons and along the coasts, although on Yap one particular type was used for war and ceremonial occasions. All are dugouts and some have a well-marked gunwale sewn on (Haddon and Hornell 1936–1938:I, 390, 392, fig. 276).

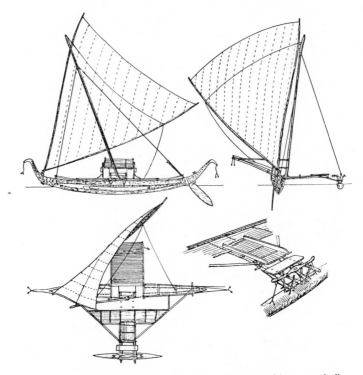

Figure 17. Yapese *Tsukpin*. A deep-sea sail canoe with a sewn hull, used seasonally for catching flying fish, this canoe had white cowries strung by cords from its bird-beak extremities. Source: Neyret 1969:23. (*Courtesy Les Amis des Musées de la Marine*)

The one place where large paddling canoes were outstanding, although of course not exclusive, was Palau. One such type was the giant war canoe, the *kabekl*, a dugout whose length ranged from forty-eight to fifty-eight feet and which carried as many as thirty-two paddlers besides the steersman. The hulls were ornamented with festoons of snowy egg cowries and their exteriors wrought to the finest possible finish. In this same island cluster, some of the sail canoes were often, if not usually, paddled (Haddon and Hornell 1936–1938:I, 430–434, figs. 310, 311). Yet, though Palauan canoes had so many suitable traits, it cannot be overlooked that all of them were single outriggers without incurving ends.

At long last, Table 2 brings together all the positive and negative findings for the six places suspected by authorities of being Drake's Island of Thieves. There is more than reasonable doubt about them. All have been victims of contradictory identification.

Table 2. How Six Caroline Islands Meet Criteria as Drake's Island

| Clues | Suspects | | | | | |
|---|---|---|---|---|---|---|
| | Palau | Yap | Ngulu | Ulithi | Sorol | Woleai |
| 8° N latitude | Yes | No | Yes | No | Yes | Yes |
| Population of 2,200 | Yes | Yes | No | No | No | ? |
| Double outriggers | No | No | No | No | No | No |
| [Double outlayers] | [No] | [No] | [No] | [No] | [No] | [No] |
| Cane floats | No | No | No | No | No | No |
| Dugouts, one-piece | Yes | No | No | No | No | No |
| Glossy hulls | Yes | No | No | No | No | No |
| Twin ends | Yes | Yes | Yes | Yes | Yes | Yes |
| Incurving ends | No | No | No | No | No | No |
| Shell ornaments | Yes | Yes | No | No | No | No |
| Large paddling canoes | Yes | No | No | No | No | No |
| Nudity | Yes | ? | ? | ? | ? | ? |
| Lengthened earlobes | Yes | Yes | Yes | Yes | Yes | Yes |
| Long fingernails | No | ? | ? | ? | ? | ? |
| Blackened teeth | Yes | Yes | No | No | No | No |
| Betel-nut chewing | Yes | Yes | ? | No | No | No |
| Slings | No | Yes | ? | Yes | ? | Yes |
| Darts | Yes | Yes | ? | Yes | Yes | Yes |
| Thieving tactics | Yes | Yes | ? | Yes | ? | ? |

? = unknown or inconclusive

## chapter six

# The Marianas Reexamined

HOW WOULD THE MARIANAS have fared if they had not been summarily dismissed from the start by reason of their high latitude? That is, assuming that for some unaccountable reason both Fletcher and John Drake had made a mistake in reporting the parallel of the first landfall made by the *Golden Hind* after leaving the Farallons, could other circumstances be incriminating enough to indict either Guam or Rota? There is the nagging possibility that Magellan's *ladrones* might after all be Drake's "theeves."

The Marianas present a situation unlike that of the western Carolines, where there was little acculturation until recently. The Chamorros lost their indigenous culture far earlier than any other Micronesians and were almost exterminated by the Spaniards in the process. On this account, modern ethnographic studies, which anyway number but a few, are of little help. They deal with a people vastly unlike those who were first exposed to the relentless campaign of missionization and subjugation that began when Father Diego Luís de Sanvitores founded his mission in 1668 at Agaña on Guam. As a consequence, ethnohistorical accounts, too, unless they are at least two centuries old, have to be treated with some caution.

## PIGAFETTA'S ACCOUNT

The early ethnohistorical sources for the Marianas are good—better, indeed, than for any other islands of Micronesia—and begin with a narrative by Antonio Pigafetta, a patrician of Vicenza who had volunteered to accompany Magellan in order to see "the great and wonderful things of the Ocean Sea." His notes constitute the first ethnographic account of an Oceanic people and tell us, among other things, that the natives of Guam and Rota, which were the islands at which the *Trinidad*, *Victoria*, and *Concepcion* stopped, had some all too familiar proclivities.

> The captain-general wished to stop at the large island and get some fresh food, but he was unable to do so because the inhabitants of that island entered the ships and stole whatever they could lay hands on, so that we could not protect ourselves. The men were about to strike the sails so that we could go ashore, but the natives very deftly stole from us the small boat that was fastened to the poop of the flagship. Thereupon, the captain-general in wrath went ashore with forty armed men, who burned some forty or fifty houses together with many boats, and killed seven men. He recovered the small boat, and we departed immediately pursuing the same course. Before we landed, some of our sick men begged us that if we should kill any man or woman to bring the entrails to them, as they would recover immediately. (Blair and Robertson 1903–1909:XXXIII, 95)

The tactic of friendliness, to be used so often as a ruse by the neolithic peoples of Oceania in their desperate efforts to acquire ferrous and other European artifacts, makes its first appearance.

> Those people seeing us departing followed us with more than one hundred boats for more than one legua. They approached the ships showing us fish, feigning that they would give them to us; but then threw stones at us and fled. And although the ships were under full sail, they passed between them and the small boats [fastened astern], very adroitly in those small boats of theirs. We saw some women in their boats who were crying out and tearing their hair, for love, I believe, of those whom we had killed. (Blair and Robertson 1903–1909:XXXIII, 97)

So the Chamorros, as they were later to be called, had stone slings as well as the swift canoes that were to excite the imagination and praise of many mariners to come.

In Pigafetta's notes there is even a hint as to the betel nut and perhaps also the blackening of teeth, prefaced by a straightforward remark about male nudity.

> They go naked, and some are bearded and have black hair that reaches to the waist. . . . Their teeth are red and black, for they

think that is most beautiful. The women go naked except that they
wear a narrow strip of bark as thin as paper, which grows between
the tree and the bark of the palm, before their privies. (Blair and
Robertson 1903–1909:XXXIII, 97)

Pigafetta was obviously so impressed by the canoes that once
again he talks about them and in so doing gives us some valuable
clues as to what a Marianas proa was like more than four centuries
ago.

Their amusement, men and women, is to plough the seas with those
small boats of theirs. Those boats resemble *fulcelere*, but are narrower, and some are black, [some] white, and others red. At the side
opposite the sail, they have a large piece of wood pointed at the top,
with poles laid across it and resting on the water, in order that the
boats may sail more safely. The sail is made from palm leaves sewn
together and is shaped like a lateen sail. For rudders they use a
certain blade resembling a hearth shovel which have a piece of wood
at the end. They can change stem and bow at will [literally: they
make the stern, bow, and the bow, stern], and those boats resemble
the dolphins which leap in the water from wave to wave. (Blair and
Robertson 1903–1909:XXXIII, 99)

Here, then, in simple terms is the flying proa of Micronesia: a canoe
painted in the usual colors—except that they do not seem to be in
combination—with an outrigger, a lateen sail, and a hull capable of
being reversed when changing direction. It is worth noting that
women are mentioned as sailing in the canoes, but probably only as
passive passengers.

### CORROBORATING WITNESSES

Subsequent commentators on the actions, appearance, and artifacts of the natives of the Marianas tend to corroborate all that
Pigafetta says he saw in 1521, occasionally adding some relevant
facts which he did not touch upon.

We can begin with the high population implied by the number of
canoes which came out to pay their respects to Magellan. No one
would dispute that the population of either Guam or Rota was at
that time large enough to man the hundred or more canoes sailed by
the natives. The wonder of it is that there were not many more
boats than that.[1]

The martyred Jesuit, Diego Luís de Sanvitores, estimated the population of Guam alone to be 50,000 when he arrived to set up the first permanent mission in 1668 (García, April 1937:20–21). On the basis of various estimates of the population of the Marianas made by the Spaniards, Freycinet thinks that in the old days there were 35,000 people on the island of Guam and 8,000 on nearby Rota (Freycinet 1827–1839:II, 327–328). Despite the unreliability of projections back in time, it is apparent that Guam and Rota had enough people at the time of Drake to qualify as the abode of the thieves. Of this there can be no question, despite the almost incredible decimation of the populace in the years immediately following upon Sanvitores' evangelical exertions.

Enough early reports of nudity among the Chamorros leaves no room whatsoever for doubt about their state of undress. Andrés de Urdaneta, one of the senior officers on Loaisa's flagship, reached the Marianas in 1526 while en route to the Moluccas, and says that the Indians "go about naked, wearing no garments" (*Col. doc. inéd. Indias* 1864–1884:V, 17). Legazpi, another illustrious traveler on the great ocean when it was still a Spanish sea, says that when he came within sight of Guam in 1565, a large number of proas with naked men surrounded the fleet.

> These *praus* were furnished with lateen sails of palm mats and were light as the wind. . . .In each canoe there were from six to eight Indians, altogether naked, covering not even the privy parts, which men are wont to cover. (Blair and Robertson 1903–1909:II, 197–198)

Still another early witness is Juan Martinez of the *San Gerónimo*. When the acting captain, Rodrigo del Angle, took his vessel to the lee side of Rota in 1566 it was met by a large number of canoes whose men were *desnudos de todo punto* (*Col. doc. inéd. ultramar* 1885–1932:III, 437). Francis Pretty, with Cavendish at Guam in 1588, similarly says that the natives who sailed out in canoes were "all naked" (Hakluyt 1598–1600:III, 817).

A secondhand but nevertheless authentic early statement appears in *Historia . . . de la China* (1586). Here, relating the experiences of some Franciscan priests in the Marianas, the author, Juan Gonzalez de Mendoza, mentions the complete nudity of the men and most of the women (Blair and Robertson 1903–1909:VI, 138). Writing a century later, García wrote in 1683 of the Chamorros:

"Their costume is that of the state of innocence . . . only the women cover as much as modesty requires with an apron or *tifis*" (García, April 1937:36; cf. Le Gobien 1700:47). This statement appeared in his annual report on the work of the Jesuits in the Marianas. The next year's annual report was written by Father Emmanuel de Solórzano, superior of the Jesuit mission in the Mariana Islands, and in it he says that a special effort was made during the year "to introduce linen [to the natives] to cover the shameless nakedness of all these islands" (Repetti 1940:256). Apparently there was still some nudity at that time.

Early Dutch explorers are corroborative of all that has been said about nudity. When Olivier van Noort arrived at Guam in 1600 on the *Mauritius* while encircling the globe it was observed that the women wore only a leaf to cover their privies, while the men wore nothing at all (Figure 18) (Noort 1602:33–34). His compatriot Joris van Spilbergen observed in 1616 that "they go about quite naked, except that some wear hats made of straw, and that the women cover their privy parts with some leaves" (Spilbergen 1619:84 and pl. 16). The chronicler of the Nassau Fleet is in agreement (*Jour. Nass. Vloot* 1631:103).

When Freycinet was on Guam in the last century the people were by then of course modestly and amply clothed, but he understood that. "Formerly the natives were often completely nude" (Freycinet 1827–1839:II, 308). In the Atlas of his account of the voyage he made around the world there is an engraving made in 1818 by Jacques Arago, the artist on his expedition, and in it are depicted men and women in nature's garb, the drawing being made on Guam but based on hearsay (Figure 19). A much earlier illustration (Figure 18) in Olivier van Noort's *Description du . . . Voyage* (1602) shows three inhabitants of the Ladrones, one a woman with long tresses wearing no more than a very small leaf to preserve her modesty, the other two being men wearing only hats. This is based on firsthand observations, at a time when the native culture had hardly been disturbed.

As for the stones mentioned by Pigafetta, they were of course not hurled merely like a baseball or cricket ball; they were propelled with tremendous force by the aid of slings. Slings are mentioned by many subsequent writers. Urdaneta tells us that when Legazpi's ships arrived at Guam in 1565 the natives tried to get the

Figure 18. Nude Chamorros. Olivier van Noort reported that Chamorro men went completely naked when he saw them in 1600. Source: Noort 1602:34. (*Courtesy The Huntington Library, San Marino, California*)

Figure 19. Natives of the Marianas. This retrospective engraving depicts complete nudity among the Chamorros. Source: Freycinet: 1827–1839:atlas, pl. 63. (*Courtesy Special Collections, UCLA Library*)

Spaniards to enter their village, yet "all the canoes and those in them, had their arms, which consisted of shields, bundles of throwing-sticks, slings, and egg-shaped stones" (Blair and Robertson 1903–1909:II, 110). Legazpi himself tells of "hardened clubs, stones, and slings (which comprise their weapons, and they manage very skilfully)" (Blair and Robertson 1903–1909:II, 199). Mendoza, who it will be recalled narrated the experiences of some Franciscans in the Marianas, wrote in 1586 of the deft use of the sling (Blair and Robertson 1903–1909:VI, 138). Writing in 1683, the historian Father García says that "they can throw stones from a sling with such dexterity and strength that they are able to drive them into the trunk of a tree" (García, April 1937:38; cf. Le Gobien 1700:55). His biography of Sanvitores contains many instances of the use of stones by the Chamorros in their bloody skirmishes with the Spaniards, as when on one occasion they penetrated the roof of the church and the residence (García, March 1938:35).[2] Rogers accurately tells of fired clay "stones" (Rogers 1718:367).

For those who like their evidence in more tangible form than mere words, a visit to the venerable Bernice P. Bishop Museum in Honolulu should prove warmly rewarding, for there in a collection of Marianas artifacts one can see more than 4,700 worked slingstones (*atupats*). They are made of white and crystalline limestone, baked clay, fine grain basalt, soft sedimentary green rock, coral, and marble. Archaeologists found most of them on the surface or just below the surface. Some were found in caches buried to a depth of three feet below the surface. "The uniformity in type of the stones in each recorded cache suggests that the slingstones were made by specific groups of belligerents and stored for ammunition" (Thompson 1932:49). Presumably, the principle of ethnological analogy as well as that of genetic continuity are fully operative in this instance.

As to the presence of John Drake's "darts" in the Marianas there again is the question of meaning. The literature usually refers uncommittedly to the "spear," which of course may be either a throwing weapon or a thrusting one. For instance, Pigafetta discloses that the natives encountered in the Ladrones "use no weapons, except a kind of spear pointed with a fishbone at the end" (Blair and Robertson 1903–1909:XXXIII, 99). Along similar lines, Urdaneta tells us: "They have no other weapons than spears—

some with points hardened with fire, and some having heads made from the shin bones of dead men, and from fish-bones" (Blair and Robertson 1903–1909:II, 35). Describing a gruesome episode in which a young Spanish roustabout had wandered into the mountains too far from his companions, Legazpi tells how the boy had been torn to pieces by Indians, "giving him at least thirty lance thrusts through the body" (Blair and Robertson 1903–1909:XXXIII, 200). Among some of the other ethnohistoric documentation are the accounts of Sanvitores (García, April 1937:38) and Mendoza (Blair and Robertson 1903–1909:VI, 138), but for the finding of barbed spear points of human bones in archaelogical sites we are indebted to Laura Thompson (1932:52, fig. 23, pl. 11, C). All this seems like sufficiently conclusive evidence of the presence of darts in the aboriginal Marianas. In addition we have an interesting statement from Safford (1903:500) that the old Chamorros "often had contests of spear throwing," and although he cites no sources for his statement we are probably safe in assuming that he had such a source when he penned these words.

The hint given by Pigafetta concerning betel-nut chewing must be given serious consideration in the light of comments by others. Freycinet tells us that "From time immemorial betel has been a necessary item to the inhabitants" (Freycinet 1827–1839:II, 321). Of course, the French circumnavigator was in the Marianas three centuries later than Pigafetta, so he cannot qualify as convincingly as he would if he had been there earlier. But García, the biographer of Sanvitores, tells us in his *Vida y Martirio de . . . Sanvitores* (1683) that when a passerby is invited into a house, "they bring out *buyo* (betel nut) which is a plant that they like very much, and keep in the mouth, like tobacco" (García, April 1937:36). García compiled his history from numerous Spanish sources, including manuscripts by Sanvitores himself. The betel habit was reported to be "still universal among the natives of Guam" at the turn of the century (Safford 1903:502).

Archaeology once again comes to our aid in the form of eighty-six Guamanian skulls in a collection at the Bishop Museum. They are said, on the basis of stratigraphical and cultural evidence, to be pre-Spanish or early post-Spanish in age, and were examined in detail by Dr. R. W. Leigh, an army dentist. His report tells us that the buccal surfaces of the anterior twelve or fourteen teeth of the Chamorros are discolored, with the shade varying from orange to blackish brown. Some of the staining was purposeful, but in the main the staining observed by Leigh was incidental to the betel-chewing habit. "The arresting feature of the teeth of the Chamorros is the discoloration from betel chewing. . . . Other than children, only six adult males had unstained teeth; these persons were probably ascetics" (Leigh 1929:267).

The early blackening of teeth, again only hinted at by Pigafetta, is confirmed by García, even though he merely says, "they color their teeth black, believing this a great adornment to their beauty" (García, April 1937:21; cf. Le Gobien 1700:48). Writing much later, Freycinet is more specific: "Formerly the women used to dye their teeth black with certain kinds of herbs" (Freycinet 1827–1839:II, 311). He says nothing about the men. Inasmuch as García wrote at a time when the practice was still extant, and yet did not mention a sex difference, we can assume that the men, too, blackened their teeth. This is important, for it was men, not women, who came out to greet Drake.

Dr. Leigh, the dentist previously referred to, does not make an unequivocal statement about blackening when describing the stained teeth in old Chamorro skulls, for he writes only of discoloration varying from orange to blackish brown. Yet in his summary he does say that "staining the teeth an orange to black color was customary" (Leigh 1929:272). Only here does he use the word "black," and his description is not really definitive.

Pigafetta's original observations on the well-publicized thievishness of the Chamorros is supported by others. Urdaneta has expounded on it at length (Blair and Robertson 1903–1909:II, 110–111) and Legazpi, still another of the firsthand witnesses, has done so in a lesser way (Blair and Robertson 1903–1909:II, 198). The historian Mendoza supplies further comments (Blair and Robertson 1903–1909:VI, 138). So does the Dutch explorer van Noort (Noort 1602:33).

## A REBUTTAL

It seems almost an affront to intrude upon this string of evidence with anything serving to throw doubt on the "guilt" of the

Marianas. However, in the interests of justice certain incongruities must be weighed against the affirmative findings.

Negative evidence cannot be used one way or another in trying to establish a connection between two cultures, yet it seems significant that Pigafetta, who was a remarkably keen observer for the times in which he lived, makes no mention of either greatly distended earlobes or excessively long fingernails. He was obviously interested in the appearance of the natives, having left fuller notes on the subject than those quoted above. Yet he is silent on these two traits, which Fletcher of course had singled out. Was this not because he could not report what he did not see?

García, who had at his disposal actual letters and records belonging to Father Sanvitores, together with other old documents, makes no mention of long lobes. Neither do Urdaneta, Legazpi, Pretty, Le Gobien, Rogers, Freycinet, Arago, Kotzebue, or Chamisso. The only authority I have encountered who asserts the presence of long lobes is Thompson (Thompson 1945:10), but as her source she cites the "Famous Voyage," presupposing that it deals with Guam.

On the subject of fingernails, Urdaneta, Legazpi, Pretty, García, and Le Gobien join Pigafetta in being significantly silent on the subject, as do all other early writers. Again, the only authority who accepts the presence of long nails is Thompson, who uses the "Famous Voyage" as her source (Thompson 1945:10).

But the real blow against the charge that the Chamorros were Drake's annoyers is the familiar one of the canoes. In Pigafetta's description, quoted earlier in full, he makes reference to what anyone would have to recognize must have been a single outrigger canoe, the outrigger being on the windward side, "the side opposite the sail." In referring to the float as being "pointed at the top" he is speaking of the median ridge running along the upper surface. Fletcher's canoes could not possibly have had this bevel if the floats were made of cane or bamboo.

The canoes seen by Pigafetta and Magellan were the same as those described later in the same century by Esteban Rodriguez, chief pilot of Legazpi's flagship, who makes a point of saying that because the Chamorro canoes were made up of pieces of wood tied together with rattan, one man had to be engaged in bailing out water because they were not caulked. He adds that the canoes were covered with a coating of colored earth, lime, and coconut oil (*Col. doc. inéd. ultramar* 1885–1932:II, 388). The important feature here, not mentioned by Pigafetta, is that the canoes were sewn together out of several pieces of wood. This is a distinctly Micronesian type of construction not in accord with Fletcher's description of the canoes that Drake saw.

Urdaneta, originally with Loaisa and now a friar making another crossing of the Pacific, this time with Legazpi, says much the same as Rodriguez; "[Their canoes are] very neatly and well made sewed together with cord, and finished with a white or orange-colored bitumen, in place of pitch" (Blair and Robertson 1903–1909:II, 110).

The painting of Marianas canoes, noted by Pigafetta, Rodriguez, and Urdaneta, is verified by García, who says:

> Their boats are very light, small and pretty, painted with a kind of bitumen which colors the hills of Guam red. It is mixed with lime and coconut oil, and beautifies their boats greatly. (García, April 1937:36)

Drake's "thieves" did not finish off their canoes in the same way as did Magellan's "thieves." They did not merely paint them; instead, they gave them a gloss. Here again, there is an important difference in detail. It cannot be overlooked that paint was a characteristic feature of the Chamorran canoe.

Pretty, who chronicled Cavendish's voyage around the world, adds a distinguishing feature to the Marianas proas as he saw them in 1588. He says that the native men had their hair tied up in one or two knots at the crown, and that this was "much like unto their images which wee saw them haue carved in wood, and standing in the head of their boates like unto the images of the deuill" (Hakluyt 1598–1600:III, 817–818). He confirms that the boats were single outriggers: "their heades and sternes are both alike, [and] they are made out with raftes of canes and reedes on the starrebordside, with maste and sayle" (Hakluyt 1598–1600:III, 818). It is significant that Pretty, a gentleman-at-arms with Cavendish, at no time makes the suggestion that the Ladrones, as he calls them, were Drake's islands.

The Dutchman van Noort was met with as many as two hundred canoes at one time, with two, three, or five men in each. The craft were neatly compact and about fifteen or twenty feet long, and one and one-half feet broad, and could sail against the wind (Noort 1602:34). This information is skimpy but it seems to offer no support for the kind of canoes described by Fletcher.

A drawing (Figure 20) in van Spilbergen's account of his voyage around the world in 1614–1617 (Spilbergen 1619: pl. 16) deserves mention. It depicts, among other things, two kinds of Ladrones canoes, labeled "G" and "H" respectively. An explanatory statement accompanying the plate says of "H" that they "are their ships, or canoes, in which they sail," and it is easy to see that we have here the typical and highly admired flying proa, with its large pandanus sails, high endpieces, single outriggers, and so on. Of the canoes marked "G" we are told that they are "the canoes, which they row; and the things which are attached to the sides are for keeping them balanced." Many of these canoes are shown and it is easy to see that they differ little from the flying proa, which is exactly the situation found in the Carolines, even today. These sailless canoes have single outriggers and twin high endpieces; but they show no sails or masts and are in some instances noticeably smaller. Most carry three and four persons and in at least one instance there is a bare-breasted woman. The sail canoes are not depicted as carrying larger numbers of natives than the paddling canoes. I think that it is likely that most of the canoes depicted without sails are simply those that have lowered them for the time being, this being easily accomplished together with the lowering, too, of the masts, which are of course easily dismountable on Micronesian canoes. Surely, one cannot on the basis of this drawing identify the "H" canoes as double-outriggered dugouts of the kind described by Fletcher.

Even better accounts than the above may be used to deny any supposed link between Fletcher's canoes and those of the Marianas. Easily the most detailed of the earlier descriptions of the Marianas proa is that of William Dampier, the brilliant English buccaneer who not only circumnavigated the globe three times but established an enduring reputation as a fine hydrographer, as well as a reporter of natural history and of men encountered in strange lands. It would take up too much space to quote him in full, so it will have to suffice to give only the gist of his account of the Guamanian

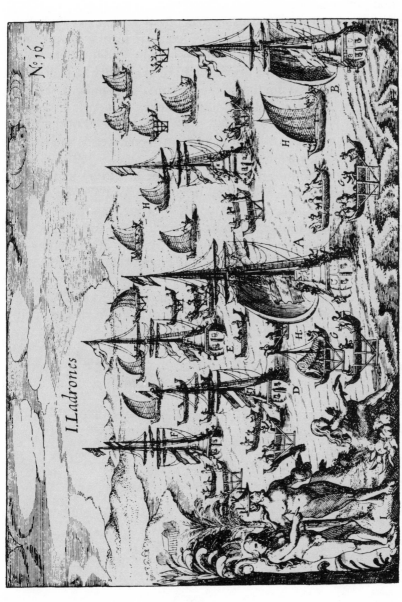

Figure 20. Marianas Canoes Seen by Spilbergen. When Joris van Spilbergen's fleet stopped at the Marianas in 1616 the Dutch saw both paddling and sailing proas. Source: Spilbergen 1619:pl. 16. (*Courtesy The Huntington Library, San Marino, California*)

proa as he saw it in the year 1686. The bottom was like that of a little canoe and was about twenty-six or twenty-eight feet long. Both sides of the boat were carried up to about five feet high with narrow plank. There was a mast in the middle, supporting a lateen sail. Parallel to the "belly side" of the boat was a log of light wood, almost as long as the boat itself and sharp as a wedge at each end. It was made firm and contiguous to the boat by bamboos reaching about six or eight feet from the side. "The use of them is to keep the great Boat upright from oversetting. . . ." Each end of the canoe could serve as a head or a stern, and by reversing ends and shifting the sail, tacking was made unnecessary (Dampier 1697:298–300). Dampier says nothing about either paint or glossy surface, incurved or outcurved ends, shell ornaments, or paddling canoes. The floats of the proas were of wood, not cane, and the outriggers were single, not double. He remarks on the tremendous speed of the little canoes while under sail. The projection of the booms was more than that estimated by Fletcher. Funnell (1707:228–229) corroborates most of this.

Other accounts, though detailed, add nothing new. Giovanni Francesco Gemelli Careri, an Italian doctor of civil law with a propensity for global travel, describes the Marianas proa as he saw it in 1696 (Churchill 1704:IV, 485), but he adds nothing that would indicate that it was anything other than a single-outriggered, lateen-sailed, Chamorro flying proa. His little sketch of a proa

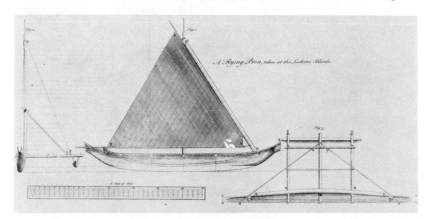

Figure 21. Flying Proa of the Marianas. Chamorro canoes were single-outriggered and equipped with lateen sails. This sketch made in 1742 by Brett conforms to the description given by Pigafetta as he saw them in 1521 when with Magellan's fleet. Source: Anson 1748: pl. 38. (*Courtesy The Huntington Library, San Marino, California*)

Table 3. How the Marianas Meet
Criteria as Drake's Island

| Clues | Marianas |
| --- | --- |
| 8° N latitude | No |
| Population of 2,200 | Yes |
| Double outriggers | No |
| [Double outlayers] | [No] |
| Cane floats | No |
| Dugouts, one-piece | No |
| Glossy hulls | No |
| Twin ends | Yes |
| Incurving ends | No |
| Shell ornaments | No |
| Large paddling canoes | No |
| Nudity | Yes |
| Lengthened earlobes | No |
| Long fingernails | No |
| Blackened teeth | Yes |
| Betel-nut chewing | Yes |
| Slings | Yes |
| Darts | Yes |
| Thieving tactics | Yes |

bears this out (Churchill 1704: 457). The privateer Woodes Rogers had a canoe presented to him in 1710 by the governor of Guam and took it back to England. His description and enthusiasm are typical (Rogers 1718:367), conforming to that of others. Commodore George Anson, the last of the Elizabethan-style "privileged plunderers," reached Tinian in the Marianas in 1742 with a badly decimated scurvy-ridden crew; yet despite being preoccupied with refitting his sole surviving ship, the *Centurion*, under trying circumstances, he had one of his lieutenants, Peircy Brett, dismantle a captured proa in order "to delineate its fabric and dimensions with greater accuracy" (Anson 1748:339–343). Brett's sketch is a fine one and has often been reproduced (Figure 21). No one could look at it and imagine that it depicted a canoe belonging to Drake's thieves.

The Marianas canoe, then, spoils any effort to make Drake's gadflies out to be Chamorros. There is not even a hint of an incurving endpiece or of decorative shells. The paddled dugout, if present, was wholly subsidiary to the flying proa.[3]

Table 3 summarizes the complete findings for the Marianas. It bears a strong resemblance to the Caroline checklist.

So we leave the aboriginal Chamorros as we found them—black-toothed and naked, chewing on their wads of betel and occasionally hurling slingstones and spears at one another. They do not seem to have had distended earlobes, so that with their nudity they had to find some other means of carrying about small items. They also appear to have lacked long fingernails. Certainly they did not have glossy, double-outriggered canoes, but did marvelously well in getting about with their multipieced flying proas. They were numerous enough, to be sure, but they lived in the wrong place to make this or anything else count.

## chapter seven

# *Mindanao*

UNLESS ONE HAS by now attributed a Mandevillian taint to the
Fletcher account of Drake's voyage across the Pacific and yielded
to discouragement, a final locale should be investigated.

When first I became drawn into the fascinating problem of the
identification of the Island of Thieves it struck me, as an anthropologist, that some crucial cultural traits mentioned by Fletcher
could not be Micronesian and perforce had to be Malaysian. I was
later encouraged in my conviction that Malaysia was worth exam-
ining by a theory expressed by Andrew Sharp that Drake's landfall
was in the Philippines (Sharp 1960:48–50) (Map 6).

It is known of course that Drake stopped at Mindanao before
pushing on to the Moluccas. At least, Fletcher says he did. The
question is whether or not he had already been to its more northerly
eastern shore before stopping farther south on the coast to take on
wood and water.

Sharp's theory has more to it than I have revealed and, taking
recognition of the statement about Mindanao, includes a stop by
Drake at Davao Gulf. But the major thrust of his argument is that
Drake first landed at Mindanao rather than some Micronesian
island. After making a few introductory statements it is to this
matter that I shall first address myself. Later I shall go into the
ramifications of his proposals.

## THE ISLAND OF MINDANAO

The Malaysian culture area, which as I have said has cultural
traits of interest to us, is the westernmost of the Pacific culture

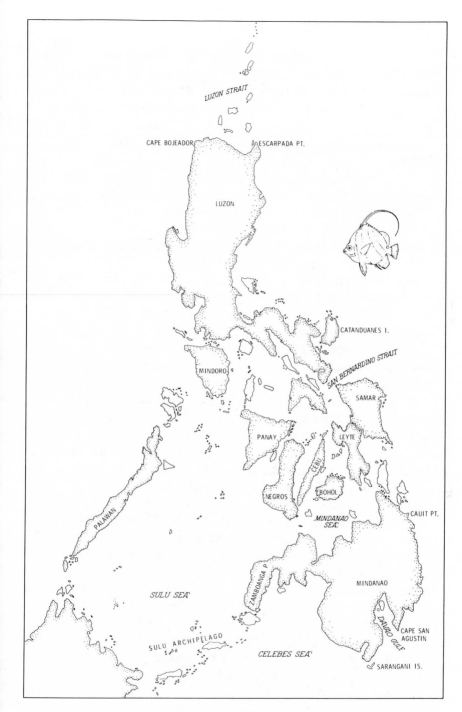

Map 6. The Philippines

areas. It straddles the equator and has a very distant outpost in Madagascar. Those of its constituent islands lying south of the equator—Sumatra, Borneo, Celebes, Halmahera, Java, and the Spice Islands—are automatically eliminated from our search. Of the islands north of the equatorial line, Taiwan is too far distant from the parallels mentioned by Fletcher. There remains the Philippine archipelago.

At the eastern limits of the archipelago, only the island of Mindanao lies at the latitudes mentioned by Francis Fletcher and John Drake. Furthermore, it is a large island, about the size of Indiana, and serves as a barrier to the few other Philippine islands situated at similar latitudes because they cannot be reached from the east without running up against its coastline.

If Drake indeed made his first landfall at Mindanao (Map 7) it would have to have been in the vicinity of Bislig Bay or Lianga Bay, for these alone are situated at suitable latitudes. They are located on the eastern side of a cordillera that extends for 250 miles along the coast of the island and descends sharply into the sea. At the head of each bay lies a lowland area; otherwise the coast is marked by rugged mountains.

Before Drake anchored there, Mindanao had been visited by a succession of Portuguese and Spaniards, and we shall have frequent occasion to refer to most of them in the ensuing investigation. If we accept the statements of Antonio Galvão, who was Portuguese governor of the Moluccas and author of a major work chronicling the discoveries of the world up to the year 1555, the first of these was Francisco Serrão. As we have already noted, Serrão had been sent out from Malacca in 1511 by the Portuguese viceroy of India on an exploratory expedition. After coasting many islands of the Banda Sea and loading his ship with spices at Banda, he headed back toward Malacca, but a storm separated his vessel from the others. The boat, a newly purchased junk, was wrecked but Serrão succeeded in reaching the island of Mindanao in 1512 with nine or ten of his companions (Galvão 1563: 35b–36b). Unfortunately, he provides us with no geographical or ethnological information and does no more for us than establish the possible priority of the Portuguese in the Philippines.

Magellan's *Trinidad* and *Victoria*, after the captain-general had

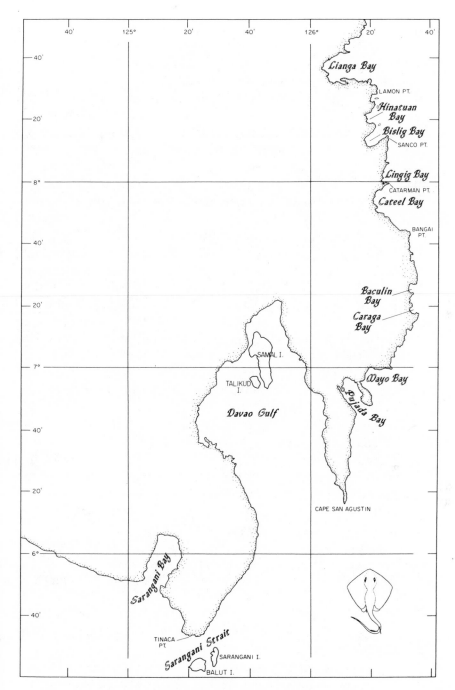

**Map 7. Mindanao—East and South Coasts**

lost his life at Mactan, went to Mindanao twice in 1521. Here, as we shall see, the records have some usefulness.

Two of García de Loaisa's ships, the *Santa María del Parral* and the *Santa María de la Victoria*, anchored there independently of one another in 1526, the latter vessel possibly stopping at Bislig Bay, a place that of course greatly interests us.

Soon after, Alvaro de Saavedra's *Florida* went to Mindanao twice, in 1528 and 1529, being careened on a small island near the very bay where Loaisa's two ships had stopped. Unfortunately, accounts of his voyage have little usefulness for us.

Another Portuguese visitor (Serrão was the first) was Francisco de Castro, a remarkable lay missionary. He had been sent in 1538 by the aforementioned Antonio Galvão from the Moluccas to Mindanao and other islands nearby to convert the natives to Christianity. Six kings, together with their wives, children, and subjects, received the waters of baptism (Galvão 1563:68b). Galvão, who is our source for this adventure, gives us no details useful for our purposes.

Ruy Lopez Villalobos' fleet of six vessels stayed at Mindanao for a month in 1543, and later in the same year his *San Juan de Letran* circled the whole island.

That amazing duo, Alonso de Arellano and Lope Martín, who had detached their *San Lucas* from Miguel López de Legazpi's westbound fleet and had reached the Philippines ahead of the eventual conqueror of the archipelago, remained on Mindanao for more than a month in the year 1565 before probing other islands of the archipelago and speeding back to Mexico on what was the first eastward traverse of the Pacific.

Another of Legazpi's ships, the *San Juan*, while searching for Arellano and Martín, had some experiences with Muslim traders at Butuan, on the north coast of Mindanao. Later, in November of 1566, it came upon part of a Portuguese armada from India (which claimed it was based at Mindanao), its immediate mission being to frighten Legazpi away from the archipelago; however, its original assignment had been to help the Portuguese quell an uprising in Ambon, a center of the spice trade. No consequences followed upon this confrontation, in which Legazpi himself was not involved as he had not gone to Mindanao.

After Legazpi had entrenched the Spaniards in the Philippines, visits to Mindanao were routine (Schurz 1939).

## THE DEVICES OF DETECTION

Aside from geography and demography, the only evidential devices available for searching out an answer to the Drake question are ethnography and ethnohistory. However, for an area of the size and importance of Mindanao, much less is at hand than one might expect.

This is especially true of ethnography, where anthropologists have spent disappointingly little time on the so-called wild tribes—peoples not so highly accultured by intruding civilizations as to have lost their cultural identity. The east coast of Mindanao has been especially neglected, yet it is the place most relevant to our search. All this is in marked contrast to the Mountain Province of Luzon, where work has been intensive; but unfortunately the Ifugao, Bontoc, Kalinga, Apayao, Ibaloy, and Kankanay, as well as ethnolinguistic peoples of the province of Abra, are not particularly comparable to the ones encountered by Drake. Some pygmies have been studied in Mindanao but they are mountain folk whose location and way of life are even more disparate from the areas under discussion than those of the interior peoples of Luzon. I do not say that ethnography is absolutely without beneficial information; it is only that it has infinitely less to offer than the intensive work done in tiny Micronesia over the last century of time by German, Japanese, and American anthropologists. In order to compensate for the dearth of data from eastern Mindanao it has been necessary to enlist help from other parts of the island and from other islands, too, particularly the Visayas.[1]

The historic accounts, on the other hand, provide more useful information than the ethnographic ones. The best observations are those of early European explorers, administrators, and missionaries, all of whom had a vital interest in the natives because they saw them as instruments for the fulfillment of economic and proselytizing ambitions. Special mention must be made of Antonio Pigafetta, Magellan's chronicler. Later commentators often have written in greater detail than he but they tend to stress nonmaterial culture, especially government, the family, and religion, all of which have less usefulness for us than material culture, which is what Fletcher and John Drake were concerned about.

There may well be Arabic writings about which I am unaware. If they do exist they might conceivably contain valuable information because of the depth of Muslim penetration throughout much of Mindanao. However, the particular part of the island in which we are interested was never Islamized

Chinese sources exist but are of very limited use in supplying clues to the Drake mystery. Prior to the Ming dynasty they are vague and disappointing, and before A.D. 982 they are merely presumptive and refer for the most part to the South Seas in general rather than any place that can be identified specifically with the Philippines. There are early and frequent references to the "Country of Black Teeth," but intriguing as this may sound it is unlikely that the land referred to is in the Philippines, as some have suggested.[2]

The first Chinese datum apparently referring specifically to the Philippines appeared in A.D. 982 but is too brief to be of use. Of several subsequent documents, two are somewhat lengthier and belong to the Sung and Yuan dynasties. The Sung record is Chau Ju-kua's *Chu-fan-chih*, dated c. 1225. The second or Yuan record is Wang Ta-yüan's *Tao I Chih Lüeh*, dated 1349. We shall have occasion to refer to them later.

Of the potential of archaeology I have said nothing simply because it scarcely exists. In the few instances in which I shall use archaeological findings I shall do so mostly to embellish the data from ethnography and ethnohistory.

Having made these brief remarks on the sources and devices of detection, let us now proceed to ascertain how much they can be of assistance to us.

### THIEVING TACTICS

What can we discover as to the *modus operandi* of the natives of the Philippines in situations of confrontation with Europeans? The Magellan episode might come to mind as a start, but despite the fact that the great explorer lost his life at one of the islands he was not the victim of treachery or intended thievery. He died while doing battle against a native king who had openly defied the authority of the sovereign of Spain. He and the local king had arranged for the fight at Mactan Island and there is even a suggestion of what is customarily thought of as chivalrous combat. So we must turn elsewhere for the kind of clue that we are seeking.

Can it be found when the second Spanish expedition across the Pacific arrived at Mindanao? Details are lacking but Urdaneta tells us that when the flagship of Loaisa's fleet anchored in 1526 at what must have been Lianga or possibly Bislig Bay, the natives there tried to cut the ship's cables and were only prevented from doing so by the vigilance of the Spaniards (*Col. doc. inéd. Indias* 1864–1884:V, 18). All that we can be sure of is that the indigenes of this interesting part of the island of Mindanao were aggressive but not necessarily treacherous.

Saavedra comes next. Some natives came out to his vessel after it had anchored in the vicinity of Lianga Bay on the eastern coast of Mindanao. The natives, who refused to go aboard the *Florida*, were persuaded by the use of signs to fill up some containers with water and come back to the ship with them. The king, named Catonao, later came on board with his son-in-law, who was also a chief, as well as with three other persons and a child, his son, whom he carried in his arms. Later, the natives tried to cut the ship's cables and pull the ship to shore but they did not succeed because they cut only one cable and overlooked the other (*Col. doc. inéd. Indias* 1864–1884:V, 76–78; cf. Navarrete 1825–1837:V, 479–480). We have here an instance of treachery after an initial show of friendship, but the example is a weak one. The natives were initially reluctant to come on board at all, and when they tried to beach the Spanish vessel in the dark they botched up their effort almost ludicrously, and the Spaniards on their part did not react with hostility, possibly because they had been aware of the maneuvers against them. The example also suffers because the natives involved not only had kings with gold crowns but also mines, cutlasses, cannons, corselets, and other sophisticated accoutrements (*Col. doc. inéd. Indias* 1864–1884:V, 79–80).

The Villalobos expedition in 1543 encountered several instances of what the Spaniards describe as outragious treachery by the indigenes. In a report to the viceroy of New Spain, Captain García Descalante Alvarado, the emperor's factor and the authority on the expedition, writes as follows about the people of Sarangani, off the southernmost tip of Mindanao:

> These people are all treacherous, and they do not keep faith or know how to keep it. They observe the peace and friendship they have contracted only so long as they are not prepared to do anything else; and as soon as they are prepared to commit any act of roguery they do not hesitate because of any peace and friendship that they have made. Those who carry on trade with them must conduct themselves very cautiously. Certain Spaniards who trusted in them were killed treacherously, under pretense of friendship. (*Col. doc. inéd. Indias* 1864–1884:V, 124)

Descalante Alvarado had led an attack on the natives of Sarangani and undoubtedly was writing with the passion of a Spanish officer unable to reconcile himself to the reluctance of the people to go along with the intentions of the intruders. Nevertheless, reports of duplicity are so common that they must be given some credence. However, as a *modus operandi* for thievery, such treachery as encountered by Descalante Alvarado is not very specifically described.

These same Spaniards, frustrated at Sarangani in their quest for food, dispatched a ship to nearby Mindanao to make peace and arrange terms of trade. It was received with an outward show of friendliness, but when a boat with six men was sent ashore, there sallied forth toward it many proas filled with men armed for battle. Seeing that the ship could not send help to the Spaniards, the natives attacked the visitors, killing one man and badly wounding the other five as they escaped (*Col. doc. inéd. Indias* 1864–1884:V, 125). Again, we see that there was duplicity but it was not designed to facilitate theft.

Treachery on the part of the natives at Mindanao is perhaps better illustrated by the harassment encountered in 1565 by Arellano and the crew of the *San Lucas*. While anchored in a cove in Davao Gulf, the natives had given the Spaniards every indication that they wanted to be friendly and to trade. Their young chief Viban had even offered to prick some blood ritually from his chest to show his friendship. Arellano had declined the proffered gesture, but Viban was not offended and caused wine to be brought for the visitors to drink. Gifts were exchanged. Later, Viban came back with two hundred followers bearing pigs, fowls, cooked dogs, rice, yams, honey, wax, sugarcane, incense, wine, oranges, lemons, and plantains. When later he again came, he had women and girls with him. And so it went. But some days later, after Viban had once more visited the cove with his lesser chiefs and their wives, he returned with some game taken in a hunt. The Spaniards were given to understand that he was now about to go off on another hunting trip. However, the next night some dogs aboard the *San Lucas* began to bark, having been aroused by a number of people on shore and by three large canoes creeping toward the vessel. Alerted, the Spaniards got their guns and harquebuses ready, and the canoes turned away and disappeared behind a point of land. It was agreed that apparently the natives had planned to cut the ship's cable and let it go ashore, where it would be vulnerable to attack. The next morning the same canoes that had disappeared the night before returned toward the ship, with Viban in one of them. An older chief accompanied him, and Viban seemed to pay deference to him. The *San Lucas* then put out to sea, sailing out of Davao Gulf on March 4, 1565 (*Col. doc. inéd. ultramar* 1885–1932:III, 47–48). Although the natives were unable to carry out their plan, they obviously had followed a familiar pattern, namely, trying to place a coveted European ship in a helpless tactical situation. Nevertheless, their *modus operandi* cannot be said to be distinctive enough to suggest that it was similar to that of Drake's thieves.

Up till now the testimony about Philippine duplicity has come entirely from a long procession of men writing about Spanish expeditions and it comes as a welcome change to hear from an Englishman, Captain Philip Carteret, even though he made his appearance almost exactly two centuries later. During his circumnavigation of the world in the *Swallow*, he anchored in 1767 in a small cove east of Tinaca Point, which is the southernmost tip of Mindanao, and there experienced such sudden hostility from the natives that he named the place "Deceitful Bay," although geographers know it as Balangonan Cove. At the sight of this vessel the inhabitants of the town of Batulaki had fired two great guns—only as an alarm, probably—and sent out three boats which chased the *Swallow*'s boat as it probed the coast in search of the bay. After the ship had been anchored, a small canoe was seen nearby but, having contented itself with looking over the visitors, it returned to the town. At nine o'clock at night the Englishmen were suddenly surprised by the hollering of a number of men onshore abreast the ship. Carteret surmised that their hideous shouts were intended to frighten them. The next morning he sent the longboat onshore to fetch some casks of water, and a number of men rushed out of the woods, with one of them holding something white which Carteret took for a signal of peace, a custom possibly learned from the Spaniards or Dutch. The men in the longboat were received in a very friendly manner and were told that they should go to see the rajah in the town. However, the Englishmen wished to get some water first, and this they did without interference. A native who seemed to be in authority over the rest was so admirous of a silk handkerchief being worn by the officer of the party that he was given it. An amicable agreement was reached to do some trading, and Carteret's men were told that they could acquire all the provisions they wanted. But as the Englishmen went on with their work they noticed that hundreds of armed men had posted themselves in parties along the beach. The natives hauled into the woods a canoe which stood under a shed on the beach, as if they were afraid it might be stolen. These men were armed with muskets, bows and arrows, long picks or spears, broadswords, krisses, and shields. For the remainder of the day they made menacing gestures against the visitors. When Carteret sent some men ashore with a white flag to speak to the people, he gave them instructions to go to a clear part of the beach—where they could not be attacked to disadvantage—but not to land. When the natives saw that nobody went out of the boat, one of them with a bow and arrow in his hands came out of the woods making signs for the boat to come where he was, which would have been within range of the arms of the concealed men. Not trusting the boat to be so near them, Carteret ordered it to return. He avoided the temptation to teach them "better manners," as he put it, because he still wanted to go to the town of Batulaki, but weather prevented him from doing so. Taking advantage of the winds he set sail for the passage between Borneo and Celebes (Wallis 1965:I, 205–208).

Carteret makes it clear that he was wary of the natives even before this unpleasantness. He remarks that when he first anchored he wanted to get up some guns he had in the hold of the ship, "knowing how little scrupulous ye people are in thes parts to cutt off all ship[s] they can master" (Wallis 1965:II, 354). He felt bitterly that the Dutch were in Batulaki and were responsible for the attack on him, but Helen Wallis, who has edited his accounts, thinks that this was not the case and that the people of Batulaki, anxious to preserve their precarious independence of both the Dutch and the Spanish, had by 1767 simply become suspicious of all European intruders except ordinary traders (Wallis 1965:I, 75). For us the important point is that while it is true that treachery may have been manifested, the objective of the natives was not theft but the repelling of a ship of the Royal Navy, which they interpreted as constituting a threat to their well-being and freedom. We fail to find here the apparent greed manifested by the people on Drake's Island of Thieves.

Looking back on all these examples, engrossing as they may be, I must conclude that they provide an unproductive scent and must be set aside.

### DARTS

In his second deposition John Drake mentions that the natives of the Island of Thieves carried "darts" in addition to stones.

If we think of the dart as a light spear, then it is almost ubiquitous in the western Pacific and is not discriminatory. However, if early explorers and others had made no mention of the spear for Mindanao it would be disturbing to any claim that Mindanao was Drake's island. Fortunately, references to spears and darts are ample and a few of the early ones may be cited.

Pigafetta, writing in Italian, noted that the people of Zuluan whom Magellan met on Humunu (Homonhon) used *lanse*, or spears, ornamented with gold, and *facine* or darts (Blair and Robertson 1903–1909:XXXIII, 110, 113).

Among the arms used by the natives whom the men of Loaisa's *Santa María de la Victoria* met in the vicinity of Lianga Bay after Loaisa had died, there were spears as well as canes "with fire-hardened points with many barbs which they can throw very far" (Oviédo y Valdés 1557:no page no.).[3] Urdaneta, who was on this ship, tells us that at the port of "Bisaya" (Bislig?) on the east coast of Mindanao the natives were bellicose and among other weapons had *azagayas*, or light spears (*Col. doc. inéd. Indias* 1864–1884:V, 18).

In his account of Saavedra's stay in Mindanao, Nápoles mentions that among the arms of the natives were *lanzas*, or spears (*Col. doc. inéd. Indias* 1864–1884:V, 79). From this account we cannot tell if the spears were hurled or not.

The presence of the dart is strongly suggested by Descalante Alvarado, who in narrating Villalobos' stay on Mindanao mentions that among the offensive arms of the inhabitants "of these islands" were *lanzas* and *azagayas* (*Col. doc. inéd. Indias* 1864–1884:V, 123; cf. Blair and Robertson 1903–1909:II, 69). By his use of terminological differences he makes a distinction between two kinds of weapons and, incidentally, leads us to suppose that Urdaneta's above use of the word *azagaya* implies a distinction from heavier spears.

Finally, writing of the Philippines as a whole, Legazpi comments that "lances with iron points, one and one-half palms in length" were among the weapons generally used (Blair and Robertson 1903–1909:II, 201). He also mentions the use of lances on Bohol (p. 206) and a nearby island (p. 209), and says he sent half-a-dozen lances to King Philip II of Spain (p. 234). But best of all for our purposes he tells us that when his Armada of three ships went to Cebu in April of 1565 for the purpose of making a settlement there, the natives proved hostile and in the battle that ensued they took to "hurling their lances by divisions of threes" (Blair and Robertson 1903–1909:II, 213).

All these sources seem to confirm the presence in Mindanao of darts of some kind, and even though this type of clue is weak, because it is not mentioned by Fletcher and is not very discriminating, it is at least satisfied.

## THE SLING

Ethnohistorical references to the use of stones as weapons in the Philippines are ample enough, but one cannot be sure that slings were employed to wing them on their way. The sling of course cannot on that account be ruled out, especially since ethnohistorical reports for the Carolines and Marianas often make reference to the use of stones without specifying the use of slings; yet we know that for these places there is ethnological and even archaeological evidence that the sling was indeed used.

For the Philippines, such conclusive proof is lacking. On the other hand, it will be recalled, Fletcher never said that the stones hurled at the English at the Island of Thieves were dispatched with the help of slings. It is an assumption made by me, and it may well be that such an assumption is unwarranted. The instances that follow, then, are equatable with the Fletcher account in that both similarly mention stones without mentioning slings.

As usual, Pigafetta supplies the earliest testimony, saying that when Magellan and his party were being engaged at Mactan Island in what was to prove to be a mortal battle, they were assaulted not only with arrows, bamboo spears, pointed stakes, and mud, but *pietre*, or stones, as well (Blair and Robertson 1903–1909:XXXIII, 178, 179). After Magellan had been shot through the right leg with a poisoned arrow, he ordered a retreat, which ended in a flight. Six or eight men remained with the captain-general. Writes Pigafetta: "The natives shot only at our legs, for the latter were bare; and so many were the spears and stones that they hurled at us, that we could offer no resistance" (Blair and Robertson 1903–1909: XXXIII, 178, 179).

Another very early mention of what may or may not imply the use of the sling comes from a statement by Descalante Alvarado in his account of Villalobos' ill-fated expedition. He says that the Spaniards had trouble with the natives at Sarrangar (Sarangani), who defended themselves "with small stones, poles, arrows, and mangrove cudgels . . ." (*Col. doc. inéd. Indias* 1864–1884:V, 121).

When Legazpi reached the Visayan island of Samar in February 1565, he was frustrated in his frantic efforts to find food supplies because the inhabitants were wary of the Spaniards. He and some monks, together with a number of sailors and soldiers, tried to make friends with the people of the village of Cuniungo. As they approached shore in the ships' boats they were met with hostility, and after deciding to retreat they were showered with stones (*Col. doc. inéd. ultramar* 1885–1932:II, 261).[4] Later, after Legazpi had left the island of Bohol and reached Cebu, he sent a party in a boat to make peace with the natives on behalf of the king of Spain. The people would not let them land because they said that their own king was not present, so they stoned the boat, causing the camp master to return to the flagship to report to the general what had happened (*Col. doc. inéd. ultramar* 1885–1932:II, 421). While still on the island of Cebu, in the vicinity of which Magellan had been killed, the Spaniards made some punitive expeditions to help a local chief named Tupas. On the first of these raids a party of Legazpi's men, while attempting an assault on a well-defended position on a slope, had to face a hail of pebbles (*riesgó de muchos guijas*) (*Col. doc. inéd. ultramar* 1885–1932:III, 123), but unfortunately there is no way of knowing if the pebbles were hurled with the aid of a sling.

Lastly, in his *Adventurous Armada* Andrew Sharp tells us that the Spaniards on the ship's boat of the *San Gerónimo*, the small galleon sent out from Mexico in 1566 in response to Legazpi's plea for help, were assailed with stones and spears when they went ashore for water and supplies on a small island where the ship had anchored after passing through the San Bernardino Strait (Sharp 1961:151).[5]

## *NUDITY*

The men who manned the canoes that accosted the *Golden Hind* were twice described by young John Drake as being "naked," but he did not elaborate on this point, on which Fletcher is entirely silent.

In our search for nudity it is necessary to rely upon accounts describing not the east coast of Mindanao but the north coast, as well as other islands. Fortunately, Pigafetta comes to our aid, without however being decisive.

Magellan had anchored his vessels off the uninhabited island of Humunu (Homonhon) southeast of Samar, in order to rest his invalids on land. Pigafetta, in writing that the people living near the island went naked, obviously uses the word in a loose sense, for he adds the remark that they wore "a cloth woven from the bark of a tree about their privies, except some of the chiefs who wear cotton cloth embroidered with silk at the ends by means of a needle" (Blair and Robertson 1903–1909:XXXIII, 109). This is the first of a series of disconcerting uses of the word for nakedness.

At the Visayan island of Zubu (Cebu), Pigafetta visited the king in his palace, seated on a mat on the ground "with only a cotton cloth before his privies, and a scarf embroidered with the needle about his head . . ." (Blair and Robertson 1902–1909:XXXIII, 147). Later, the prince took the foreigners to his own house, where four girls were playing instruments, and they "were naked except for tree cloth hanging from the waist and reaching to the knees" (Blair and Robertson 1903–1909:XXXIII, 151). This statement has the virtue of lucidity because it explicitly qualifies what in this particular instance is meant as nakedness. Pigafetta then adds statements suggestive of complete nudity when he writes that "some were quite naked" and that "the prince had three quite naked girls dance for us" (Blair and Robertson 1903–1909:XXXIII, 151).[6] Further on he writes that the queen came with great pomp to hear mass and that "A great number of women accompanied her, who were all naked and barefoot, except that they had a small covering of palm-tree cloth before their privies . . ." (Blair and Robertson 1903–1909:XXXIII, 161). Once more, still writing about Cebu, he says: "Those people go naked, wearing but one piece of palm-tree cloth about their privies" (Blair and Robertson 1903–1909:XXXIII, 171).

Pigafetta does give a conclusive instance of complete nudity. After Magellan was killed on the little island of Mactan off the east coast of Cebu, the survivors of his expedition burned one of their ships, the *Concepción*, off the island of Bohol because there were too few men left to work it. They sailed south to northern Mindanao, where the king came out to the vessels and went through a blood pact ritual with the foreigners as a token of closest friendship. Pigafetta set out for shore alone with the king in a *balanghai* in order to see the island, and as they were entering a river "the king removed the cloths which covered his privies, as did some of his chiefs; and began to row while singing past many dwellings which were upon the river" (Blair and Robertson 1903–1909:XXXIII, 199). Subsequently he adds the more general statement that the "people go naked" (Blair and Robertson 1903–1909: XXXIII, 205). The significance of the first observation is that it suggests the possibility that men on Mindanao may have gone completely naked when manning their canoes.

Later, Pigafetta went to a small, almost uninhabited island to the southwest, Cagayan Sulu, where the people, who were Muslims banished from an island called Burne, "go naked as do the others" (Blair and Robertson 1903–1909:XXXIII, 207). On the island of Palawan, admittedly far to the west of Mindanao and therefore of questionable significance, Pigafetta likewise found that the people "go naked as do the others" (Blair and Robertson 1903–1909: XXXIII, 211).

Subsequent commentators seem to have been afflicted with Pigafetta's ambiguous use of the word for nudity. Thus, when Legazpi arrived at the Visayan island of Samar from Guam in 1565 he was visited by some chiefs and their followers. They were described by Esteban Rodriguez, his chief pilot, as wearing gold earrings but being *desnudos*, except for a loincloth that covered their private parts (*Col. doc. inéd. ultramar* 1885–1932:II, 395).

Some generalized but contradictory remarks about nudity in the Philippines have been made by Francisco de Sande, who sailed from Acapulco to the Philippines in 1575 to assume the governorship of the archipelago. In a report to the king of Spain he says that the people of the islands are "naked, and barefoot," but then he adds without any awareness of the ambiguity of his description that they wrap a cotton cloth around their loins (Blair and Robertson 1903–1909:IV, 67). In a later report to the king he again says that the natives go naked, yet in the same breath offers the information that they know how to raise silk and cotton to spin and weave into clothing (Blair and Robertson 1903–1909:IV, 98).

Carelessness of this kind is so common in the old records that one is justified in asking if John Drake really had been thinking of total nudity. Some further and final examples ought to increase any doubts that may have arisen in one's mind. They seem to support the obvious suggestion that in those times the idea of nudity was somewhat relative.

The sixteenth-century Boxer codex, for instance, tells us that Visaya men "usually go naked, and wear nothing on the body except a cotton cloth . . . which with a few polished turns they wrap around their waist and between the legs so as to cover the private parts and posteriors . . ." (Quirino and Garcia 1958:397). The unidentified compiler of the codex[7] probably visited the Visayan islands but we do not know which islands they may have been. Anyway, once more the Spanish word *desnudos* is used in a sense short of complete nudity.

A provocative but again inconclusive statement was made in 1609 by Bartolomé Leonardo de Argensola, who says that the reason the region of the Pintados is so called is "because the Indians at that time went about naked, and with their bodies adorned and painted [tattooed] in various colors" (Argensola 1609:164). What interests us here, of course, is not the tattooing prevalent at the time of Legazpi, which is the period referred to by the writer, but the remote possibility that the Pintados (Visayans) were naked—that is, utterly naked. Argensola does not resolve the problem any more than do other writers.

Captain Pagés, who visited Samar in 1768, says: "In the remote parts of the country, and especially at a distance from the missionaries, persons of both sexes appear almost naked" (Pagés 1791–1792:I, 205).

None of all this is intended to imply that the natives of the Philippines were uniformly clad in few or no clothes at all. Indeed, there are numerous descriptions of people wearing ample garments. The earliest seems to be in the Yuan dynasty document mentioned earlier in the section on the devices of detection. It is pre-Hispanic in time. In it Wang states that on San Tao, which some modern scholars identify as the coast south of Cape Engano (Luzon), "All wear a single garment" (Wu 1959:108). The men and women of Ma-yi, a place not specifically identified but probably an island or island group in the north, are said to "wear a blue cotton shirt" (Wu 1959:108). On Min-to-lang, which may be Mindanao, both men and women "wear short black shirt, and the blue cloth petticoat" (Wu 1959:109). At Ma-li-lu, not identified, "all wear short shirt of blue cloth, and tie around them a red cloth turban" (Wu 1959:109). Finally, in Su-lu, identified as Sulu, the people are said to trade with the Chinese for cotton cloth (Wu 1959:109).

One could argue that none of these people belong to the northeastern coast of Mindanao, and that certainly they represent inhabitants exposed to Chinese influences. Such a protest seems to be counteracted by some observations made by Urdaneta, who was on the *Santa María de la Victoria* when it reached Mindanao on October 6, 1526, and anchored at a port called Bizaya. He states that the natives wore clothing of cotton and silk, and garments of satin cloth from China (*Col. doc. inéd. Indias* 1864–1884:V, 18). It comes as a shock to know that geographers have more or less identified Bizaya as being Lianga Bay or possibly Bislig Bay, the very places that Sharp's theory would favor as being in the area of Drake's landfall. This is the approximate area, too, where Saavedra later landed, and his chronicler, Nápoles, likewise describes the natives of the place as wearing very fine cotton cloth (*Col. doc. inéd. Indias* 1864–1884:V, 79).

Another early report of ample clothing refers to an area much farther south and is less jarring on that account. Arellano, whose small *San Lucas* sighted Mindanao on January 29, 1565, at 9 degrees, found anchorage the next day in Davao Gulf and tells us something about the dress he saw on both men and women. The day after he anchored, says Arellano, two or three natives appeared on the beach and pilot Lope Martín went ashore with a few men. The natives wore cloth head coverings and breeches and carried daggers in their belts. Later, after the foreigners had returned to their ship, a finely dressed young chief appeared on the beach and waved to the ship. Arellano and Martín went ashore with a small party of their men. Arellano reports that the chief, named Viban, wore a dagger in his belt. Native spiced wine was drunk and gifts were exchanged. On the following day Viban returned with more than two hundred followers who bore all sorts of foods. The next day when Viban once more put in an appearance he was accompanied by his brother and two other chiefs, with their wives, who were attended by some girls. The ladies wore long skirts, elegant bodices, and attractive bonnets (*Col. doc. inéd. ultramar* 1885–1932:III, 27–34 passim). Obviously, this was something of a state visit demanding a display of finery, and it would be interesting to know how these people were dressed in routine circumstances. The two or three natives first encountered on the beach apparently wore nothing more than head coverings and breeches.

To sum up this evidence it would seem clear that one cannot discount Mindanao only because of reports of clothing worn by the natives. South Sea islanders who set out in canoes with adventure on their minds are apt literally to shed their clothes and be stripped for action, with little use for more than a possible loincloth. Certainly, silks and satins would be incongruous with their purpose. Recall, too, the king and his chiefs, who removed the cloths from their privies when they and Pigafetta sailed up a river on the island of Mindanao. And the reader is once more reminded that *The World Encompassed* and the "Famous Voyage" never mention nudity. Only John Drake does, and he may have meant something less than complete bareness.

## DISTENDED EARLOBES

Another of the culture traits mentioned by Fletcher, the enlarging of holes made in the lobes of the ears, is widespread in the Malaysian culture area and is noticeably present in the Philippine archipelago. That the practice extended back in time to at least the arrival of Magellan is attested to by Pigafetta for an unspecified island near Homonhon, where the Spanish vessels had anchored. He writes,

> There are people living near that island who have holes in their ears so large that they can pass their arms through them. Those people are caphri, that is to say, heathen. (Blair and Robertson 1903–1909:XXXIII, 109)

Homonhon, it will be recalled, is north of Mindanao, near Samar. Unless Pigafetta was guilty of gross exaggeration, the lengthening of the lobes was comparable to that in the Caroline Islands.

However, subsequent accounts by other reporters are more modest in their descriptions. Indeed, Pigafetta himself says merely of the naked girls whose prince had arranged at Cebu for them to entertain the foreigners that some "had large holes in their ears with a small round piece of wood in the hole, which keeps the hole round and large" (Blair and Robertson 1903–1909:XXXIII, 151). He fails to describe the ears of the men.

A variation in the piercing of ears is reported in the Boxer manuscript, which stresses that numerous ornaments could be worn in the lobe because it had so many holes (Quirino and Garcia 1958:406–407). The natives in question were the Visayans of the period around 1590.

Gemelli Careri, who traveled in the Philippines in 1697 but often used the accounts of others in his descriptions of the peoples of the archipelago, informs us that "in some countries" both men and women delighted in wearing pendants in their ears, and the bigger the hole in the ear was, the handsomer it was counted. Some had two in an ear (Churchill 1704:V, 447).

Large holes are reported also by the missionary Juan Francisco de San Antonio who spent twenty years in the Philippines during the first half of the eighteenth century. He says that by then the "civilized" people had adopted the custom of the Castilians in

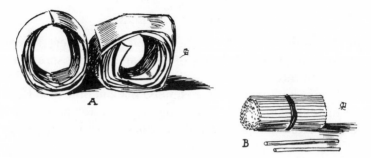

Figure 22. Bagobo Ear Stretchers. "A" are twisted leaves that act as a spring; "B" are small sticks which are increased from time to time. Source: Cole 1913: fig. 5.

piercing the lobes of the ears but that others, especially in the mountains, had large holes in which they placed pendants and gold earrings (Blair and Robertson 1903–1909:XL, 328).

On Mindanao specifically there are various examples, although none are for the east coast under scrutiny. Late in the last century the Bukidnon of the north central part of the island are reported to have been wearing a large ear ornament called a *balaring*, which was a plug of wood at each end of which was a circular plate of brass, copper, silver, or engraved gold. The hole of the ear was greatly stretched to allow the plate to go through (Sawyer 1900:341).

Modern ethnographers have reported that enlargement of the lobes was still being practiced in recent times by contemporary tribes on Mindanao. The Manobos of the eastern part of that island, especially in the Agusan Valley, are said to pierce the earlobes of both sexes and enlarge the aperture (Garvan 1941:55–56). The valley is inland from the eastern coast at approximately the latitude of the head of the Davao Gulf. The Bagobo, one of the so-called wild tribes of the west coast of the gulf, enlarged the ears of both men and women—at least, in the early part of the present century—to permit the insertion of ear plugs. One method was to put a piece of twisted banana or hemp leaf in the earlobe of the child, the leaf acting as a spring which continually enlarged the opening. The other method was to fill the opening with small round sticks, adding more from time to time, until the desired result was obtained (Figure 22) (Cole 1913:59). Living south of the Bagobo, but located in the mountains on the west side of Davao Gulf, are another "wild tribe," the Bila-an, whose men and women both wear large wooden ear plugs (Cole 1913:134).

It should be obvious by now that these various examples portray the enlarged lobe as essentially a means of holding an ornament, whereas Francis Fletcher in his account does not mention ornaments. On the other hand, as we have previously seen, the enlargement of the hole in the Carolines was essentially an end in itself, the insertion of ornaments being somewhat secondary and occasional. Nevertheless, the Philippine examples that have been offered technically satisfy the criterion of distension, even though imperfectly.

## LONG FINGERNAILS

While Fletcher left much unsaid about the "theeves" who harassed Drake, he was sufficiently attracted to the long fingernails of some of them that he not only mentions them but states their approximate length, one inch.

References in the literature to long fingernails as a Philippine cultural trait are rare. Of the Mindanayans of Mindanao, Dampier made this observation in 1686: "They have a Custom to wear their Thumb-nails very long, especially that on their left Thumb, for they never cut it but scrape it often" (Dampier 1697:326). However, the people he described were Muslims living around Illana Bay, far from the east coast of Mindanao. P. M. F. de Pagés, a French naval officer who visited the non-Islamic natives of Samar in 1768, wrote: "Thick short fingers, and long nails on the middle and little ones, are esteemed highly becoming, insomuch that I have observed them on different persons two full inches in length" (Pagés 1791–1792:I, 203).

Allowing the nails to grow long can never be a luxury permitted to all the men of a community. It is too impractical. Indeed, for this reason the Chinese regarded it as a mark of genteelness in which only the aristocracy and gentry could afford to indulge. Those men among Drake's annoyers who had long nails may have represented a special class or category. It may well be that the failure of the literature to report the custom, except in the instance of Dampier and Pagés, stems from its limited occurrence, thereby escaping the attention of observers. For these reasons I am inclined to discount it as a truly significant clue.

## BETEL-NUT CHEWING

The next clue, the betel-nut-chewing habit, can be demonstrated beyond the shadow of a doubt to have been an old and widespread culture trait in the Philippines. Although it is not necessary to rely on archaeological finds to prove this point, they are available. Ming and Sung jarlets with prepared lime inside have been found in grave goods, and it has been inferred that the discolored human teeth and shell containers found in Palawan caves and belonging to a period about 2500 B.C. provide indications that the practice extends back to the neolithic period (Scott 1968:39; Fox 1970:62, 65, 109). If this evidence is not sufficiently conclusive, there are less controvertible ones.

Thus, the presence of the betel in pre-Hispanic times seems amply established by Chinese records. We know that the nut was one of the products bartered with China by the Philippines during the Sung dynasty (Hirth and Rockhill 1911:160, 214). It was thought to have medicinal value and to prevent belching. The source of this information is Chau Ju-kua, who in the thirteenth century was inspector of foreign trade in Fukien. His remarkable book *Chu-fan-chih*, or "Description of Barbarous Peoples," is a valuable source of information on the ethnography of the countries and tribes known through the sea trade carried on by Chinese and Muslim traders in the Far East. The author does not say anything at all about the Filipinos' own use of the betel, but it is reasonable to assume that it was being chewed in the classic manner with betel-pepper leaves and lime.

Wang Ta-yüan's *Tao I Chih Lüeh*, published in 1349, corroborates the presence of the betel in May-yi, this time during the Yuan dynasty. Ma-yi is generally identified as being the islands of Mindoro and Luzon, and by extension is applied to the whole Philippine archipelago (Wu 1959:109).

In addition to the archaeological finds and Chinese records, we have the statements of the delightfully perceptive Pigafetta, the first European to mention the practice of betel-nut chewing in the Philippines. Writing of the island of Masaua (modern Limasawa), off the southern coast of Leyte, he tells us:

> Those people are constantly chewing a fruit which they call *areca*, and which resembles a pear. They cut that fruit into four parts, and then wrap it in the leaves of their tree which they call *betre* [betel]. Those leaves resemble the leaves of the mulberry. They mix it with a little lime, and when they have chewed it thoroughly, they spit it out.

It makes the mouth exceedingly red. All the people in those parts of the world use it, for it is very cooling to the heart, and if they ceased to use it they would die. (Blair and Robertson 1903–1909:XXXIII, 132–133)

History has two picturesque passages concerning the use of the betel in the Philippines. Early in the seventeenth century the theologians of the College of Manila often gave their expert opinions on actual moral problems upon the request of the authorities, or fellow Jesuits working in the missions, or private persons. Their decisions for the period 1602–1636 have been preserved, and among them is a response to a query as to whether one breaks the law of fasting by chewing the betel. No, said the moralists. Chewing two or three preparations does not break the fast because the quantity is too small; only a portion of the betel is swallowed, the rest being saliva and uncleanliness (Costa 1961:356). The other passage concerns a proposed Japanese college in Manila, where young Japanese could be trained as priests and then sent back to their native land to serve among their oppressed Christian brethren. Accordingly, an ordinance was issued by the governor in 1624 setting in motion such a project and providing for a regular income for the institution by various means, one of which included a government monopoly of betel and tobacco. The furore raised in Manila was overwhelming because it affected everyone who smoked or chewed the betel. The *audiencia* rescinded the ordinance, which had other objectionable provisions, too (Costa 1961:370–371).

Morga supports the above when he describes in some detail the betel complex as it existed on Luzon during the latter part of the same century (Morga 1868:280–282).

The widespread use of the nut in the Philippines is most heavily documented by the Jesuit historian Juan José Delgado (1697–1755) in his remarkable encyclopaedic work *Historia general sacro-profana, política y natural de las Islas del Poniente, Llamadas Filipinas* (Delgado 1892:667–668, 774).

The Augustinian historian Father Zúñiga (1760–1818) makes some observations on the custom of chewing the betel and adds the interesting comment that "even many Spaniards adopt it with great avidity" (Zúñiga 1966:7).

In addition to these more generalized reports, there fortunately are specific references to the use of the betel nut on the island of Mindanao, and these may be examined briefly. The first reference is given by Captain Dampier, who visited Mindanao in 1686. He chewed some of the betel nuts and said that the old ones but not the new ones cause great giddiness in the head of those not used to chewing them. He adds, inaccurately, that the nut makes the teeth black (Dampier 1697:318–319). Moving down in time to the present century, the anthropologist Fay-Cooper Cole says of the Bukidnon of north-central Mindanao, who live on a high plain, that continued betel chewing discolors the teeth (Cole 1956:29). He observed these people in 1910. He also found that the Bagobo, one of the so-called wild tribes of Davao Gulf, were chewing betel almost constantly when he visited them, also in 1910. So were the Manobo of east Mindanao seen by Garvan (1941:18). For the Bagobo, Cole describes in some detail the method of preparing the wad, and depicts the boxes and tubes (Figure 23) used for carrying the materials (Cole 1913:70, 71, fig. 14, and pls. XVIIa and XLI).

## BLACKENED TEETH

The deliberate blackening of teeth for aesthetic purposes is well known in the Philippines, thereby giving further credence to the Mindanao hunch. Antonio de Morga, who was lieutenant-governor of the archipelago late in the sixteenth century, tells us about the practice as it existed on the northern island of Luzon, saying that the black color of the teeth is perpetual but ugly to look at (Morga 1868:270).[8] His opinion of course was not shared by the natives.

The next to comment on blackened teeth is the Boxer codex, which informs us that the Visayans of the times were accustomed to blacken or redden the teeth with a certain juice or herb (Quirino and Garcia 1958:417) and that the Tagalogs do likewise (p. 426), but one is left in doubt if the blackening, at least, was the accidental result of chewing the betel nut or a deliberate effort, using some other material. Perhaps the compiler of the codex was unable to make a distinction between the two.

The same kind of ambiguity is to be seen in a statement made in

1604 by the Jesuit Pedro Chirino to the effect that "all cover their teeth with a varnish, either lustrous black or bright red—with the result that the teeth remain as black as jet, or red as vermillion or

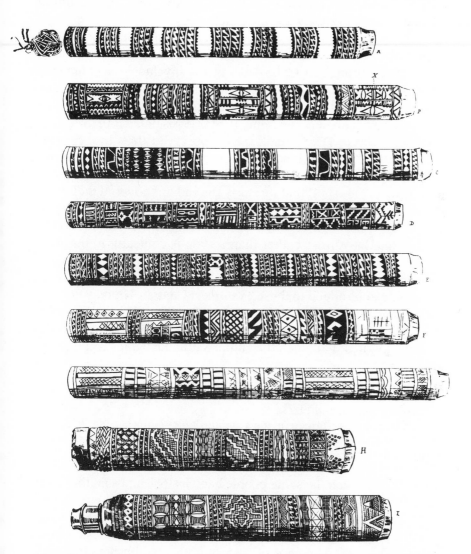

Figure 23. Bagobo Lime Tubes. These incised bamboo containers are also used for tobacco. Source: Cole 1913: fig. 14.

ruby" (Blair and Robertson 1903–1909:XII, 187). Were there indeed two separate and purposeful kinds of cosmetic coloring? If so, this would be the only reference in the literature to reddening of which I am aware. I exclude of course any red coloring resulting as a side effect from chewing the betel.

Later writers leave us in no doubt; they tell of the straightforward blackening of the teeth. For instance, the Jesuit pioneer missionary Francisco Colín says in his invaluable seventeenth-century work *Labor evangélica* that the natives of the islands covered their teeth "with a heavy coating of black ink or varnish which aided in preserving them" (Colín 1900–1902:I, 60). Speaking of women only, Dr. Gemelli Careri observed that they covered their teeth "with a black dye to preserve them" (Churchill 1704:447). The Franciscan writer Juan de San Antonio relates in his *Crónicas* (1738–1744) that formerly the Indians covered their teeth "with ink or a varnish of a black color" (Blair and Robertson 1903–1909:XL, 327). Whether or not Colín and San Antonio really had in mind a varnish rather than a stain is conjectural, but most likely the blackening was due to the penetration of some kind of dye into the enamel.

More can be added to these examples. Captain Thomas Forrest, describing the Muslims in the area around Illana Bay in the southwest of Mindanao as they were when he saw them in the eighteenth century, writes that when the sultan's granddaughter came of age she had

> her beautiful white teeth filed thin when stripped of the enamel, in order to be stained black.
> This rite is performed on the Mindano ladies at the age of thirteen; and the ceremony is sumptuous in proportion to the rank of the person. (Forrest 1779:251)

Dampier had seen the same people back in 1688 and said that their teeth were "black" (Dampier 1697:325).

Making a leap into the twentieth century, there are reports by anthropologists of the blackening of teeth by some tribes on Mindanao. Thus, the Manobos of eastern Mindanao blacken the teeth of both sexes by rubbing a plant across them (Garvan 1941:55). Teeth are blackened by both the men and women of the coastal Bagobo tribe of Davao district. Color is obtained either from carbon, collected by holding a piece of metal over the smoke of burning bamboo, or from a powder secured from the *lamod* tree, which is put on leaves and chewed (Cole 1913:60–61). The Bukidnon of north-central Mindanao, who are on a high plain and therefore are not coastal people, blacken their teeth with a deposit formed by the burning of guava bark. The "sweat" deposited on the blade is rubbed on the teeth several nights in succession, and the process must be repeated at intervals to maintain a proper color (Cole 1956:33; cf. Sawyer 1900:342).

It is interesting that the teeth of skeltons discovered by archaeologists in ancient graves and burial caves indicate that some of them were artificially blackened or reddened (Scott 1968:35). Apparently, however, it is not possible in this instance to say if the coloring was deliberate or the result of the incidental use of the betel nut.

## CANOES

Canoes could be the *sine qua non* for identifying Drake's island, and to them we must next direct our attention.

It is infinitely regrettable but nevertheless understandable that early descriptions of Philippine watercraft stress larger vessels and say little about small ordinary canoes.[9] In the review that follows, large boats are included because even though they could not possibly have been the canoes seen by Drake they have some features that characterize the small canoes, too, especially double outriggers and bamboo floats.

Inevitably, one must begin with Pigafetta. His first mention of a native boat is brief. "On Monday afternoon, March 18, we saw a boat coming toward us with nine men in it" (Blair and Robertson 1903–1909: XXXIII, 103). All that this informs us is that the boat must have been small. It was from the tiny island of Suluan and approached Magellan when he was off the nearby island of Homonhon. Four days later these same people arrived with food "in two boats" (p. 109), but again Pigafetta offers no details. On March 28, while anchored off the coast of Limasawa the flagship was approached by "a small boat which the natives call *boloto* with eight men in it" (p. 113). Once again, no details.

Two hours later the Spaniards saw two *barangay* coming. "They are large boats and are so called [by those people]. They were full of men, and their king was in the larger of them, being seated under an awning of mats" (p. 115).[10] Obviously, the *barangay* were not the kind of boats that met Drake, and this is made even plainer when Pigafetta further describes them. He says that while he was ashore, the king showed him a *barangay*, under a bamboo covering, which was as long as eighty palms and resembled a *fusta* (p. 119).[11] It is interesting that when the Magellanic fleet sailed from Limasawa to one of the islands off the coast of Leyte, the king of Limasawa could not follow the Spaniards closely and they had to wait to enable him to catch up. The king was greatly astonished at the speed with which they sailed (p. 137). This testifies as much to the slowness of the Philippine craft as anything else, for the Spanish ships of the time were not known for their speed. And it contrasts with the Micronesian proas, which easily outdistanced European sailing vessels.

To conclude with Pigafetta. In a Visayan word list that he compiled he defines a *balangay* as a large boat and a *boloto*—usually spelled *baloto*—as a small boat (p. 197). The Visayan islands, which were the setting for the above experiences, are significant to us because their inhabitants constitute a fairly homogeneous cultural-linguistic group that by the time of Drake had spread to the northeast coast of Mindanao.

The *baloto* and the *barangay*, then, are the two boats whose native names are given by Pigafetta. It is necessary, using other accounts, to see if they have any bearing on the canoes used by the natives who were so troublesome to Drake.

Alzina (Alcina), a Jesuit who has left us a manuscript on the Visayans written in 1668, offers by far the most information.[12] A *baloto*, he says, is the Visayan name for a canoe made of a single log hollowed out on the inside, and it has various sizes, shapes, and names. It ranges in size from very large to so small that it was used by one man alone, who could carry one on his shoulders when taking it to the seashore or the bank of a river. Alzina, among whose talents orderliness and literary skills are not the most conspicuous, is not consistent in saying that the *baloto* is made out of a single hollowed-out log, for some *balotos* are, according to his own lengthy descriptions, large vessels made up of many planks and other pieces. Probably he was referring to the keel alone. Be that as it may, he informs us that some *balotos* customarily carried ten or twelve or more persons and that their outer side is hardly above water level. The surface of all the wood on the inside is smooth and polished, a fact that has relevancy in identifying the canoe type as like that of Drake's Indians. Alzina writes that the boats have double-outrigger structures whose floats are made of canes. However, he mentions a feature not hitherto encountered: large or small, the *balotos* have awnings like roofs designed to protect people from the hot sun and the rain; but they are folded up when contrary winds require it (Alzina MS trans.:134–138, 152–153, 157–158).

The little *balotos* with one or two men, says Alzina, are a remarkable and almost unbelievable thing to behold as they move along like a ball bouncing over the waves of the sea. They often fill with water, but the men lighten the cargo and bail out the water with great ease using their oars. Alzina remarks that occasionally when he was traveling from place to place in a hurry, the *baloto* he was in—large and carrying twelve or more Indians as rowers—filled with water but did not capsize because it was counterbalanced by the outriggers (Alzina MS trans.:164–165).

It is unfortunate that Alzina, who goes into considerable detail about boat building, does not specifically say that the small *balotos* did or did not have sails, and he lets us know only by inference that they had outriggers. However, his drawing of a *baloto* from which four men are fishing depicts both a sail and an outrigger on the side visible to the viewer (Figure 24). I think that the important thing is that he mentions a hollowed log, a smooth and polished inside of the hull, and the use of paddles.[13]

The *baloto*, then, does not closely correspond to the description of the canoes seen by Drake but it is not entirely unrelated, either.

The other kind of boat mentioned by Pigafetta, the *barangay*, is also described by Alzina (Alzina MS trans.:168–170). He says that it is larger than the *baloto*, and is built upon a square keel with boards added from the sides. Although he describes in some detail the paddles that are used, he is stingy about other details that might be of some use to us; in fact, he does not even specifically mention outriggers and sails. All this does not really matter, however, as the *barangay* is obviously a small ship rather than the kind of canoe we are searching for.

Figure 24. Seventeenth-Century Philippine Canoes. The legends read: "*Baloto* [four men are fishing from a canoe]; *Biroc; Panco Tilinbao; Baloto menor; Joangan, los Españoles Joanga; Las caracoas son como las Joangas, exceptas las rodas de popa i proa; Batel; Rambo ó correlan.*" Source: Alzina MS, Muñoz copy. (*Courtesy The Biblioteca del Palacio Real*)

A man whose testimony could have been invaluable in identifying Drake's island fails us. He is Andrés de Urdaneta, who was on Loaisa's flagship, the *Santa María de la Victoria*, when it was anchored in 1526 at what was probably Lianga Bay or possibly Bislig Bay on the northeast coast of Mindanao, the very area that Sharp reckons was the place where Drake made his landfall. Several times, he says, the Indians would come in very light, oar-propelled *navios* in order to cut the ship's cables (*Col. doc. inéd. Indias* 1864–1884:V, 18). In Spanish a *navio* is simply defined as a ship; it is not specific as to size and other characteristics. Urdaneta himself says nothing about the vessels' structure or size, except that they were very light. Undoubtedly these *navios* were too large to have been of the kind seen by Drake. Yet small canoes, too, rather than larger boats alone might have been coming out to harass the *Santa María*. If only we knew for sure.

Also disappointing us is another early visitor, Nápoles, who was with Saavedra's *Florida* in the same area where Loaisa's flagship had been two years before. When the ship reached eastern Mindanao in 1528 it was met by a king in a *calaluz*, described merely as a small brigantine (*Col. doc. inéd. Indias* 1864–1884:V, 76). It is difficult to envision the kind of native craft that this might be. We know that on a subsequent night three or four men came out stealthily on a *caraluz* (*sic*) and, putting the ship's anchor on their boat, tried to pull the Spanish ship ashore. They failed, but not, as they later discovered, because they had too few men. Then they cut the cable holding the anchor and had some people on shore, including three Spanish prisoners from the Loaisa expedition, try to pull the ship, without success. Another anchor behind the ship, according to the prisoners, must have been holding the vessel fast. We need not go into the comical denouement but must conjecture that the *calaluz* had to be fairly small, not only because of the few men on it but also on account of its ability to get under the prow of the Spanish vessel almost undetected when trying to cut the second cable.[14] Nápoles mentions another native craft called a *parol*, in which the king and five others, including a child in arms, came out to meet the *Florida* prior to this episode, which I have already described several pages back when talking about thieving tactics. But we have no way of knowing what the *parol* was like, unless the word means *prao*, except that it too is said to be like a brigantine (*Col. doc. inéd. Indias* 1864–1884:V, 76–78; cf. Navarrete 1825–1837:V, 479–480).

Still further frustrating is the account by Descalante Alvarado of Villalobos' stay at Mindanao. It informs us that a ship dispatched from Sarangani to Mindanao met in the Sarangani Strait many *paroas* filled with armed warriors (*Col. doc. inéd. Indias* 1864–1884:V, 125). We are left in the dark as to what the native boats were like, except to be told that they were *navios de la tierra*, hardly a description on which to build any kind of conclusion.

The parade of disappointments continues with Legazpi. His chief pilot makes numerous references to *paroas* in his "Relacion" (*Col. doc. inéd. ultramar* 1885–1932:II, 373–427 passim), but the most we can salvage is that these boats were propelled by oars and might have as many as thirty oarsmen (p. 396). Some reference is made to *canoillas pequeños* (p. 400), showing that at least there were small canoes. Here again we learn nothing about outriggers, floats, paint or lack of it, and so on.

Arellano of the *San Lucas*, the small vessel that had detached itself from Legazpi's main fleet, is of no help at all in his own "Relacion."

Following these earliest voyagers comes Antonio de Morga. Writing in 1609 about the people of Luzon he describes their large square-sailed vessels, such as *vireys* and *barangays*—the latter already mentioned by Pigafetta and Alzina above—propelled by large numbers of oarsmen and balanced with what I assume to be outlayers (Morga 1868:272–273).

At this time I feel I must take time out to explain the difference between an outrigger and an outlayer, even though they greatly resemble each other. The former rests on the water; the latter does not. A vessel with outlayers depends for its balance on the equal weight of each outlayer, much as a tightrope walker depends on a long pole held across his body. Under the stress of waves and wind, the vessel may roll; if so, one outlayer will dip into the water and prevent capsizing, while the other outlayer rises higher away from the water. In the detailed descriptions given by various writers, I fear that I cannot always tell with certainty when an outrigger is in question and when an outlayer. I also fear that sometimes when the word "outrigger" is used, an outlayer is really intended, and vice versa. Sometimes the same word is used for both, as in the Spanish use of the native word *cates*, which indubitably refers in some instances to a Philippine outrigger and in others to an outlayer. Thus, Alzina speaks of the single *cates* on Guamanian canoes; yet he uses this same term to refer to Philippine outlayers and outriggers (Alzina MS trans.:120). Later, as we shall see, Dampier makes a clear distinction between a true Philippine outlayer and a Guamanian outrigger, but refers to both kinds of apparatus as "outlayers." As a rule, outlayers never seem to be found in small- or moderate-sized canoes, but one cannot always say conversely that they occur in all the large ones. Some drawings of very large vessels seem to depict outriggers rather than outlayers, although it is not possible to be certain about this, given the poor quality of the draftsmanship.

The presence of outlayers on Visayan *barangays* and *vireys* has been noted by the Boxer codex, which describes them as being counterweights placed outside the body of the vessel on both sides. These counterweights, on which the rowers are seated, enable the vessels to travel with safety (Quirino and Garcia 1958:409). Morga, as we have seen, similarly reported the presence of outlayers on Luzon *barangays* and *vireys*. A Frenchman named de Guignes, who was in the Philippines from 1796 to 1797 describes vessels with outlayers as he observed them on the river and along the bay of Manila. The outlayers were made of bamboo, and although the sailors sat on them to counterbalance the wind, they sometimes broke and the boat would capsize, drowning the men (Guignes 1808:401–402; cf. Lane-Fox 1875:431).

Dampier, an excellent reporter, describes the boat used by the sultan of the "Mindanao people" in 1686. It was far too large and complex to have been of the type described by Fletcher, for it could "entertain 50 or 60 Persons or more," and had a small house with windows (Dampier 1697:336). What is notable about his description, however, is that it reiterates the existence of true outlayers, rather than outriggers, and specifies that the cross-pieces were made of bamboo. In his words,

Besides this [places fore and aft for the mariners to sit and row], they have Outlayers, such as those I described at Guam; only the Boats and Outlayers here are larger. These Boats are more round, like the Half-Moon almost; and the Bamboes or Outlayers, that reach from the Boat, are also crooked. Besides, the Boat is not flat on one side here, as at Guam; but hath a Belly and Outlayers on each side: and whereas at Guam there is a little Boat fasten'd to the Outlayers, that lies in the Water; the Beams or Bamboes here are fasten'd traverse-wise to the Outlayers on each side, and touch not the Water like Boats, but one, three or four foot above the Water, and serve for the Barge-Men to sit and row and paddle on; the inside of the Vessel, except only just afore and abaft, being taken up with the Apartments for the Passengers. There run across the Outlayers two tire of Beams for the Padlers to sit on, on each side of the Vessel. The lower tire of the Beams is not a foot from the Water; so that upon any the least reeling of the Vessel, the Beams are dipt in the Water, and the Men that sit are wet up to their waste; their feet seldom escaping the water. And thus, as all our Vessels are Rowed from within, these are Paddled from without. (Dampier 1697:336)

There is no likelihood that Drake saw boats with outlayers at the Island of Thieves. Such craft are simply too large and too complex to match Fletcher's description, and the main reason that they have been mentioned is merely to cover all possibilities. In addition, such large vessels may have certain other traits that might fit in with Fletcher and be found in smaller craft, so we shall continue to explore them.

To get back to Morga and his descriptions of the larger craft. He tells us about even larger vessels known as *caracoas*, *lapis*, and *tapaques*, which might have as many as two hundred rowers as well as thirty soldiers for fighting (Morga 1868:273–274). These are of course too large for the boats met by Drake, except that the *caracoas* have been said by a later observer to be sometimes quite small, as we shall soon see. One wishes that Morga had elaborated upon his statement that the people "use canoes made of one very large tree" (Morga 1868:272). Unfortunately, he gives no details whatsoever. If nothing else he confirms our conviction that the *barangay* is too large for our requirements.

Too large, too, was the *caracoa*, and some additional proof of this may be seen in several accounts. Thus, a work by Argensola published in the same year as Morga's book describes the *caracoa* as a sort of vessel using oars, being open and bigger than the Spanish bark and steered by two rudders, one ahead and one astern (Argensola 1609:17). A later English translation of his book has an excellent drawing of a Moluccan *corcoa* that does not appear in the

Spanish edition, and it shows not only several scores of men either paddling from outlayers or standing up holding spears, but also a conspicuous cannon (Argensola 1708:61).

The meticulous Alzina has something to say about the Visayan *caracoa*. It greatly resembles, he says, the brigantines of Spain and is best for war fleets, but is smaller and carries gangplanks, great *cates* (outlayers?), large awnings, and *burcilantes* (Alzina MS trans.:173). He provides a drawing of a vessel which he says is like a *caracoa* although it is called by another name: *joangan, los Espanoles joanga*. This vessel is large and has a tripod mast, rectangular sail, outlayers, decks, awnings, and a high arched stem and stern whose appearance is that of a tight incurving spiral (Alzina MS 1668).[15] In this description and drawing there is nothing really suggestive of the canoes encountered by Drake.

We may look into an extended description of the boats of the Lutao or Orang Laut that has been given by Francisco Combés, S.J., in his *Historia de las Islas Mindanao, Iolo, y sus adyacentes* (1667). The Orang Laut were and still are atypical, being a Muslim people scattered along the coasts from Johore to the Philippines and Borneo. Often referred to as the Sea Gypsies, they spend most of their time at sea on endless voyages of trading and sea piracy. As seen by Combés in the southern islands of the Philippine archipelago, their boats were quite large, being built up of planks, some of which were tied together with rattan. The smaller of these vessels were rowed by crews of sixty or more men, and Combés saw a large one manned by three hundred hands. *Cates* ran on both sides of their boats from stem to stern, being made of three or four bamboos as thick as the arm or even larger, their purpose being to buoy the vessel and keep it safe. These boats were crescent-shaped, with only a small part of their narrow keels in the water (Combés 1667:62–63).

There is no possibility that Drake met up with these Sea Gypsies and their war vessels, but Combés' description serves to remind us once more of the presence in the Philippines of double-outriggered or double-outlayered boats, propelled with paddles, and having a crescent shape. The floats were made of bamboo.

I dislike roaming all over the Philippines like this for documentary descriptions of Philippine watercraft but I have already complained that I am forced to do so by necessity. And so I offer

Captain John Hunter's account of his sanguinary encounter in August of 1791 with the natives of Hummock Island (Balut) in the Sarangani group off the tip of southern Mindanao (Hunter 1793:248–256). His ship, the *Sirius*, was first met by a canoe with twelve persons aboard, and then later that same evening and in the ensuing days by a larger boat and several canoes of undescribed size. On board the large boat was a raja and a "considerable number of people," and the craft was covered with an awning of split bamboo. During the *Sirius'* attack on the natives, Hunter "saw the Raja pulling at an oar himself" as he was trying to escape being shot by the Englishmen (p. 255). Obviously, Hunter's account is not useful, not only because it fails to describe the canoes but also because it concerns natives who were too clothed and too sophisticated to have been Drake's thieves.

Perhaps the first truly accurate and detailed descriptions of Philippine watercraft can be attributed to Admiral Paris, who in his classic study *Essai sur la construction navale des peuples extra-Européens* (1843) depicts in words and drawings the canoes he observed in Manila Bay about 1830. The *banka* is small enough and is an oar-propelled dugout, equipped with double bamboo outlayers; but unfortunately its fore and aft are dissimilar and its leaf shelter is designed for passengers (pl. 75; p. 68). Paris also describes a dugout canoe with two bamboo outriggers, a spritsail, paddles, a large oarlike rudder, and a leaf shelter (pl. 71; p. 68). A fishing canoe, not unlike the last mentioned, is also depicted (pl. 74; pp. 67–68). So is a much larger one, having a wide and lengthened stern (pl. 74; pp. 67–68). Both the latter have two booms for each float, as do all the others mentioned. On a huge cargo canoe of about sixty tons with two masts, double outriggers with bamboo floats, a cabin, and other complexities (pls. 70, 71; pp. 66–67) there is no need to comment; it is really a small ship. The same may be said of the flat-bottomed *casco* (pls. 72, 73; p. 67), which obviously is an offshoot of the Chinese junk. Not only are Paris' canoes found too far away from Mindanao, they do not correspond sufficiently to Fletcher's description, except for the outrigger structure.

We are now left, finally, with twentieth-century studies of Philippine watercraft. Although they are essentially ethnographic and not ethnohistorical in character and reflect a situation more than three centuries later than the time of Drake, they have the merit of stressing smaller craft.

The first of these studies, "Austroinsulare Kanus als Kult- und Kriegs-Symbole," by Müller-Wismar (1912), contains almost nothing that is useful for our purposes, even though it covers the whole of Austronesia. He deals with the canoes of Sulu (figs. 32, 55), Zamboanga (fig. 56), and Cebu (fig. 57) with outrigger construction in mind, but only very briefly and from a special point of view (Müller-Wismar 1912:244). Among his fifty-eight illustrations of canoes and parts of canoes, only those depicting the Solor and Alor type in the lesser Sundas is suggestive of an incurving endpiece (fig. 27). One need not be reminded, however, that the Sundas are not in the Philippines.

Hornell's monograph *The Outrigger Canoes of Indonesia* (1920) is a far better study, being the first adequate and connected account of the outriggers of Malaysia, most of the information being collected firsthand by the author during a visit to the then Dutch East Indies. However, Hornell did not visit the Philippines, getting his information from photographs and notes sent to him by the director of the Bureau of Science, Manila, and by a Colonel O. C. Waloe. He states: "Unlike the outriggers of Polynesia and of India and Ceylon, those of Indonesia [including the Philippines] are of the double type with few and unimportant exceptions" (Hornell 1920:43). Hornell distinguishes two subtypes of Philippine canoes —the Philippine and the Sulu. The Sulu subtype centers in the Sulu Islands. Its range extends approximately as far north as Sindangan Bay on the Zamboanga Peninsula of Mindanao, eastward as far as Sarangani Island, and on the south includes the whole of the islands in the Sulu and Tawi-Tawi groups (Hornell 1920:76).

According to Hornell, the true Philippine outriggers are of an extremely simple design marked off sharply from the highly complex and ornate pattern favored in Sulu. They vary in size from small dugouts to large built-up boats having one or two sails. The hull is the same throughout in its design, having as a base a hollowed-out log or dugout, with plank sides raised upon the edges in the larger boats. The outrigger booms, made of tough wood, are normally two in number; their outer ends on either side are secured by neatly made rattan lashings to the upper surfaces of from one to five bamboo poles that form the float. The booms do not pass through the body of the boat but lie upon the upper edges, secured thereto by rattan lashings (Hornell 1920:76).

The Sulu subtype is much more elaborate in detail and the

owners are lavish in its ornamentation. The hull consists of a dugout, and the sides are raised by two washstrakes. The ends are bifid. The prow has a lower and an upper projection, and the latter has a board attached to its upper edge, prolonging it upward. The bifurcated stern is much more elaborate and shows great artistic skill in the carving of the handsome ornamentation of both the horizontal and the upwardly sloping branches. The upper branch of the stern consists of two lateral and slightly divergent wings of perforated woodwork, carved in a bold foliate pattern. There are three or four booms making up the outrigger frame, directly attached to a bamboo float on each side of the canoe (Hornell 1920:77). Obviously, the Sulu subtype is too elaborate to correspond to anything described by Fletcher, especially because of its bifid ends, so we are left to evaluate the previously described Philippine subtype.

What is favorable in the Philippine subtype are: two outrigger booms with bamboo floats and a dugout hull which is built up with washstrakes only in the larger canoes. What is unfavorable is that nothing in Hornell's text nor in his plates indicates the ends of the canoe to be incurving in a semicircle, to be twin ended, or to have shell ornaments. Apparently, the canoe hulls were left unpainted, and might have been "burnished." Over three centuries had elapsed since Drake's voyage and it is possible that some changes in the type of canoe described may have taken place, but I have the feeling that these canoes were too large and too different in profile to have been what Drake encountered.

Continuing our review of the literature chronologically, the next pertinent work is Nooteboom's *De Boomstamkano in Indonesie* (1932). It devotes much of a whole chapter to Philippine outriggers but enlightens us very little, being content for the most part to cite skimpy references to a series of fairly modern travelers, commentators, and the like.

More recent is the sweeping review of Oceanic canoes that appeared over a period of many years in the French journal *Triton*, later absorbed by another maritime journal, *Neptunia*. The author is the Jesuit priest Jean-Marie Neyret, and although portions of his writings are based on firsthand observation and experience, especially in Melanesia, the ones relevant to our inquiry (Neyret 1970a:1–12) are drawn from the works of previous writers, namely,

Paris (1843), Hornell (1920), and to a lesser extent Trogneux (1889).

The merits of Neyret's coverage of Philippine canoes are that he deals principally with small craft and complements Hornell's preoccupation with outrigger structure with Paris' interest in rigging. The shortcomings are: He deals with canoes observed during the last one- and one-half centuries; he has no firsthand knowledge of Philippine craft, and, except for Paris, his sources are themselves secondhand—not necessarily a serious flaw, however; his coverage, as he is the first to admit, is perforce incomplete, no thorough study of Philippine canoes having ever been made; and finally, his treatment of Mindanao canoes encompasses only the Sulu subtype as found in Las Palmas in the western part of the island and is not at all concerned with the Philippine subtype found on the eastern coast. Reluctantly, I must conclude that admirable as it may be, Neyret's study has little utility for our purposes.

Summarizing our knowledge of Philippine canoes, and trying to project back to the ethnographic present, we can say that aside from large vessels approaching the size of ships, they are characterized as having in common the double outrigger of the general Malaysian culture area. If one insists on double outlayers, these too are found, both in Magellanic and recent times. Floats are made of bamboo, consisting sometimes of single canes and sometimes multiple ones fastened together. Most often the canoes are dugouts of one piece. The hulls are not described as being painted; rather, when mention is made of their finish they are said to be smooth and polished. Twin ends exist, although they are not very common, there being no need because of their double-outrigger construction to reverse the canoes when tacking. Here and there throughout the archipelago there are canoes with spiral and even crescent-shaped heads and sterns. Most canoes have sails, although paddling canoes are not uncommon, and even where sails are employed there often is high reliance on paddling and rowing. Of all the traits that interest us the only one lacking is the use of shells suspended as ornaments from the ends of the canoes. It would be difficult to suspend them from the tight-spiraled endpieces seen in some craft. Prows and sterns of great height would be needed for the suspension, but such high fore and after endpieces do not appear to characterize ordinary-sized canoes.

It is not really proper, however, to depict Philippine canoes in terms of selected traits; great variability characterizes the archipelago. If we narrow our search to the eastern coast of Mindanao, we do not get much satisfaction from the literature. As already noted, early Spanish sources make brief references to the *calaluz* and *parol* in the general area of Bislig Bay, but there is not enough to inform us about vital details. Modern writers are silent altogether on eastern Mindanao except for Hornell's assertion that there the Philippine or true subtype prevails, a style which more readily approximates the description by Fletcher than does the Sulu subtype with its elaborateness, lavishness, bifid ends, unidentical head and stern, and triple or more outrigger booms rather than two alone.

A final evaluation of all the evidence of canoe characteristics will be held in abeyance until a future section. For the present, however, it can be said that many more relevant features, especially the double outrigger and the bamboo float, are to be found in the Philippines than in Micronesia.

## SOME DEMOGRAPHIC REALITIES

There remains to consider the matter of population, which I have purposely deferred until now because my findings came late and have something of the nature of a climax to the building list of disappointments.

Incredible as it may seem, there is every reason to believe that eastern Mindanao fails to meet the demographic criterion that I have set up for the Island of Thieves. The coast in the vicinity of 8 degrees latitude was especially sparsely populated. Indeed, the whole of the Philippine archipelago, in contrast to the present-day population of about 40 million inhabitants, may at best have had only about 500,000 people around the time of Drake. This estimate, as well as some highly convincing information, comes from the historical study of the population of the Philippines made by David P. Barrows, who argues cogently that real growth did not manifest itself until about two centuries after Magellan's visit. Much of what I have to say in the paragraphs below comes from his section on Population in the *Census of the Philippine Islands* of 1903, volume I.

The gist of his argument is that native settlements were few at the time of the first Spanish visitors, and that reports show time and again that the weary and hungry trans-Pacific voyagers had considerable difficulty in finding victuals to replenish their exhausted stores, not so much because of the hostility of the natives as the real lack of foodstuffs in a sparsely populated area. Barrows furthermore makes use of a rough census reported in 1591, which I shall have reason to refer to later. To his arguments may be added one of my own: never did large fleets of canoes come out to meet the ships of the earlier Europeans; indeed, often no canoes at all were seen by the voyagers.

To begin with the matter of provisions, our first example is that of Magellan, whose wanderings through the Visayas are best explained by his desperate need for food supplies, which were sorely lacking on Homonhon and Limasagua, to say nothing of the unpopulated islands in the vicinity. On being told that he could supply his men and ships on any of three other islands—Leyte (?), Mindanao, and Cebu—he set sail for the last-named. Pigafetta makes no mention of sighting people or towns on the five islands the vessels passed en route, nor of procuring any food, except one of the huge fruit bats of the islands. When the Spanish fleet sailed to the Sulu Sea after Magellan's death, the first island they reached, Cagayan Sulu, was almost uninhabited and the Spaniards were unable to get provisions there. In desperation they continued westward until they reached the 275-mile-long island of Paragua (Palawan), where at long last they found a sufficiency.

Skipping over the years and coming closer to the time of Drake we have the example of Legazpi, whose difficulties have been so aptly and concisely described by Barrows that I shall quote him.

> The experiences of Legaspi's fleet (1569–1571) [sic] in searching for populous coasts and acquiring supplies of food was almost a repetition of those of the voyagers who had preceded him in the years earlier in the century. The little seas which divide the islands of the southern Visayas were then rarely disturbed by the passing of native proas. Most of the islands contained neither inhabitants nor clearings. . . . The little island of Limasagua, which had been quite populous in the time of Magellan, was almost deserted. "It contains," wrote Legaspi, "less than twenty people." Settlements, with a few exceptions, were small. Some, which were dignified with the name of towns, contained no more than twenty or thirty people.

Then, as in Magellan's time, Cebú was the most populous of these southern islands. . . . Here, after effecting a settlement, Legaspi, having sent back to New Spain more than half of his expedition, held on from the first of June, 1565, until August of 1568, when reenforcements arrived from Acapulco. During this period of more than three years he had probably less than one hundred and fifty men, not a large force to sustain had there been any considerable population in the Visayan Islands, yet the record of these three years is one of almost constant experience of scarcity of food and of expeditions sent out to the neighboring islands, Leyte, Bohol, Mindanao, and Panay, to forage for provisions. (*Census of the Philippine Islands* 1905:I, 417–418)

Even more valuable in demonstrating the spareness of population throughout the archipelago at the time of Drake is Barrows' use of old population estimates. Apparently the earliest estimates were made by an anonymous soldier who participated in Legazpi's conquest of the archipelago, and it is notable for its detachment. In 1572 he prepared a manuscript, "Relación del Descubrimiento y Conquista de la Isla de Luzón y Mindoro" (printed in Retana 1895–1905:IV, 1–37). The writer, who from time to time deprecates the estimates of the population made by others, gives personal estimates of various islands, regions, and towns, including Manila, and almost invariably revises these earlier estimates considerably downward. Of Mindanao, he says that it was poorly populated. Even the regions known to be the most heavily populated, such as Cebu and Manila, had only a few thousand souls (*Census of the Philippine Islands* 1905:I, 418–420).

More detailed and systematic than this are the census figures contained in a manuscript, "Relación de las Encomiendas existentes en Filipinas el día 31 de Mayo de 1591," which appears to be the earliest complete enumeration of the islands, made on the basis of encomiendas (printed in Retana 1895–1905:IV, 39–73).[16] Those who escaped the encomienda system were the mountain "Igorot," the forest Negrito, and the Moros. The census included all the rest and thus encompassed the great bulk of the population. About 667,612 souls were reported to the king in 1591, and even this is too high for Barrows. It interests us that the jurisdiction of Cebu, which included Cebu itself, as well as Masbate, Burias, Leyte, Negros, the settlements of Cagayan and Butuan in northern Mindanao, both coasts of Samar, the little islands of Camotes, Mactan, and so on, had 65,000 souls, a very small population for so large an area. The great peninsula of Surigao in northern Mindanao had no settlements at all (*Census of the Philippine Islands* 1905:I, 422).

Barrows cites further population estimates and censuses, by Chirino, Morga, Zúñiga, and Buzeta, but they pertain to a time postdating Drake and will not be discussed here, albeit they tend to corroborate all that has been said above about the thinness of the population.

Turning now to my own line of argument, in perusing Portuguese and Spanish accounts of initial and subsequent European contacts with coastal indigenes I had often been struck by the fact that either no native canoes were encountered or only a few, as compared with the numerous ones that purportedly greeted Drake at the Island of Thieves. To be sure, some of these were very large but never really numerous. This was true in the case of Serrão, Magellan, Loaisa, Saavedra, Castro, and Villalobos, the first visitors.

While I could illustrate my point with any of the accounts of early voyages, I have chosen to describe the experiences of the *San Lucas*, captained by Arellano. This tiny ship, which had been met with a great number of canoes at Truk in the Carolines, saw neither a canoe nor a human being when it reached Mindanao. The following day, some people did put in an appearance and they continued to visit the *San Lucas* for the several weeks that it remained in the gulf. Subsequently, while coasting Mindanao clockwise, the ship encountered a very large native vessel on the south coast, and then many native vessels in the islands near Zamboanga (a Muslim area), but apparently nothing at all on the north coast. Passing between Bohol and Cebu it encountered no canoes. No mention of vessels is made for the coast of Leyte or any of the numerous islands seen en route to San Bernardino Strait, although north of Samar the *San Lucas* passed a large sailing canoe whose crew cried out "capitan" and "pilote" (Sharp 1961:30–51).

It should not be overlooked that when Drake himself stopped for wood and water at Mindanao at what must have been Davao Gulf, he apparently saw neither human beings nor canoes, but even if he had they must have been few in number, for they are not mentioned by either Francis Fletcher or John Drake.

Mindanao, then, as all accounts indicate, was one of the lightly populated islands of the Philippine archipelago at the time of

Spanish entry, and the eastern littoral was especially devoid of people, despite the propensity of Filipinos to occupy coastal regions. For, with more than 85 percent of the region occupied by uplands, the lowlands "are confined to a few small river estuaries and delta lands at the heads of Pujada, Cateel, Bislig, Lianga, and Lanuza bays, at the northern end of graben-like Lake Mainit, and on several of the islands lying off the north-eastern coast" (Wernstedt and Spencer 1967:517). Even to-day, large stretches of the east-ern coast are unpopulated. The northeast monsoon may be a factor in all this.

Table 4. How Mindanao Meets Criteria as Drake's Island

| Clues | Mindanao |
| --- | --- |
| 8° N latitude | Yes |
| Population of 2,200 | No |
| Double outriggers | Yes |
| [Double outlayers] | [Yes] |
| Cane floats | Yes |
| Dugouts, one-piece | Yes |
| Glossy hulls | Yes |
| Twin ends | No |
| Incurving ends | ? |
| Shell ornaments | No |
| Large paddling canoes | Yes |
| Nudity | ? |
| Lengthened earlobes | Yes |
| Long fingernails | ? |
| Blackened teeth | Yes |
| Betel-nut chewing | Yes |
| Slings | ? |
| Darts | Yes |
| Thieving tactics | Yes |

? = unknown or inconclusive

There is, then, no reason whatsoever to believe that Drake could have been met at 8 or 9 degrees of latitude by about a hundred canoes carrying approximately 800 men, and that about 2,200 souls lived in the vicinity.

## VERDICT ON MINDANAO

The time has come to make a judgment on this last remaining island. As a comparison of Table 4 with Tables 2 and 3 will show, there is more evidence pointing to Mindanao as Drake's island than any place in Micronesia. Yet there are doubts that frustrate a resolution to the problem.

To be sure, this large island has a striking canoe feature, double outriggers and even double outlayers, as well as cane floats with two booms, glossy and unpainted hulls of one piece, occasionally incurving ends, and a predominance in early Spanish times of paddling and rowing in the smaller craft, as opposed to sailing. Micronesia does not.

Mindanao keeps stride with Micronesia in betel-nut chewing,

blackening of teeth, distended ear lobes, darts, and even a certain *modus operandi* in thieving from vessels, so that it cannot be dismissed on this account. It also matches Micronesia in the hurling of stones in skirmishes, although it is not certain if the sling was employed.

Yet, certain characteristics disturb us. For instance, while nudity (mostly incomplete) has been reported, it seems to have been decidedly subordinate to the wearing of clothing, often described as very ample even when natives were visiting Spanish ships newly arrived at the island or elsewhere in the archipelago.

Again, although the occurrence of long fingernails also has been reported, it is only for the Muslims around Illana Bay, some distance from the northeast coast, and for the natives of the island of Samar.

Most crucial of all the ethnic traits is the canoe, and although Mindanao falls within the classic region of the double outrigger, its canoes do not have the hanging shell ornaments that caught the eye of Fletcher, nor do they ordinarily have truly twin ends or consistently incurving endpieces, despite the sporadic existence of spiral or crescent-shaped hull profiles. If it has been possible to come up with a composite canoe that embodies all the more important features mentioned in the Fletcher account, this has only been done by considerable tugging and straining. A canoe type composed of elements drawn from disparate originals is an eclectic canoe, hardly worthy of being considered a definitive piece of evidence. Certainly, it is not possible to say with any assurance that a fleet of such canoes appeared off the coast of eastern Mindanao to greet the *Golden Hind*.

Then, of course, there is that other and surprising source of doubt, the demographic verities. When first I embarked on this investigation of the Island of Thieves I never dreamed that population would prove to be a stumbling block to the acceptance of Mindanao. But I think I have shown conclusively that the area around Bislig Bay was too sparsely populated to have mustered enough men to man the number of canoes said to have surrounded Drake. I think I have shown, too, that this is reflected in the scarcity of food supplies and the paucity of boats reported in the early Spanish accounts. The whole of the Philippine archipelago was lightly populated, but the east coast of Mindanao was especially devoid of souls. I cannot possibly envision about eight hundred men in a hundred canoes suddenly emerging from a bay such as Bislig or Lianga. It is only by reconciling ourselves to the possibility of a light population density for Mindanao that we can understand why the English documentary sources make mention of neither natives nor canoes in Davao Gulf when Drake stopped at what must have been that place to take on wood and water.

The obvious reaction on the part of the reader will be to ask if, having eliminated the Marianas, the Carolines, and the Philippines, there never was then an Island of Thieves. Was it a figment of Fletcher's imagination? No. There must indeed have been such an island, according to separate witnesses not in a position to influence one another's testimony. However, its identity cannot be proven beyond a reasonable doubt.

Yet, as when a jury has rendered a verdict of Not Guilty or better still the Not Proven of the Scots, it is permitted for a person to have and to express his own private opinions. He may speculate and he may suggest, and that is what I propose to do in the remaining pages. This may seem anticlimactic, yet in the interests of history and the historical methods, as well as plain curiosity, I feel constrained to pursue the matter still further with the conviction that I can come up with a final and valid statement concerning the whole episode with which we have been engrossed. After all, some unanswered questions remain, particularly how so strong a Malaysian trait of culture as the double-outriggered canoe with its glossy hull and bamboo floats entered onto the scene.

Pertinent to my speculation is a consideration of the places immediately visited by Drake after he had shaken off the unwanted hospitality of his ungracious hosts. Accordingly, the next chapter deals with the "foure Ilands" reached by his history-making vessel.

## chapter eight

# "*Foure Ilands*"

THE GEOGRAPHIC IDENTIFICATION of the "foure Ilands standing in 7 deg. 5 min. to the Northward of the line" is not as simple and straightforward as one might hope. Indeed, it is a difficult question.

*The World Encompassed* tells us that these islands were encountered after the *Golden Hind* had left the Island of Thieves and had sailed "without sight of land" from the third of October until the sixteenth, a period of almost two weeks. According to the book, Drake spent five days coasting the islands "and then anchored and watered vpon the biggest of them called Mindanao" (Drake 1628:84).

Unfortunately for us, there are not four islands at the latitude mentioned, thus compounding the problem. Wagner tries to resolve it by taking John Drake's statement—that an island was encountered at 7 degrees and that a day was spent there taking on wood and water—to mean that the island was the southernmost of the Pelew (Palau) group or "possibly Songosor, which, however, is further south than 7°" (Wagner 1926:500 n.3).

There are many weaknesses in Wagner's argument, which of course requires acceptance of his belief that Drake never went to Mindanao at all and that the Island of Thieves was Yap. He overlooks Fletcher's statement that there were four islands in all and that Drake coasted them for five days or so. If he is going to rely on Drake's young cousin, he overlooks John's second deposition, wherein it is stated that the island where wood and water were taken on was large and was called Bosney.[1]

If, taking the first of Wagner's possibilities, the island in question was the southernmost of the Palaus, it would have to have been Angaur. But Angaur is disqualified on more than one count. For one thing, it is not distant enough from the Island of Thieves, if the latter is identified as Yap, or any other place in the western Carolines, for that matter. Angaur is approximately 260 nautical miles west of Yap. To accept it requires willingness to accept an average run of only 20 nautical miles per day for the *Golden Hind*, or an average speed of less than one knot. A more serious obstacle to the acceptance of Angaur is that it is a smallish island, with a land surface of only 3.5 square miles, so it would not have taken five days to coast it. Moreover, this elevated coral island is not part of a group of four, even though it is near some other small islands. The only thing favoring it is its latitude close to 7 degrees.

As for Songosor, better known as Sonsorol, it is even further out of the question than Angaur, and for many of the same reasons. It consists of two tiny coral islands, these being Sonsorol itself and the smaller island of Fana nearby. Sonsorol is a little over a mile in length and about one-half mile in breadth, so it would not have taken five days to coast both it and its satellite. Anyway, why would Drake have wanted to coast it at all? As for the distance from Yap to Sonsorol, Sonsorol is about 150 miles farther southwest than Angaur, but even this is not far enough for a thirteen-day voyage. Worst of all, its latitude of 5°19′ N is much too southerly for either Fletcher or John Drake.[2]

## OPTICAL ILLUSIONS

It is my contention that the four islands were not really four islands but two peninsulas in Mindanao plus two islands lying between these peninsulas.

The idea was first implanted in my mind by Andrew Sharp in his splendid book *The Discovery of the Pacific Islands* (1960). In it, as we have previously noted, he suggests that Drake's first landfall was at Mindanao itself and that Drake then coasted its eastern shore until he anchored in Davao Gulf, and that what he saw as four islands were really the east and west sides of the gulf, and two islands in the upper part of that gulf (Map 8). I have printed Sharp's argument verbatim below, but in reading it the reader should know

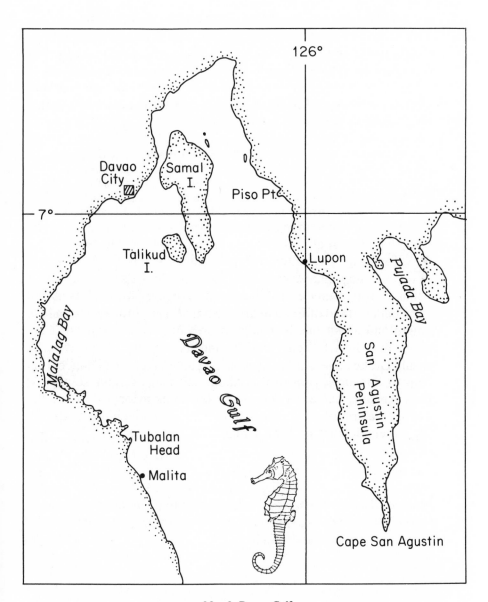

126°

Davao
City

Samal
I.

Piso Pt.

7°

Talikud
I.

Lupon

Pujada Bay

Malalag Bay

Davao Gulf

San
Agustin
Peninsula

Tubalan
Head

Malita

Cape San Agustin

Map 8. Davao Gulf

that he unfortunately used Vaux's 1854 edition of *The World Encompassed* as his source for the Drake voyage, as have virtually all writers for more than a century.[3] This famous edition incorrectly states that after his first landfall the English privateer sailed "within" sight of land for thirteen days (Vaux 1854:136), whereas the original editions of *The World Encompassed* clearly say "without."[4] Sharp's argument is as follows:

> The natural interpretation of these data would be that the ship spent all the time, from its first landfall until anchoring, at no great distance from the east coast of Mindanao, which extends from well north of 8 degrees to well south of 7 degrees 5 minutes. The references conform with the view that Drake came to the east coast of Mindanao in latitude 8 degrees north, where there are some islets on the coastal reefs, that he drifted in calms as described and stood off making slowly south, without recognizing he was near a continuous coast, that he came in to the main coast again in the vicinity of latitude 7 degrees north near the peninsula making the east side of Davao Gulf, came round it into Davao Gulf, and anchored on the west side of Davao Gulf near the two islands in Davao Gulf, Samal and Kud, dominating the view to the north, the "four islands in 7 deg. 5 min." being thus the east side of Davao Gulf, Samal, Kud, and the west side of Davao Gulf, where the travellers at their anchorage would be told that they were at Mindanao. Coming out of Davao Gulf they would come to Sarangani at no great distance to the south, and thence go on to the Moluccas. (Sharp 1960:49–50)

In order to accept the Davao area as the locale of the four islands it is not necessary to accept the east coast of Mindanao as the locale of Drake's first trans-Pacific landfall. Nor, consequently, is it required to conjecture, as Sharp has done, that Drake sailed down the eastern coast until he met up with these four islands. The Davao possibility can be treated separately even if a non-Philippine island is favored as the Island of Thieves.

## A SURVEY BY SEA AND AIR

Restive over the possibility of testing Sharp's ingenious hypothesis, I made a trip to Mindanao in 1966 to see if the land connecting the east and west sides of the gulf might indeed be invisible if one did not sail far up into the head of the gulf. I decided to employ both a motor-powered outrigger canoe and a light plane—the first to keep me at water level, the other to put me at a level approximating the height of a ship's mast. The reconnaissance is perhaps best described in chronological sequence.

We departed Davao City at 9:45 A.M. on Thursday, September 8, in the *Digna*, a double-outriggered *banka* that I had chartered for the occasion. It interested me to see that each of its two floats consisted of three 27-feet lengths of thick bamboo lashed together. I noted that it was of 3.36 gross tonnage and 2.30 net tonnage. As I have said, it was motor-driven. I was accompanied by Father Gerald Nagle, M.M., who graciously served as my interpreter and verified all the observations made on the eastward journey across the gulf. My route was planned to take me from Davao City on the northwest shore of the gulf to the small town of Lupon on the opposite shore, skirting as close as possible the southern edges of the islands of Talikud (Kud) and Samal, mentioned by Andrew Sharp.[5]

My notes, which I shall cite throughout, state that the skies were very clear, except for occasional clouds and a somewhat hazy horizon. At position No. 1 (See Map 9), indicated on an outline map I had previously prepared in my notebook, the *Digna* was off the west coast of Talikud, the time now being 10:45 A.M.

The two islands divided the upper part of the gulf into what I chose to call in my notes the west arm and the east arm. At 11:20 A.M., position No. 2, I noted that the west shore of the gulf was "still clearly visible even with some haze." We were about one-quarter mile off the tip of Talikud, approaching the channel separating it from Samal.

Position No. 3 was reached at 12:30 P.M. We stopped for ten minutes at a little barrio that I was told was called Pangubatan, so that food could be bought for the crew. By now, despite an almost cloudless horizon in that direction, the west shore of the gulf could not be seen, but the east shore was visible, despite low-lying clouds.

Position No. 4 was reached at 1:30 P.M., being about one-third of the way across the open stretch of water between Samal Island and the town of Lupon. I wrote: "Can see Samal very clearly, can see Lupon moderately well, but definitely cannot see any land in the background between Samal and the east arm of the gulf." I made a note to the effect that I considered this to be the crucial stretch,

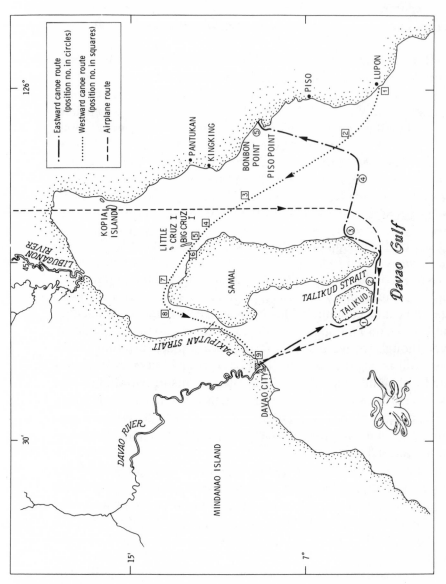

**Map 9. The Author's Canoe and Plane Routes**

knowing how important it was to know that the land connecting the east and west sides of the gulf could not be sighted.

Position No. 5, a place on the east coast called Piso Point, was reached at 2:55 P.M. and a landing was made there because the water at nearby Lupon to the immediate south was too rough.

After staying overnight at the Maryknoll mission, I undertook to make the return trip the next day, September 9, but this time without Father Nagle. We left Lupon under a "bright and sunny" sky, with some low-lying clouds. This time I labeled the point of departure, position No. 1. The time was 9:30 A.M. I entered the following comment in my notebook: "Even more than yesterday does the east side of the gulf look like a detached island [detached from the west side], with the open water between it and Samal Island looking clear and devoid of any visible background [of land]."

Position No. 2, 10:15 A.M. I made a mental note of the fact that the *Digna* seemed to be returning to Davao City by a route somewhat north of that taken on the previous day, but I thought that this might be a temporary maneuver because of some current. At any rate, the canoe captain and his crew spoke no English whatsoever and I spoke no Philippine dialect, so there was no use in inquiring. Even though we were a little farther north than yesterday, there was "still no sight of land in [the] background between [the] east side [of the gulf] and Samal." I attributed this to two things—the distance to the north end of the gulf and the presence of some haze.

The eastern coast of Davao Gulf was increasingly covered with haze as we moved farther and farther north in the open stretch of water between it and Samal Island. I noted that this eastern coastline was indented by a series of ridges that almost gave the impression that the coast was discontinuous, consisting of a series of small islands; but I was aware that the impression was a false one. At 10:35 A.M. I noted that this coast seemed to end abruptly at a low plain (Bonbon Point?), which had trees visible to a sharp eye. I also noted that two tiny islands were visible to the northeast of Samal. These were the Cruz Islands. I was later to ascertain that the southern of the two was called Big Cruz Island and was about 1¼ miles long and 220 yards wide, with a height of 90 feet at its southern extremity. About ¾ mile to the north of it was Little Cruz Island, about 700 yards long and about 110 yards wide, with a height of 42 feet (U.S. Hydrographic Office 1956:422). These small islands, I thought, could not have been seen by Drake as he crossed Davao Gulf.

At 10:50 A.M. I became convinced that we were returning to Davao City by a course north of Samal, and tried to indicate by gestures and words of protest that we were to return by the same route by which we had come yesterday; but to no avail. Fortunately, this turned out to be a most felicitous departure, for after all I had already been convinced that the connecting background could not be seen at sea level, and here I had the opportunity of testing the whole matter at a much more northerly point.

Position No. 3, 10:55 A.M. The head of the gulf was still not visible.

Position No. 4, 11:20 A.M. Although approaching close to the Cruz Islands there was "still no sign of the background."

Position No. 5, 11:35 A.M. Abreast of the eastern gulf town of Pantukan, where smoke could be seen billowing up in the hills behind it. Yet, there was still no sign of the head of the gulf, even though the west coast began to come in sight. I noted, significantly, that it seemed without doubt as if the east and west coasts were not connected.

Position No. 6, 11:55 A.M. We were now between the Cruz Islands and Samal. For the first time I was able to see the "mainland" connecting the east and west coasts. The land was "very low-lying with some trees barely visible." I noted that I could not see any of the high land (the Olagusan Uplands and the Central Mindanao Highlands) that I knew were located farther inland from the low, flat coast (the Davao Piedmont).

Position No. 7, 12:25 P.M. We had left the Cruz Islands behind and were nearing the northern tip of Samal. "Now we can see a continuous coastline from the east to the west coasts, but by no means is it completely obvious; there are a couple of stretches where the shoreline is barely visible."

Position No. 8, 1:00 P.M. We had now "rounded [Samal] and [were] heading home—to the south."

Position No. 9, 2:15 P.M. Docked at Davao.

The *banka* trips had proven to me that at sea level, unless one skirted the north of Samal, it was not possible, even for a person with normal distance vision, to see the coastline connecting the two arms of Davao Gulf. There is no intimation that Drake ever went that far north; we assume that he crossed the gulf just south of Samal and Talikud.

Sea level, however, is not mast height; consequently, I was anxious to test my canoe findings against observations taken from a plane. On Saturday, September 10, 9:21 A.M., I left the airfield at Davao in a Piper Super Cub with a Filipino pilot who spoke good English and could follow my directions in flight. We first headed for the northeast coast of Mindanao, as I was anxious to observe the Bislig-Lingig area where Sharp speculated that Drake might have made his first landfall. It would constitute a digression for me to reveal at this point my findings and impressions about the possibility that I would there find the Island of Thieves, so for the present I shall concern myself only with the return flight in which I again tested the peninsulas-as-islands theory.

At 11:35 A.M., with a slightly hazy horizon, we were heading south not far from the east coast of Davao Gulf. At an altitude of 2,000 feet and a latitude approximately only one-fourth the distance from the head to the mouth of the gulf, well before reaching the latitude of Lupon, the north coast began "receding from view."

Shortly afterward, having turned sharply from a southerly to a westward direction at almost the latitude of Lupon, the north coast was barely visible at 1,500 feet and "could even be confused with [the] darker coloration of [the] water, due to [the] light-dark patterns of sunlight."

Dropping to 100 feet and flying westward over the open water between the east coast and the island of Samal, the north coast was not visible. The latitude was that of the southern tip of Samal.

Still flying westward at 100 feet and looking northward from the south coast of Samal, the view to the north was completely blocked by the island.

Continuing to fly at 100 feet but now at the south coast of Talikud, the view north was likewise obstructed by the island.

Once more, then, it was evident that even at mast height a person cannot see the head of Davao Gulf at the latitude of the southern shores of Samal and Talikud. The east and west coasts appear to belong to separate islands, with two smaller islands between them.

Although I had been unable to plan my water and air trips to coincide in time with Drake's dates for the voyage, I was not too far off—forty-six and forty-eight days earlier, if one converts from the Julian calendar by adding ten days for the Gregorian system, which had not yet gone into effect.

## CARTERET'S BLUNDER

Through a wonderful instance of serendipity, I later came upon an obscure account in the history of exploration which gives much credence to the speculation that the configurations of the Mindanaoan coastline are deceptive enough to lead a mariner into imagining he is seeing something which in truth is something else. Philip Carteret, in 1767, after a perilous voyage through the Strait of Magellan and westward across the Pacific while in search of the Terra Australis, headed for Mindanao with his sick and decimated crew because he thought deer were available there near a deep bay in the southern part of the island. But his frantic search met with nothing but bitter frustration. He had sailed into Pujada Bay (Wallis 1965:II, 348–350). The bay, a small one, is located east of Davao Gulf, from which it is separated by Cape San Agustin.

What had caused Carteret to fail in his effort to find relief for his ravaged scorbutic men? The answer lies in an earlier account by Dampier of an island he referred to as St. John's. Dampier had been in the vicinity in 1686 and 1687 and was under the misapprehension that Mindanao was two islands—Mindanao on the west and St. John's immediately to the east. He had told how on his first voyage he had sailed from St. John's to Mindanao, where he had found an ample supply of deer at a savanna near a deep bay in the southern part of the island. He called the inlet the Bay of Deer (Dampier 1697:347–348).

A brilliant analysis of the blunder, which was an extension of a series of much earlier blunders on the part of explorers and cartographers, has been made by Helen Wallis, who recently edited Carteret's log and other documents bearing on his circumnavigation of the world. I take the liberty of quoting extensively from her notes rather than from Carteret himself, who was an understandably confused man when drawing up his own observations while at sea.

She begins by saying,

Nearly all the mistakes in Dampier's description of Mindanao to which Carteret drew attention can be traced to a single misapprehension on Dampier's part: the belief that Mindanao (as it really exists) comprised two islands. To the east lay the Island of St John's, which was in fact the south-eastern peninsula of Mindanao. The island of "Mindanao" to the west of St John's consisted of the southern and western peninsulas of the true Mindanao.

Thus when Dampier on 21 June 1686 arrived at the "Island of St. Johns," he was [really] standing off the eastern coast of Mindanao, and when he steered away for the "Island of *Mindanao*", lying "about 10 leagues distant from this part of *St. Johns*", he was crossing not a strait, as he supposed, but Davao Gulf. All the places in his description were correspondingly displaced. The "Bay of Deer", which in his reckoning lay to the north-west of the "southeast" point of Mindanao, Cape San Agustin, was actually northwest of Tinaca Point, the southerly point. If Carteret had realized this, he could hardly have failed to recover the bay at the first attempt. (Wallis 1965:II, 361)

In short, the "Bay of Deer" was really Sarangani Bay, whereas Carteret had been looking for it on the actual east coast of Mindanao. This does not imply that he knew there was no such place nearby as St. John's; but in his time, more was known about the true contours and size of Mindanao, and St. John's had been relegated to the status of a small-sized island, usually just northeast of the true Mindanao. For him, St. John's did not enter into the picture.

Frustrated at Pujada Bay, Carteret later mistakenly thought he had found the "Bay of Deer" northwest of Cape San Agustin. After crossing Davao Gulf in disappointment, he encountered hostility from the natives of the coastal town of Balangoan just east of Tinaca Point, so he resumed his course for Batavia. As he did so he saw to the west a deep bay which he correctly identified as Dampier's "Bay of Deer," but now it was too late for him to pause in search of the venison which had eluded him because of the inaccurate description available to him (Wallis 1965:I, 74).

Dampier's misconception about the configuration of Mindanao can be traced back to much earlier errors. Says Wallis,

Dampier's mistake had its origin in a curiously persistent cartographical error. Since 1574 San Juan had been marked as a large island off the east coast of Mindanao. The origin of this error lay in a displacement of the islands of San Juan (also called San Antonio), which were discovered and named by Espinosa in the *Trinidad* in 1522, and were probably the Sonsorol Islands. Thus Friar Santistéban of Villalobos's expedition, 1542, wrote of Mindanao, San Juan and San Antonio as if they were adjacent islands, and described how he sailed between them. In c. 1575 Lopez de Velasco in his MS. map of the East Indies showed San Juan as a north-easterly appendage of Mindanao; in his text he named it "Isla de Buenas Señales ó Sant Juan", thus identifying it with Pigafetta's "Acquada da li buoni Segnialli", which was the island of Malhón or Homonhón. (Wallis 1965:II, 361)

Wallis then proceeds to attribute these seemingly foolish mistakes to the same kind of visual aberrances that I am imputing to the Fetcher assertion that Drake "fell with foure Ilands."

Since the east coast of Mindanao is clear of islands, it may seem strange that this non-existent "San Juan" should survive the observations of many navigators. Its survival arose from the common mistake of seeing peninsulas as islands, and bays as straits. Almost from the beginning the irregular shape of Mindanao had caused confusion among navigators and cartographers. (Wallis 1965:II, 361–362)

Wallis cites certain cartographers and others besides Dampier who had been confused in one way or another by Mindanao's irregular shape: Descelier (1546), Gastaldi (1561), Seller (1675), Moll (c. 1710), de Mannevillett (1745, 1753), Bellin (1756), Herbert (1758), Alves (1764), and in later years even the renowned Burney (1803). Wallis continues:

Dampier therefore was doing no more than interpret the evidence of his own eyes in the light of contemporary maps when he described his voyage along the coast of St John's and Mindanao. Carteret had no suspicion of Dampier's misapprehension, for the island was much less conspicuous on the maps of the mid-eighteenth century. It was usually shown as a small island off north-east Mindanao, near the entrance to Surigao Strait. (Wallis 1965:II, 362)

As I have said, I was unaware of the history of the St. John's illusion when I made my trip to Davao Gulf, so I was greatly encouraged through Wallis' publication to find that the mistake had been perpetuated for over two centuries by explorers, cartographers, and geographers.

## NAUGHT AT DAVAO GULF

Aside from navigation and geography, what makes the four islands further appealing in terms of the identification I have applied to them is that almost nothing happened there.

This would be consistent with the light coastal population that has characterized this part of Mindanao. The records do not reveal that Drake met with any people or canoes, although he may very well have done so; but if he did they were perhaps so inconsequential as not to deserve mention. Moreover, Drake apparently took no steps to acquire food—only wood and water—which could either signify that he had a sufficiency of nutriments or that he simply did not find them readily available.

The lower Davao Gulf did have some Moros living in a few settlements scattered here and there on the coasts. They were tribesmen who had relatively recently been converted to Islam; they had not yet had time to develop towns and pirate fleets, as had their fellow Muslims in the kingdoms of Magindanao and Sulu.

The rest of the people were pagan tribes, chiefly Manobo (also known as Kulaman),[6] Mandaya, and Bagobo groups living without villages in upland areas away from the coasts. A people known as the Laoc, said to be a small degraded division of the Tagakaolo tribe living in the interior mountains of the so-called Sarangani Peninsula, migrated at some unrecorded time to the east side of the gulf and settled near Cape San Agustin (Cole 1913:158, 159).

The experiences of early explorers would seem to support the view that the shores of Davao Gulf were not bustling places. The Portuguese, Serrão and Castro, do not seem to have entered the gulf, nor did the Spaniards Loaisa, Saavedra, and Villalobos after them. Arellano, however, did anchor his *San Lucas* in a cove inside the mouth of the gulf in 1565. It may be significant that although he ordered a volley to be fired, no Filipinos showed themselves. This might have been through fear but it was just as likely due simply to the absence of anyone in the vicinity. The Spaniards went ashore and gathered water and firewood. Not until the next morning did anyone appear—only two or three men who shouted as they worked their way down through the jungle to the beach from a hill opposite the anchorage. From their actions one would have to assume that they were anxious to meet the visitors and that they had not seen them the previous day. They went back over the hill, only to return with thirty or forty men and their chief, whom we have already mentioned in the preceding chapter when discussing the question of treacherous tactics. His name was Viban and he was very young. At one time Viban came back with two hundred men and a variety of foods and wine, and later brought with him some women and children. One night, after the Spaniards had been there for over a month, three large canoes crept up on the *San Lucas*. The Spaniards, interpreting this to be an effort to cut the ship's cables, made their arms ready, and the canoes turned away. The next morning Viban returned toward the ship with the three canoes, but the wary Spaniards decided that it might be wise to sail out of the gulf, which they did (*Col. doc. inéd. ultramar* 1885–1932:III, 29–36, 45–49; Sharp 1960:39–41, 47–48).

Subsequent to Arellano, there seem to be no records of penetration into the gulf until Drake made his appearance, so that we have no further information regarding the early situation. Little has ever been known of the early occupancy of the Davao Gulf area. Later records tend to lose their value because they come after increasing Islamization and Hispanization, as well as population expansion.

Nevertheless, one cannot help but note that when in 1686 Dampier rounded the southeastern tip of St. John's island—actually Cape San Agustin in Eastern Mindanao—he saw a canoe of natives near the shore and sent out one of his own canoes to talk to them, but the men beached their canoe and fled into the woods. He says they could not be "allured to come to us, altho' we did what we could to entice them; besides these Men, we saw no more here, nor sign of any Inhabitants at this end." Dampier then crossed the gulf to the other side and although he coasted to within a league of the shore he found no canoes or people, try as he might (Dampier 1697:309).

To return to Arellano. We may assume with some confidence that the natives he met were Manobo (Kulaman), Mandaya, Bagobo, or even Laoc Tagakaolo, rather than Moros. Undoubtedly, the Moros had influenced them but not converted them. An incident narrated by Arellano would seem to confirm this. He says that Viban, upon meeting the Spaniards at the beach for the first time, waded in, took a little water in his hand, and made the sign of the cross, undoubtedly as the result of contact with the Portuguese in the Moluccas. Had he been a Muslim, even a superficial one, he would hardly have performed so characteristic a Christian gesture.

Which of the so-called wild tribes were encountered by Arellano cannot be established. If we assume that the captain, having rounded Cape San Agustin in order to enter the gulf, anchored in a cove located just inside its mouth, geography would seem to favor the little-known Laoc Tagakaolo people, who however may not yet have settled the area from the Sarangani Peninsula.[7] Otherwise, geography would probably favor the Mandaya, who not only occupy both slopes of the mountain chain that borders the Pacific Ocean from about 9 degrees north to almost the tip of Cape San Agustin but who also come down to the east side of the gulf and even extend to the head of the gulf. The Bagobo and Manobo (Kulaman) are likewise essentially mountain people, but located on the west side of the gulf rather than the east. Both show some coastal occupancy, with the Bagobo centering around high Mount Apo higher up into the gulf, and the Manobo (Kulaman) farther south, as far as the tip of Sarangani Peninsula.

However, we know more about the Bagobo than any of the other Davao tribes and for this reason will use them as our model in testing my reasons for arguing that the natives whom Drake could have encountered would not have been very conspicuous. This does not do great violence to the ethnographic facts, for not only are the physical features and dialects of the tribes of Davao District similar, "the cultural agreements are even more noticeable" (Cole 1913:201).

Let us pursue this excursus with some specific traits. Thus, mention by Arellano of chiefs and lesser chiefs is not inconsistent with what we know of the *datu* and petty *datu* of the Bagobo and the culturally similar Mandaya (Cole 1913:95 *et passim*).

Polygyny seems implied by some of Arellano's statements in describing visits by the chiefs and their wives with the Spaniards. Compare this with the recent situation among the Bagobo, where "A man may have as many wives as he desires and can afford" (Cole 1913:103). Polygyny used to be common throughout the Davao region.

Also consistent with Arellano is the fine dress of the men and women noted throughout Davao District about the turn of the century. Bagobo men have been especially singled out as the most handsomely dressed of all the wild tribes of the Philippines. They wear decorated kerchiefs around their heads, and often an elaborately beaded or embroidered coat which is generally open in front. Their hemp cloth trousers scarcely reach to the knee. They wear two belts—one to hold the trousers, the other to support the fighting or working knives which each man carries (Cole 1913:57). This description closely resembles that given by Arellano.

The wives and their attendants—brought to visit the Spaniards by Viban, his brother, and two other chiefs—were well dressed, wearing long skirts, elegant bodices, and handsome bonnets said to be reminiscent of those worn on the heads of peasant Spanish women. Compare this with Cole's description of a narrow tube skirt made like a sack, and an embroidered jacket worn with a close neck, decorated with various attachments of complicated designs in shell or metal disks or beads (1913:57–58). Cole, however, makes no mention of Manobo (Kulaman) head coverings, except for decorated wooden combs, the ones for festive occasions being more elaborate than everyday ones (1913:59). On the other hand he does describe a head covering worn by Mandaya men when on the trail. It consists of a little "palm bark" hat which is strikingly decorated with painted designs, "betel wings," and chicken feathers, and lacks utility (Cole 1913:167:fig. 47). This is strongly paralleled by some very elegant and many-colored palm headdresses given by the women to Arellano, his pilot, and his second in command; they must have been just as nonutilitarian.

As for the Filipinos' gifts to the Spaniards of pigs, chickens, dogs killed for food, rice, *millo* (maize?), yams, honey, wax, sugarcane, incense, wine, oranges, lemons, eggplants, and three kinds of plantain, all could have been available either through local resources or trade.

The highly agreeable sweet wine drunk by Arellano may have been what Cole describes as a wine made from sugarcane, whose juice is boiled with the bark of certain trees and lime juice (1913:85). The only difference here is that to Arellano the wine appeared to be spiced with cinnamon and ginger. But note that one of the alcoholic drinks of the culturally related Mandaya is made by boiling strained honey with a plant called *palba*, similar to ginger, and allowing it to ferment (Cole 1913:186).

The natives' preoccupation with iron, noted by Arellano, is prevalent among the Bagobo. Cole makes frequent mention of iron and says that the knives made by them "are in great demand and often travel inland" (1913:92).

The obvious eagerness of the people to trade is confirmed: "The Bagobo is a keen trader. . . . In early days, Chinese and Moro traders brought gongs, jars, plates, and other crockery, as well as many other articles now among the prized heirlooms of wealthy men or occupying an important place in the ceremonial life of the tribe" (Cole 1913:91–92). This would account for their many fine porcelain pots painted in various designs, and for their ironware, of which Arellano made careful mention.

Two or three "Indians" who were tied up and evidently offered for sale or barter to the Spaniards are reminders of a practice that was still extant early in the present century, when a moderate form of slavery persisted among the Bagobo, Manobo (Kulaman), and Mandaya (Cole 1913:96, 155, 182). The crueler, sanguinary side of slavery among the Bagobo and Manobo (Kulaman) is given by a Jesuit missionary, Mateo Gisbert, in a series of letters written in 1886 (Blair and Robertson 1903–1909:XLIII, 234, 242, 246–247, 247 n.108, 248–250).

Cole has remarked that the Bagobo made no use of boats until recently because of the considerable distance of their habitat from the sea (1913:90). I do not think that we can exclude the possibility that they had some coastal settlements from which they might have been driven by Moro encroachments. But consider this alternative possibility: The seemingly hostile canoes described by Arellano made their belated appearance over a month after the *San Lucas* had anchored in the gulf, and Viban was now accompanied by an older chief to whom he appeared to pay deference. Where had the canoes been all this time? Did they belong to the older man? If so, where did he come from? I speculate that word regarding the Spanish visitors eventually reached more distant places, and that Viban's sudden change of attitude may have been inspired by his superior, who could have come, let us say, from the head of the gulf where coastal Mandaya called Pagsupan (Cole 1913:165) lived near the Tagum and Hijo rivers, both of which debouch into the gulf.

As for the bloodletting sign of friendship offered by Viban but declined by Arellano, such use of blood constitutes a well-known ritual in the Philippines, the most famous being the compact between Legazpi and Sikatuna, a local chieftain on Bohol. It dramatized a treaty important in Philippine history, sealing the "eternal brotherhood of the Faith," and has been commemorated in momument and painting. The two men mixed together each other's blood and drank it. The Boxer Codex of 1590 contains a brief but useful comment on the role of the blood compact in alliances or peace treaties (Quirino and Garcia 1958:393). Among the Bagobo, the blood compact consists of the cutting of each principal's wrist until the blood flows freely, and each participant drinks the other's blood; or, their blood may be caught and mixed in a dish from which they then drink (Cole 1913:95).

To conclude, it is my contention that the nonevents at the four islands are significant. Drake could easily have missed meeting up with any natives because the tribes in the Davao area were essentially noncoastal. Moreover, they were undoubtedly few in numbers, which was especially true of the islands of Samal and Talikud. Dampier encountered only a canoeload of men in the gulf. Recall that Arellano had no success raising anyone at first, and only two or three men the next day. They had to go back over the hill to fetch some others. Apparently, the largest number of people brought along by Viban was two hundred men, and if he controlled a much larger number than that, which he doubtlessly did, they remained behind in their upland settlements.

Arellano was in the cove for well over a month. Drake, on the other hand, coasted his four islands for only five days. If the English captain began on the Pacific side of the eastern peninsula of the gulf at 7°5', then entered the gulf proper, passed the southern shores of Samal and Talikud, and finally stopped at "Mindanao" (the west coast) for wood and water, he was more or less on the go all the time. He might have been undetected by most natives, and shunned by others, especially if they had but a few canoes.

As for the evidence of Arellano that the natives had pigs, fowl, cooking dogs, rice, and other foodstuffs, which they presented to the Spaniards, this was after they had been dealing with them for some days. We have no way of knowing if Viban rounded them up with difficulty or whether they were readily available. In any event, when Drake's men went ashore they came back with only wood and water.

## WHAT THE FOUR ISLANDS IMPLY

If Sharp and I are right in the hypothesis that the four islands encountered by Drake were in reality two peninsulas and two islands in the Davao Gulf area, what does this signify?

A minor implication, which may quickly be disposed of, is that it lends credence to the assumption that Fletcher was not in error when he said that the *Golden Hind* afterwards sailed past the Sarangani Islands off the southernmost tip of Mindanao. I mention this because Wagner (1926:173) has expressed some misgivings on this point.

More importantly, the identification of the four islands as being the Davao Gulf area provides geographical and nautical arguments for the rejection of the Bislig-Lianga coast of Mindanao as the locale of Drake's first South Sea landfall. If, for the sake of argument, we were to go along with Sharp's suggestion that the *Golden Hind* did indeed hit the coast first in the Bislig-Lianga area, it would be asking too much of us to accept that he could have lost sight of the Mindanaoan coastline on his way south to Davao Gulf.

It is demanding too much, too, for us to believe that it took thirteen days for Drake to reach the area of the gulf from the Bislig-Lianga vicinity, from which it is separated by only about 160 miles. True, John Drake talks about nine days, but even that is too long. Bear in mind that the tender *San Lucas* made almost exactly the same alleged run in less than one day on January 30, 1565, starting at 9 degrees, or about 69 miles farther north than 8 degrees. The winds were very favorable.

It might be argued that either adverse winds or a dead calm could have frustrated the *Golden Hind*, but the documents make no mention of this. However, I must admit that in view of their consistent miserliness with meteorological details, except in spectacular instances, such a possible omission is not necessarily significant.

On the other hand, as with the rest of the southern Philippines, widespread seasonal variations are less important for Mindanao than for the northern islands and areas closer to the Asiatic main-

land. The southwest and northeast monsoons are not as strong or
persistent. More noticeable are the relatively local climatic variations, which overshadow the seasonal changes, and even they are
generally less pronounced over open water than over the inland
and coastal areas. The actual winds may be quite variable during
the season (U.S. Hydrographic Office 1956:24–25).

For the east coast of Mindanao specifically, between Cauit Point
and Cape San Agustin about 182 miles to the south, the situation is:
"For 6 months (May to October), the prevailing wind is southwest
. . . while in October [the winds] change from southwest to north"
(U.S. Hydrographic Office 1956:327).

Those meteorological monsters of the sea, typhoons, rarely
affect eastern Mindanao. Gales may be experienced during the
northeast monsoon, but fewer than from July to part of September.

If Drake's Julian calendar date of October 16 for reaching land is
converted to the Gregorian method of reckoning, it will be obvious
that the *Golden Hind* would have been favored, if indeed it had
reached the east coast of Mindanao, by being ten days deeper into
the incipient period of northerly winds and a like amount of time
past the period of gales.

Currents favor a ship coasting south. "A constant southerly
current has been observed on the east coast of Mindanao at a
distance of over 4 miles from the shore," and "there is a constant
southwesterly current off Cape San Agustin" which "attains a rate
of 1½ knots" (U.S. Hydrographic Office 1956:328, 329).

In sum, Drake most likely would not have been impeded by
adverse winds if he indeed sailed southward along the coast of
Mindanao, and he might even have been speeded by any favorable
northerly airflow that might already have established itself in October. The ocean current, too, would have been in his favor.

Aside from my skepticism that Drake could have lost the east
coast of Mindanao and that it would have taken him thirteen days
to sail down the coast to the four islands, I have further reason to
reject the northeast coast as the locale of the Island of Thieves. It
emerges from my aerial survey of the region, made during the same
flight undertaken to test the Davao Gulf theory.

At the time that I flew over the coast I was fully prepared to
believe that the ethnographic data that I had been massing was
persuasive enough to identify it as the mystery place. Even after

the reconnaissance was completed I still clung to the opinion that my search had been successful. But I had a lingering and uneasy feeling that the results had not been as convincing as I had hoped. Let me recount the salient details of my flight in the Piper Super Cub.

We arrived at Lamon Point, 8°28' N, on the east coast of Mindanao at 10:25 A.M. Looking north I could see Lianga Bay a few miles away at about 8°35' N. Although we did not fly over the bay I could observe some tiny islands within it.

Proceeding southward from Lamon Point to Bangai Point at 7°44' N, I observed in succession the following coastal features: Port Lamon, Hinatuan Bay, Bislig Bay, Sanco Point, Lingig Bay, Catarman Point, and Cateel Bay.

The islands observed off the coast between Lamon Point and Cateel Bay were: Bagasinan I., Mahaba I., Tigdos I., Manomawan I., Maowa I., Mancharon I., Mawes I., Majangit I., and Hamuan I. There were numerous other islets that were even smaller than these and consequently were hardly worthy of notice. All were observed at a height of 2,500 to 3,000 feet.

After reaching the vicinity of Bangai Point, which defines the lower limits of Cateel Bay, we headed back over the Pacific Cordillera to Davao Gulf. The airline distance we had covered from Lamon Point to Bangai Point was approximately fifty miles.

What impressions did I form as a result of this leg of my flight? All the islands seemed too small and wild to qualify as the Island of Thieves. There were few signs of human habitation. Some islets had coconut palms and a few had cultivated strips. For the most part the others were covered with trees and bushes, and sometimes fringed with mangroves.

I considered the possibility that the islands were not important in themselves. However, none of the bays, including Bislig, which I had searched out most eagerly of all, gave me the impression that they were capable of supporting a dense population and a large fleet of canoes.

If I did not immediately reject the eastern part of Mindanao upon the completion of my aerial survey, it was for two reasons. First, I thought that conditions in the sixteenth century might have been different—that there might have been a heavier occupancy of the land. Second, I was still under the illusion that the ethnographic evidence was too overwhelming to ignore and that the small number of contradictions would disappear when enough further research had been made. The deficiencies eventually found in the list of cultural traits were to dispel all that. So were the old Spanish demographic records.

The final and most important implication of my identification of the Davao Gulf area as the four islands is that, in combination with the rejection of the Bislig-Lianga area as the Island of Thieves, it rekindles the nagging possibility that Drake's first landfall was after all in the Carolines, for at 8 degrees north of the equator the only other land besides the Philippines would have had to be in Micronesia.

Moreover, a run of sixty-eight days' duration is more consistent with a California-to-Carolines run than a California-to-Mindanao one because of the slowness of the ships of the time. The *Golden Hind*, a cross between a warship and a merchant vessel, carried ten or fifteen tons of artillery and arms, and when it left the California coast it was groaning with booty, especially twenty-five or thirty tons of silver and gold.

## TIME AND THE OCEAN

The question of time for the run from California is important and interesting enough to deserve that special space be given to it.

It is true that two early vessels completed the trans-Pacific crossing in a time comparable to Drake's, the first example being the *San Lucas*, which with stopovers made the trip from Mexico to Mindanao between November 20, 1564, and January 29, 1565, a period of about seventy days. For the first eleven days it had had to hang back because it was sailing in convoy with three others of Legazpi's ships, which were much slower than it. After detaching itself from the main fleet it reached the Marshall Islands and stopped briefly; then reached Truk, where it stopped overnight; and subsequently had a skirmish with the natives at Pulap Atoll, and another at Sorol Atoll. Admittedly, the ship was small and obviously built for speed. Perhaps it was too exceptional a craft to be used for purposes of comparison.

The only other swift passage was that made by Thomas Cavendish in 1587–1588 in the 120-ton *Desire*. Leaving Baja California and having favorable easterly and northeasterly winds at his disposal, he reached the Philippines in fifty-six days, having been delayed only by a few hours' stop at Guam. He had the advantage of not being encumbered with bullion to the extent that Drake had been, nor with such heavy ordnance. Although I am not familiar with the details of his ship's characteristics, it may be assumed that even with the passage of less than a decade from the time Drake left England, there had been advances in naval architecture, especially since the *Golden Hind* evidently had not been built in England and was hardly a new vessel.

Other early vessels made the westward crossing to the Philippines in longer time, but they cannot always be compared adequately with Drake's ship because of differences in point of departure, course, time of year, delaying stops en route, and ship characteristics. The starting point for Magellan and two of Loaisa's ships was the Strait of Magellan. Magellan spent about 108 days in reaching the archipelago, including a three-day stopover in the Marianas. Loaisa's flagship, the *Santa María de la Victoria*, required about 133 days, including a six-day stop at Guam, and his *Santa María del Parral* needed approximately 159 days.

Departing from Mexico and tarrying for nine or ten days in the Marshalls, Saavedra's *Florida* took approximately 90 days for the crossing to Mindanao. Also departing from Mexico, with brief stops en route in the Marshalls and at Fais, Villalobos' fleet consumed about 94 days. It took Legazpi 85 days to cross from Mexico to Samar, but included in that were a half-day stop at Meijit in the Marshalls and a twelve-day stop at Guam. The case of the *San Gerónimo* is atypical but interesting. Sent in 1566 from Acapulco to the Philippines to join Legazpi, it used 153 days to reach the vicinity of the *embocadero* or San Bernardino Strait; but en route it had experienced mutinies against four successive commanders, had stopped at Ujelang in the Marshalls, and had shuttled back and forth five times after sighting Guam. It was so old and had become so battered at sea that it had to be broken up when it reached the archipelago (Sharp 1961:115 *et passim*).

Some years after Drake's voyage, five vessels of Admiral Joris van Spilbergen's fleet, sailing for the Dutch East India Company, left Navidad near Acapulco on November 20, 1615, and speedily reached Cape Espiritu Santo on the Philippine island of Samar sixty-seven days later, although they did not cast anchor in Manila harbor until early March 1616. They had been in the Marianas for two days.

It is tempting, because there were so many of them, to compare the *Golden Hind* with the Manila galleons and the length of time it took them on their return passage from Mexico to the Philippines. One must bear in mind, however, that the type of vessel referred to as a galleon varied in type over the years. Originally, it was slim and seems to have been designed, not necessarily in Spain, as a protest against the broad carracks or *naos* of the early si:.teenth century, and only later did the Spanish variety assume the familiar image of a highly decorated vessel riding high out of the water (Landström [1961]:112–113). English, Flemish, and Dutch galleons were not as exaggerated as this, and were essentially men-of-war.

The Manila galleons were cumbersome trading ships with broad beams and high forecastles and poops. Their tonnage varied a good deal, as did their size. A law of 1593 limited their tonnage to three hundred each, ships with more than double that displacement having been in service before then. In time, tonnages reached as high as two thousand. Outward bound from Acapulco, their Philippine cargo having been discharged, they traveled light, almost in ballast. They carried artillery, but not a good deal. The galleons sailed alone, without convoy, and, once they had reached the right latitude for catching the trade winds in a zone south of Acapulco, went in a direct line to the Marianas. They usually cleared the Mexican coast late in February or sometime in March, the best season of the year for timing a favorable arrival in the Philippines to avoid typhoons (Schurz 1939:279). Despite these advantages, they were slow sailers.

Sailing with the northeast trades between 12° and 14°N, these westward-bound galleons ordinarily took about three months to make the passage from Acapulco to Manila, of which two months were spent in reaching the Ladrones,[8] about fifteen days more in reaching the San Bernardino Strait, and another fifteen in reaching Cavite on Manila Bay (Schurz 1939:281). The time varied a good deal, however, and when it was necessary to make the passage through the tortuous *embocadero*, as it almost invariably was, the time consumed could be a matter of four to six weeks, so it is necessary to bear this in mind when calculating sailing time. It is for this reason that I prefer, when possible, to figure time of arrival off nearest land, usually Cape Espiritu Santo. This seems only fair in view of the fact that Drake did not have to negotiate a similarly treacherous channel in crossing the Pacific to reach the Island of Thieves. In the examples that follow, the reader is cautioned, therefore, to make a mental subtraction whenever I am unable to ascertain the date of arrival off the San Bernardino Strait. He is also cautioned that although it is customary to speak of virtually all vessels that sailed between Mexico and the Philippines after Legazpi as "galleons," the term is used loosely with respect to both ship structure and purpose. I greatly suspect that the later "typical" galleons made the traverse in much slower time than earlier vessels because of their size and structure.

Of specific early galleon crossings departing from Mexico, mention may be made of three ships under the command of the able Juan de la Isla, who left Acapulco on March 9, 1570, and on June 7 cast anchor off the small island of Maripipi (Colín 1900–1902:I, 155 n.3). Thus, it took ninety days for this part of the voyage to the Philippines, which ultimately ended at Panay and apparently did not include a stop at the Ladrones, or Marianas, but did include a passage through the *embocadero*.

Two ships left Acapulco on April 6, 1575, and arrived at Manila on August 25, having taken seventy-two days through open sea just to reach the Marianas (Dahlgren 1916:43).

As far as I can ascertain, neither of these two examples involved galleons on the regular Manila run. The crossings were prior to Drake's and were made in fairly good time.

Galleons postdating Drake could be unusually fast or dreadfully slow, although I cannot say with certainty whether all of the following instances pertain to vessels belonging to the "Manila galleon" category. In the fast group are two vessels which sailed from Acapulco on March 22, 1595, and reached Cavite 81 days later. Even faster were two "very swift" vessels which in 1610 with strong winds crossed from Acapulco to Manila in 73 days. By contrast, in 1718 it took a galleon 116 days from Acapulco to the entrance of the *embocadero*, and 22 more to Cavite. And in 1730 a galleon took 172 days to reach Mindoro (Dahlgren 1916:51, 80, 115, 117).

Obviously, there are so many variables in determining the length of time that it took to cross the Pacific that it is not possible to make strict comparisons. Yet I must repeat my contention that the *Golden Hind*, laden down with so much dead weight, probably traveled slowly and could not have reached Mindanao in sixty-eight days. It could, however, have made it comfortably to the western Carolines, many hundreds of miles closer to California.

## chapter nine

# *Faults and Flaws*

I HAVE SAID THAT it is not possible to single out absolutely a place in either Micronesia or the Philippines as being the Island of Thieves. At the same time I am convinced that the mystery island is indeed in one of these two places and that this can be demonstrated by accepting a less rigid set of rules of evidence.

The only way of reconciling my two seemingly paradoxical positions is, on the one hand, by regarding the documents bearing on the case as faulty accounts, and, on the other, by subjecting them to painstaking reanalysis. To the first of these I shall now proceed.

The shortcomings of the materials, aside from some exceptions in John Drake's two Spanish depositions, have as their source essentially four things: their composite nature, their faulty synthesis, their alteration through tampering, and their errors of fact. All of this is in addition to glaring errors of omission, about which nothing can be said except to deplore once again the loss of Drake's original records. Responsibile for some of these deficiencies is a subtle political bias, especially perceptible where England's interests were concerned.

I propose to demonstrate these inadequacies by a separate consideration of each of the major documents, and then by a comparison of each of them with the others in order to bring out discrepancies.

### FLAWS IN THE "FAMOUS VOYAGE"

All the shortcomings I have listed are to be found in the first published account of the circumnavigation, the "Famous Voyage," appearing as a later insert in Richard Hakluyt's great work on the principal voyages and discoveries of the English people. There is every reason to think that this account had at least three sources and that their unknown compiler was Hakluyt himself. In chapter 3 I went into some detail regarding this account, so here I shall limit myself to a special consideration of its sources, the way they were used, and an evaluation of their accuracy.

As Wagner (1926:238–285) has gone to much trouble to explore the origins of the "Famous Voyage," I am inclined to accept his findings and shall present them herewith. He identifies three main ingredients, in addition to some minor ones.

First, the John Cooke account.[1] Not much is known about Cooke, except that he was a witness at Doughty's trial at St. Julian. His account forms the basis for the first part of the "Famous Voyage," except for the portion dealing with the trial, which was deleted because it put Drake in a bad light and was replaced by a single innocuous paragraph. Cooke left the expedition before it entered the Pacific and returned to England, so he has nothing to say about the Island of Thieves.

Second, the "Anonymous Narrative."[2] This begins at the island of Mocha off the coast of Chile and covers the second part of the voyage. It may have been dictated, after the Drake expedition returned, by an uneducated seaman named William Lege or Legge, and written by a gentleman of Drake's party. The narrative has no direct applicability to the case of the Island of Thieves because the "Famous Voyage" fails to incorporate any of it beyond the sack of the town of Guatulco in Mexico. This is no great loss to us because the narrative, the whole of which is extant, has Drake sailing from America to Ternate in the Moluccas without sight of land, an obvious mistake. Yet to some extent it has usefulness in checking the reliability of other sources.

Third, the latter half of a manuscript by Fletcher, now lost. It would appear that from Guatulco on, no other source but Fletcher was used. In the "Famous Voyage," the wording of the ethnographic details surrounding the Island of Thieves is often identical to that in *The World Encompassed*, proving that there was a single fountainhead for these data at least. If the reader will refer back to the extracts in chapter 3 there will be no doubt of this.

Of the lesser ingredients going into the "Famous Voyage," Wagner believes that there are a few indications that some limited use was made of Fletcher's manuscript dealing with the first part of the voyage. Another ingredient is very brief and consists of some miscellaneous memoranda having no bearing on the Island of Thieves, and probably belonging, according to Wagner, to the "Anonymous Narrative" from which they in some way became separated in the volume of manuscripts that have been under discussion.[3]

There is nothing wrong per se with a composite account if it has been assembled from good firsthand documents that have not been tampered with by the distortion of certain facts and episodes, or their deliberate omission. Yet, while the "Famous Voyage" has none of the digressive interpolations and extraneous commentaries inserted in the later book published under the name of Drake's nephew, it does exercise some editorializing, especially by the expurgation of that portion of Cooke's account dealing with the Doughty affair. Defenders of Drake the hero have been bitterly critical, to be sure, of Cooke's narrative, but it is the judgment of impartial historians that it is essentially accurate. The censoring of the Cooke account, by Hakluyt or whoever else compiled the "Famous Voyage," leaves us with the uneasy feeling that we cannot always expect objectivity or accurate reporting in the rest of the work.

However, the compiler of the "Famous Voyage" was probably right in replacing the "Anonymous Narrative" with Fletcher in covering the Island of Thieves, for the former makes no reference to such a place, even though John Drake speaks of it by name in both of his depositions.

Notwithstanding its mention of the first landfall after leaving California, and a description of the natives encountered there, the "Famous Voyage" says nothing about thieving on the part of the natives nor of the reprisals taken there against them, and fails to use the appellation "Island of Thieves." In addition, it is at variance with other sources with respect to dates and elapsed time periods, a matter I shall discuss under the heading of "Discrepancies."

It makes no mention of next arriving at four islands. It says nothing of Mindanao nor the taking on of wood and water. It states, laconically, that after leaving the island where the encounter with the long-eared, black-toothed natives took place "we light vpon diuers others, some whereof made a great shewe of Inhabitants." There is no suggestion as to the identity of these other islands nor of their latitude. In brief, the "Famous Voyage" appears to have skipped over the four islands and called attention instead to some unidentified isles farther to the south. Only toward the Moluccas would there have been places capable of a great show of people. Mindanao was sparsely populated during the sixteenth century.

The account does mention various islands encountered after leaving the "diuers others." They were met just before reaching the Moluccas and they themselves form part of the confusion with which we have to deal when using the "Famous Voyage" in our investigation. Their names are given as Tagulada, Zelon, and Zewarra; but Wagner, who like myself spent much time trying to identify them, finally decided that Tagulada is the island of Tagulandang or Tahulandang, as it is now known, and Zewarra might be Siago, as the island of Siaul or Siau was then known (Wagner 1926:278 n.49).[4] He says nothing about Zelon, but elsewhere (p. 175) he had already made it out to be Siaul, and Zewarra to be Sarangani, thereby adding to the confusion; for on one page this makes Zelon and Zewarra one and the same island—Siaul—but on another they are two places, Siaul and Sarangani. This contradiction in names is not as important as the erratic positions of these islands, if Drake indeed encountered them in sequence in going from Sarangani to the Moluccas. However, if it is of any comfort to know, *The World Encompassed* jumbles similar names and positions even more.

A few more omissions, errors, and exaggerations may be pointed out before leaving the "Famous Voyage" and moving on to other documents. Three islands are said to have been found in the Strait of Magellan on the third of October (1578), whereas the month was really November.

Purposely or unintentionally, no mention is made of the disappearance of the *Marigold* after Drake's fleet had emerged out of the Strait of Magellan into the Pacific. Might this have been because of the possibility that, like the *Elizabeth*, the ship had deserted rather than foundered, as reported? Its captain had temporarily been relieved of command by Drake just before the Doughty trial.

Another omission is the lack of any reference at all to the slave girl Maria, who was taken aboard the *Golden Hind* and carried across the whole Pacific before eventually being left on a Moluccan island.

Among the exaggerations, which however are far fewer than those in *The World Encompassed*, is the glowing account of the relations between Drake and Babù (Baber, Babur), the sultan of Ternate. The document does not mention that at one point Babù had ordered the execution of the English captain for attempting to trade for cloves without his license. The "Famous Voyage" also must have been in error in relating almost ecstatically that the sultan had earlier sent word to Drake that "hee would yeeld him-selfe and the right of his Ilands to bee at the pleasure and com-mande of so famous a prince as he served."

Again, I find it hard to believe that the Javanese were "of goodly stature," as reported; everything we know about these people points to the opposite.

If it is any consolation, it should be noted that the "Famous Voyage" departs from *The World Encompassed* least of all in those portions dealing with the voyage subsequent to Drake's departure on April 16, 1579, from the port of the Mexican town of Guatalco, which he sacked. And it is less erratic than that book.[5]

## DEFECTS *IN* THE WORLD ENCOMPASSED

This leads us to *The World Encompassed* itself, a far lengthier but much padded account. The book was obviously not based on Drake's journal; it was made up from various sources, including possibly some recollections of men who had made the circumnavigation.

We are not even sure of the ultimate authorship of the book. The official compiler is Drake's nephew, Sir Francis Drake, but his real role seems to have been limited to lending his name to the volume by writing a brief "Dedication" to the earl of Warwick. It has been suggested that if a single person was behind the compilation of *The World Encompassed* it was Philip Nichols, "preacher," who in 1626 had written *Sir Francis Drake Revived*. But a single compiler is not a single source. Indeed, the title page of *The World Encom-passed* contains words to the effect that it was "carefully collected out of the notes of Master Fletcher Preacher in this imployment, and diuers others his followers in the same."

The core of the book is the first half of a manuscript by Francis Fletcher, deposited in the British Museum as Sloane MS No. 61; but the manuscript was subjected to deletions and additions, especially a substituted acount of the Doughty affair probably written by the unknown compiler of the book himself. It does not cover the voyage beyond the Island of Mocha off the coast of Chile but is here mentioned, as are most other sources, because it goes to show how much of a composite the book is.

Supplementing Fletcher and covering only the story of Captain Winter's voyage to the Strait in the *Elizabeth* and his return to England, is a fairly reliable account by Edward Cliffe, a mariner who returned with Winter. This, together with partial accounts by Nuño da Silva and Lopez Vaz, had been published in 1600 by Hakluyt and therefore was available to the compiler of the "official" account.

The remaining portion of the voyage was compiled from several unknown sources, probably and chiefly a later and revised version by Fletcher of his full account of the circumnavigation, which he intended to publish as a book but never did; this manuscript is lost.

Accusations of bias have been raised against *The World Encompassed*, notably by W. S. W. Vaux in his "Introduction" to the Hakluyt Society's reprinting of the book. He particularly assails Sir Francis Drake, the nephew, whom he charges with omitting some passages from Fletcher's manuscript and modifying others because he felt that they were "in some degree derogating from his uncle's memory" (Vaux 1854:xii). If this is true, Sir Francis did more than lend his name to the volume.

On the other hand, Vaux thinks that the tone of certain documents that he has included in his 1854 edition in the form of three appendices—probably, with the Cooke narrative, the oldest contemporary manuscript records of Drake's voyage in our possession—were "put together by some one who was not friendly to Sir Francis Drake, or who, in the quarrel with Doughty, had taken part with him against his accusers" (Vaux 1854:xiv).

Francis Fletcher has been charged by some with harboring antagonism against Drake because of the Doughty affair, but this has been debated. Nevertheless, an anonymous memorandum de-

scribes a hilarious but cruel farce in which, after the *Golden Hind*
had been freed from the treacherous shoal south of Ternate, Drake
caused Fletcher to be fastened to the forehatch by padlock. After
the ship's company had been assembled, Drake, sitting cross-
legged and with a pair of slippers in his hand, excommunicated the
chaplain from the church of God and denounced him to the devil
and all his angels, forbidding him to go before the mast on pain of
death and forcing him to wear a notice on his arm declaring him to
be the "falsest knave that liveth" (Vaux 1854:176). One can imagine the lasting effect that this prank may have had on a man
destined to be the chief source for the two major accounts of the
circumnavigation, unless Fletcher accepted it all in good humor,
which is doubtful.

At any rate, *The World Encompassed* abounds in straightforward mistakes, omissions, exaggerations, and flights of fancy. Take
the latitudes given in the book. They have been a source of puzzle-
ment to us, and Wagner has challenged them as being "extremely
inaccurate." To support his allegation he gives a list in parallel
columns of the actual latitudes of nine ports visited by the *Golden
Hind* as compared with the latitudes recorded in *The World Encompassed* (Wagner 1926:474). The differences range from as little
as 1 minute to as much as 2 degrees, 38 minutes, and 4 seconds.
Even though Wagner concedes that "there may be some question
whether the figures given were from observations made by Drake,
or anyone on the *Golden Hind*," the fact remains that the record as
we have it is not always reliable in this respect.

Another of the several instances of exaggeration or a mistake in
magnitude is the assertion that in Chile at the latitude of 22°30′ S
there was a great Spanish town called Mormorena, the truth being
that there was no town there at all and that what was really referred
to was a small nearby settlement which obtained its water from the
spring "Moreno" (Wagner 1926:105–106).

A still further instance of exaggeration revolves around the
number of Spaniards who came out of the Chilean town of La
Serena to thwart Drake's attempt to take on water at nearby La
Herradura. John Drake is noncommittal, saying "men on horse-
back came out," but *The World Encompassed* claims that there
were three hundred men—one hundred mounted Spaniards and
two hundred Indians on foot—an improbably high number. It is

interesting that the account by John Cooke, who was not there, says that there were three hundred horsemen and two hundred footmen. More credible is the figure given by Pedro Sarmiento de Gamboa, who says there were only fifty or sixty Spaniards and some Indians.[6] A secondhand account by the Portuguese Lopez Vaz, who tells us he obtained his information from Nuño da Silva, a pilot captured by Drake, says the Spaniards "sent twelve horsemen," but this seems like an exaggeration in the opposite direction.

One of the intriguing omissions in the Fletcher account may have been a deliberate attempt to suppress a scandal. John Cooke, no admirer of Drake, who returned to England with Winter on the *Elizabeth*, and therefore was not an eyewitness, said in his account that the English captain took from the captured *Cacafuego* a "proper negro wench called Maria, which was afterward begotten with child between the captain and his men pirates, & sett on a small Island to take her adventure as shalbe hereafter shewed . . ." (Wagner 1926:271). Later, William Camden made a brief reference to Maria and her inhumane abandonment (Camden 1625:426). She was also referred to by Gaspar de Varga, alcalde of Guatulco, whose port was sacked by the English (Wagner 1926:381). Even the "Anonymous Narrative" refers to her. However, Don Francisco de Zárate, an official traveling on the captured Spanish ship, is silent on the matter, even though it was from him that the girl was taken.

The story of Maria, her pregnancy, and her abandonment with two other Negroes, was long considered by a few to be a fiction created by some malicious person, until the discovery of John Drake's two unknown depositions, both of which outline the main facts (Fuller-Eliott-Drake 1911:II, 348 [356], 373 [394–395]; Nuttall 1914:31, 53).

One of Drake's admirers, unable to bring himself to see any wrong in his hero's behavior, says that after all he had "rescued these people from slavery and one of them from death, and was leaving them to a life which to them was perfect bliss" (Corbett 1899:I, 300 n.2). Life on an uninhabited island in the Malaysian archipelago—a cozy place for three! A suggestion from another admirer takes an altogether different line of reasoning, saying that

he was little likely to undermine the respect which he had established by a sordid amour with a negress. He might, more probably, have taken her to wash his fine linen and goffer his ruff with less damage to them than would be wreaked by the clumsier hands of one of his crew. (Mason 1941:175)

One hopes that the writer of these lines is not implying that Maria became pregnant from laundering clothes.

A less colorful error of omission seems to have been an incident involving Drake reported by a Spaniard named Francisco de Dueñas, in which the *Golden Hind* encountered and fired upon a Portuguese galleon, most likely in the Celebes Sea.[7] Dueñas, furthermore, tells us that Drake later took aboard two Indian fishermen to guide him to the Moluccas. *The World Encompassed* does not mention either of these two stories (Wagner 1926:173, 175).

*The World Encompassed* is not lacking in excursions into the imaginary. For instance, it tells us that along the coast where Chile and Peru meet and in the Province of Cusco, "the common ground, wheresoeuer it bee taken vp, in euery hundred pound weight of earth, yeeldeth 25.s. of pure siluer, after the rate of a crowne an ounce" (Drake 1628:56). It has been reckoned that this would amount to five ounces for a hundred pounds, no less.

Fantasy, intermingled with fairly accurate reporting, enters also into the account of the culture and behavior of the Indians encountered by Drake at the Californian bay where he put in for five weeks to repair his ship before heading for the Moluccas. The aborigines, who must have been Coast Miwok or possibly Pomo, were simple food gatherers, yet they are depicted almost as if they were members of a European monarchical society. Says one distinguished anthropologist: "All the references to the King, his Guard, the Sceptre or Mace Royal, the Crowns, and the like, are of course fancies" (Kroeber 1925:276). I find particularly annoying the alleged coronation of Drake by fawning Indians and the eager transference through him of the sovereignty of their country to Queen Elizabeth. In the words of a critic,

Fletcher's childlike credulity and love of the marvelous and extraordinary no doubt induced him to read into some very simple actions of these Indians a meaning totally contrary to that intended by them. According to him Drake accepted the crown and the chains placed around his neck as a sign that the Indians were conferring the

sovereignty of the country on him. . . . Nothing can be more certain of course, than that the Indians had no such idea, but with the
lingering feudal notions characteristic of Englishmen of the day,
Drake might have believed that the ceremony had such significance.
(Wagner 1926:147)

However, in all candor, it is not so much the imaginings of *The World Encompassed* itself which undermine our confidence as it is the fantasies of the man behind the book—Francis Fletcher. The compilers of *The World Encompassed* and the unknown author of its predecessor, the "Famous Voyage," felt it necessary to reject the wilder and more lurid of his interpolations, as well as his sermonizing and his railing against Spain and the Catholics, all of which appeared in his unpublished manuscript (Sloane MS No. 61). What must we think of a chronicler who describes (Figure 25) some playful Patagonians, whom Drake met at what is now called Puerto Deseado (47°45′ S), as giants whose women had feet like shovels and hands like shoulders of mutton, to say nothing of brows like the forehead of an elk and bags under their chins which reached down to their breasts as if stuffed with cotton? His propensity for fiction is again seen in his gruesome description of the cannibalistic fate encountered by two of Drake's landing party captured by Indians at the island of Mocha off the coast of Chile as they stepped ashore to fill their water butts. No one but he in his manuscript has recorded how the two men, Thomas Brewer and Thomas Flood, were bound and laid on the ground, with their tormentors dancing and singing around them in a circle, all the while cutting away their flesh "by gubbets" and casting it up into the air, then catching it and devouring it in a most monstrous and unnatural manner, "like doggs."

### JOHN DRAKE'S LIMITATIONS

In contrast to the "Famous Voyage" and *The World Encompassed*, John Drake's two depositions, made in 1584 and 1587, have the virtue of being free of the tamperings to which other primary documents were subjected. They could not have been influenced, moreover, by any already assembled accounts of which we are aware, for the young cousin was in England only a few months after his return on September 26, 1580, on the *Golden Hind*; for on May 1

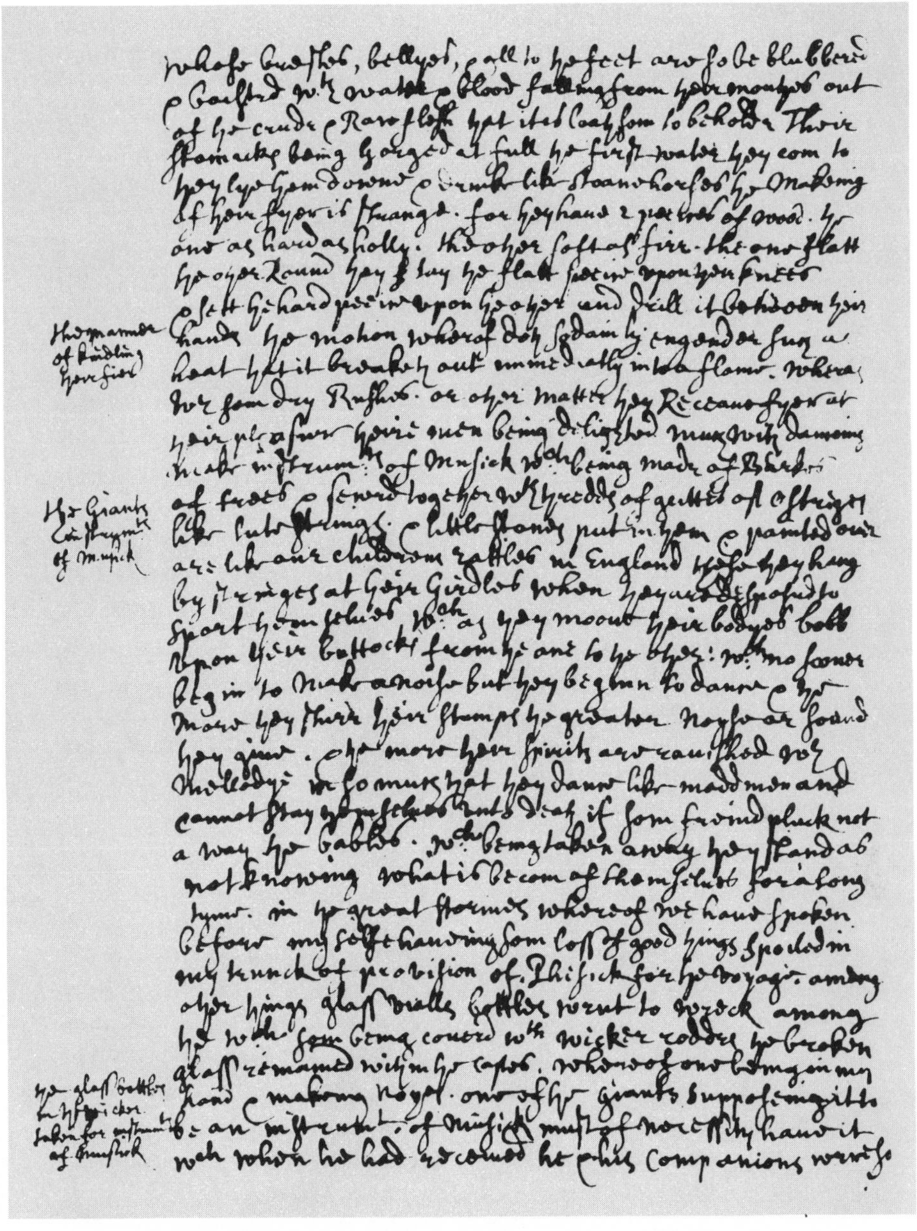

whose breastes, bellyes, & all to the feet are so be blubbered
& besmeared w^th watery blood falling from their mouthes out
of the crude & Raw flesh that itt is loathsom to behold. Their
stomacks being gorged at full the first water they com to
they lye them downe & drink like Beastes horses the making
of their fyer is strange. for they haue 2 peeces of wood. the
one as hard as holly. the other soft as firr. the one flatt
the other Round they lay the flatt peece upon their knees
& sett the hard peece upon the other and twirle it betwixt their
hands the motion wherof doth sodainly engender such a
heat that it breaketh out immediatly into a flame. wheras
we som dry Rushes or other matter they Receave fyer at
their pleasure. their men being delighted much with dancing
make instrum^ts of Musick w^ch being made of Barkes
of trees & sewed together w^th threddes of gutts of Ostriges
like lute strings. & little stones put in them & painted over
are like our children rattles in England these they hang
by strings at their Girdles when they are disposed to
sport themselves w^ch as they moue their bodyes both
upon their buttocks from the one to the other: w^ch no sooner
begin to make a noise but they begin to dance & the
more they thinke their stamps the greater. noyse are found
they give. & the more their spirits are ravished w^th
melodye: w^ch so much that they dance like madd men and
cannot stay themselves unto death if som freind pluck not
a way the bables. w^ch being taken away they stand as
not knowing what is become of themselves for a long
tyme. in the great stormes whereof we haue spoken
before my selfe hauing som loss of good things spoiled in
my trunck of provision of Phisick for the voyage. among
other things glass violls bottles went to wrack among
the w^ch som being couered w^th wicker rodds the broken
glass remained within the cases. wherof one being in my
hand & making noyse. one of the giants supposing itt to
be an instrument of Musick must of necessity haue it
w^ch when he had receued he & his companions were so

the manner of kindling their fier

the Giants instrum^ts of musick

the glass bottles in the wicker taken for instrum^ts of musick

Figure 25. Page from Sloane MS No. 61. Here Francis Fletcher describes in fanciful terms the Patagonian giants. Other imaginings occur throughout the manuscript. Source: Sloane MSS. (*Courtesy The British Library*)

of the following year he sailed away on the ill-fated Fenton expedition, and after being wrecked off the Rio de la Plata was captured by the Spaniards and never again returned to England.

But of course the depositions are weakened by having been given from memory and, possibly, a wish to mislead his Spanish captors, who had a burning desire to find out all they could about the adventures of his illustrious relative. Thus, in his first deposition young John does not even mention the Northwest Coast and the Indians of Nova Albion, a glaring omission of a part of the voyage given much space in other accounts. Both of his depositions suffer from a virtual absence of dates.

The deficiencies in John Drake's two accounts are plentiful enough and I do not wish to dwell upon them unduly, but I feel that I should give a few more examples. One of them is his assertion that the *Golden Hind* sailed to Bosney (Borneo) from the southern tip of Mindanao. This would have taken Drake much too far out of the way in his quest of the Moluccas. Anyway, John makes no mention of Borneo in his earlier deposition, having the vessel proceed to the Moluccas after taking on wood and water at an island whose name he did not know but which we have been accepting right along as a place somewhere in Davao Gulf.

He gives 4° N as the latitude of the uninhabited island where Drake stopped to clean and repair his vessel for the homeward voyage after leaving Ternate. This seems unlikely as it would have taken him north instead of southward. *The World Encompassed* gives a more likely latitude of 1°40′ S.

The last example of error which I shall notice is that John, doubtlessly for self-protection, told his Spanish captors that he did not share in the booty amassed by Drake, being given only "some articles of clothing" on his return to England. Yet he himself tells us that by order of the queen, 40,000 pesos were to be distributed to the men of the ship. Although he was not a member of the crew he was nevertheless a relative of Drake, who, together with those who had financed the expedition, received a huge share of the treasure, which has been estimated to have had a value of £600,000 or "about £18 million in the values of the 1970s" (Thomson 1972: 156). As a prisoner of the Inquisition it is understandable that he did not disclose that it was he who had been the one to discover the treasure ship *Cacafuego* at sea, thus reaping the reward of the gold chain his older cousin had offered to the one who made the first sighting. More than a few articles of clothing, indeed, would have been his when the loot was divided up in England.

## DISCREPANCIES

Gathering together all these documentary sources for purpose of comparison, they are seen constantly to contradict one another. Americans, especially Californians, would dearly like to settle the controversy surrounding the identity of the bay where Drake careened his ship preparatory to making a run for the Moluccas. The documents are so unreliable that the anchorage has been identified variously as Trinidad Bay, Bodega Bay, Tomales Bay, Drake's Bay (formerly known as Jack's Bay), Bolinas Bay, and even San Francisco Bay. The "Famous Voyage" gives a latitude of 38 degrees for the spot, and *The World Encompassed* gives 38°30', but the "Anonymous Narrative" gives 44 degrees. Anthropologists have attempted to help by identifying the Indians with whom Drake came in contact, about whose actions and customs there is an ample batch of detail in the records; but the matter has not been settled once and for all by their findings. An inscribed brass plate, discovered in 1936, fitting the description of it given in the "Famous Voyage" and *The World Encompassed* has not been universally accepted as genuine, although a small book published by the California Historical Society lends strong support for its authenticity (*The Plate of Brass*, 1953). The locale of the discovery of the plate on the shore of San Francisco Bay near Greenbrae, Marin County, is slightly indecisive because it is suspected by some to have been moved inland at some time from its original place on the Pacific coast nearby.[8] Incidentally, the "Anonymous Narrative" says the plate was "of lead."

Many contradictions among the sources are apparent in the accounts of the Island of Thieves and the islands touched at soon after leaving it. The "Famous Voyage" says that the date of arrival at the former was October 13, whereas *The World Encompassed* gives it as September 30. It has Drake leaving the night after reaching it, rather than being delayed there for three days. It gives four days as the length of time it took to reach the next islands—the "diuers others"—instead of the nine days specified by John Drake and the thirteen by *The World Encompassed* for the "foure Ilands." The length of time that elapsed in sailing between this uncertain area and the Moluccas is given as about twenty-seven days by the "Famous Voyage," twenty days by John Drake, and about twelve days by the Drake book.

Another contradiction, as well as an omission, surrounds the Maria affair. John Drake, in explaining that Maria and two male Negroes were left on an uninhabited island south of Ternate in order to found a settlement, is at variance with the "Anonymous Narrative," which by stressing the girl's advanced pregnancy implies that this was the reason for leaving her and the others behind. *The World Encompassed* chooses to ignore the whole matter. As an aside, there seems to be some merit in Antonio de Herrera's allegation in a publication dated 1606 that Drake was moved, not by the idea of a settlement, but by a desire to avoid having the three Negroes eat his victuals (Wagner 1926:334). There was a very long voyage ahead to England around Africa. To this I add my own suggestion that Drake, especially in view of the greatly lessened number of mouths remaining to be fed, may have wanted to rid himself of the trio mostly because they might be a source of embarrassment in England. In any event, such is our lack of confidence in all our documentary sources that no single one can be selected as providing a reliable statement of Drake's motivation.

The location of Maria's island, named "Crab" Island by Drake's men because of the abundance of delicious robber crabs found there, is the subject of further discrepancy. John Drake, in his first deposition, gives it as 4° N, while *The World Encompassed* places it at 1°40′ S.

John Drake says that the English never saw any natives in all the time they were on Crab Island, and that they obtained nothing more than wood, water, and crabs; but in this he is contradicted by Francisco de Dueñas, the man sent in 1581 to the Moluccas by the governor of the Philippines to ascertain sentiment about the incorporation of Portugal into Spain. Dueñas states with much credibility that all the time they were there, Drake and his men were sold food by the natives of the coast of "Ymbutan" (Limbotan) and the "Island of Zangay." Ymbutan is probably on the island of Celebes and Zangay is probably one of the Banggai group. Perhaps Maria and her companions were not so completely stranded after all, although we have no idea of what might have become of them as a result of later contacts with the natives of these places.

These are only some of the contradictions, but a few more may be added. Take the matter of dates. The "Famous Voyage" asserts that on his homeward stretch Drake first sighted the African coast on June 18 at the Cape of Good Hope, whose latitude is 34°22′, whereas the book "compiled" by Drake's nephew maintains that he first sighted land on May 21 at a latitude of 31½ degrees and passed the cape on June 15.[9]

Again, *The World Encompassed* has the triumphant vessel arriving at Plymouth on September 26, while the "Famous Voyage" has it reaching "England" in November. On this score, the "Anonymous Narrative" is of no help; it gives no date. As for John Drake and his two depositions, in the first he gives no time whatsoever and in the second says that it seems to him that they entered the port of Plymouth "in October." These confusions in dates should not be regarded as isolated examples; they are but a few out of many.

## POLITICAL CONSIDERATIONS

It has been suggested by historians that political considerations influenced accounts of Drake's circumnavigation. Elizabeth, whose country after all was not at war with Spain, could not appear to sanction the depredations of her great sea captain, so a certain amount of covering up had to be done. Drake, who was an emotional man with a loudly proclaimed dislike for both the papacy and the Spaniards, had a strong incentive to maintain secrecy regarding some of his explorations and to misrepresent others.

One possible misrepresentation of this sort revolves around the latitude at which Drake first struck the northwestern coast of America on June 5, 1579, after having left Guatulco in Mexico at latitude 15°44′ N on April 16. According to John Drake it was at 48 degrees, a highly unlikely parallel in view of the prevailing northwest winds and the distance involved.[10] The "Anonymous Narrative" likewise has Drake at this latitude, but this proves nothing. An ambiguous statement in *The World Encompassed* makes the parallel out to be 42 degrees, where it was said that extreme cold was encountered—in June, no less—and the men suffered greatly from the ordeal.[11] This book has Drake then sailing north to 48 degrees, an impossibility in view of the head winds and swells prevailing at that time of the year, and the short number of days that elapsed. The "Famous Voyage" gives a northernmost latitude of 42 degrees (43 degrees in the revised 1600 edition) and also speaks of extreme cold and a snow cover on the land, described as being not mountainous but a low plain.

All this talk of snow and high latitudes, mixed with erroneous descriptions of the coastline, appear to have been inspired by a desire to prove that the English had reached farther north than any Spaniard and consequently were entitled to claim Nova Albion by right of discovery. Contemporary accounts of the episode in England by John Stow, Blundeville, John Davis, and Camden support latitudes of between 46 degrees and 48 degrees, but none of these men had accompanied the expedition. The parallel of 42 degrees may have been the correct one but this was not enough to counter Spanish claims, for they had earlier reached this far north and perhaps a degree more. It has been suggested that in order to defend their priority to the discovery of Nova Albion and to counteract Spanish claims, the English simply decided to move the discovery up to 48 degrees (Wagner 1926:138). Some skeptics have expressed doubt that Drake ever reached the Northwest Coast at all. This may be too extreme a view but it tells us something about the kind of mistrust that *The World Encompassed* and other documents engender in their readers.

Another kind of political consideration probably enters into the descriptions of Drake's alleged coronation by the Indians of Nova Albion and their exuberant cession of their land. The English were anxious to illustrate the truth of their conviction that they were vastly superior and more humane than the Spaniards and Roman Catholicism in their relations with the American Indians. It may be significant that John Drake, a prisoner of the Spaniards and a subsequent convert to Catholicism, makes no mention of the joyful coronation.

In my exposure of the defects of the documents pertaining to Drake's circumglobal adventure I have not been trying to make a game of it by finding every possible fault. Had I done so, the list of flaws would constitute a veritable treatise in itself. What I have tried to do, by selected examples, is to convince the reader of the weaknesses of the sources and to prepare him for my ultimate conclusions.

## THE DOCUMENTS AS CONFLATIONS

Once one accepts that the documents pertaining to Drake are not sacrosanct, it becomes permissible to regard the account of the Island of Thieves as a composite, a bringing together of observations that were originally made in diverse places and made to appear as if they were one alone. There is no other way of making sense out of the documents except by an admission of their blended nature. If one insists that they refer to one place alone he is embarrassed by contradictions, such as the presence of characteristically Malaysian traits in Micronesia.

The kind of composite account that has perturbed me is the same that has confronted those seeking to solve a similar ethnohistoric problem—the identity of the Indians encountered by Drake when he prepared his vessel in a California bay for the crossing to the Spice Islands. I think that the anthropologist Robert Heizer has proven fairly conclusively that the natives were Coast Miwok or Pomo (Heizer and Elmendorf 1942; Heizer 1947; cf. Kroeber 1925:275–278). But Wagner the historian has suggested that Drake, coasting south after attaining a latitude in the forties, actually put in at two or three places and that "the writer of the original narrative or the compiler who worked on it embodied in one description those of all the Indians he met" (Wagner 1926:169). Although I think that Wagner is too arbitrary in his interpretation of the cultural data, which he thinks points to the Yurok Indians of extreme northern California, he does properly raise the specter of conflation with regard to two cultural traits—the canoe and the house type of the Indians. In a posthumous publication he argues against the San Francisco Bay area and the bays just above it: "The Indians in that neighborhood used tule balsas and did not roof their houses with boards," whereas "such canoes and houses were characteristic of the Indians further north" (Wagner 1970:15). Heizer has dealt with these two traits by saying that it is a matter of semantics in the instance of the canoe, and of misconstruing Fletcher's description in the instance of the dwellings (Heizer 1947:256–257). This may be true, but however one looks at it, the use of the word "canow" in *The World Encompassed* is in itself an intrusion borrowed from other experience.

The Fletcherian "cony" illustrates conflation in a lesser way by showing how the English chaplain combined diverse zoological features to create a small mammal that has never existed in the world of nature—or, at least, in California, where they were said to have been seen by the multitude and eaten by the Indians. He reports that

> their heads and bodies, in which they resemble other Conies[12] are but small; his tayl like the tail of a Rat, exceeding long; and his feet like the pawes of a Want or Moale; vnder his chinne, on either side, he hath a bagge, into which he gathereth his meate, when he hath filled his belly abroade, that he may with it, either feed his young, or feed himselfe, when he lists not to trauaile from his burrough. . . . (Drake 1628:80)

What the Elizabethan visitors really saw—depending on which modern commentator one selects—were either gophers, ground squirrels, or Point Reyes mountain beavers. Fletcher combined their features with those of English rabbits, which he had seen in England, although elsewhere he compares them in size with "Barbarie Connies."

I shall not endeavor to ferret out other examples of the wrongful admixing of disparate experiences; instead, I shall deal with one that comes closest to our investigative interests.

### THE SPICY INGREDIENT

To me, the most vexing of all the composites and the one that led me on the wrong scent for so long is the description of the outrigger canoes. If Drake was at the non-Philippine Island of Thieves for three days at most but had ample opportunity to notice the numerous canoes from which the natives harassed him, and was in the Foure Ilands five days but apparently encountered no canoes at all, how could his chroniclers have incorporated traits of Mindanao canoe types in their description of the pestiferous boats? The answer is obvious; they did not. Instead, they incorporated traits that were later observed in the Spice Islands or Moluccas (Map 10), which are likewise in the Malaysian culture area.[13]

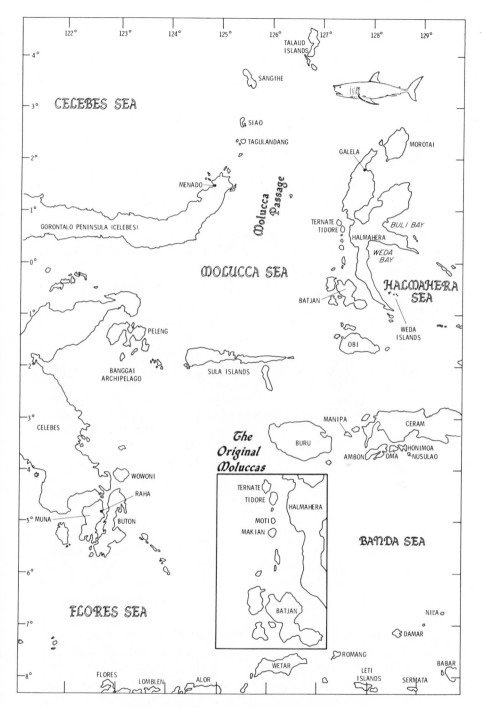

Map 10. The Moluccas and Nearby East Indies

We know that from November 3, 1579, to March 26, 1580, Drake wandered through the Molucca and Banda seas and touched the more southerly Arafura and Timor seas and the Indian Ocean, and then set his course west southwest directly for the Cape of Good Hope. He had continually encountered canoes, some big and some small, not only at sea but at such stopping places as the famed island of Ternate and other locales identified in varying degrees of exactness as either Peleng or Banggai Island, Wowoni, Dama, either Roma or Jamdena (Timor Laut), and the south coast of Java west of Panggul Bay. He also passed close to many other islands.

Fortunately, we know a good deal about the canoes of the East Indies. As far back as 1598, Willem Lodewijcksz told his readers that at the island of Pugniaton—in the Sunda Strait between Java and Sumatra—the people had "skiffs or little canoes, not a foot wide, with reeds [bamboos] on both sides" ([Lodewijcksz] 1598:16r). But he went into more detail than this when, writing of the East Indies in general, he said,

> They have certain small longboats which sail with so much speed that it is marvelous . . . being hollowed out of a single tree, very sharp in front and quite round underneath; and so that they may not overturn there are two large reeds [bamboos] on both sides, one fathom from the boat, tied to two sticks that are firmly attached to the boat; it carries so large a sail that it is amazing that the boat does not overturn and go to the bottom. ([Lodewijcksz] 1598:36r)

Indonesian canoes have not undergone much change for hundreds of years, at least when they were observed in the last century and the early part of the twentieth. Most of what we know is assembled in the previously mentioned survey by Jean-Marie Neyret, who uses such authorities as Paris and especially Hornell. For certain purposes I shall make almost exclusive use of it, not only because it is convenient but highly systematic and comparative as well. I shall concentrate particularly on the Moluccas.

Drake spent the most important part of his time in the Moluccas, especially Ternate just off the western coast of Halmahera. Although Neyret's coverage does not include this small island that was so powerful in the heyday of the spice trade, there are pertinent and valuable ethnohistorical materials that will be offered when the time comes. His survey does embrace Buli Bay and the settlements of Galela and Weda on the eastern shores of curiously contorted Halmahera itself, and such islands off its coasts as Morotai, Batjan, and Obi. Other descriptions are for the Sula group, Buru, Ambon, and Ceram, all farther southward of Halmahera than the others (Neyret 1970c:1–10).

A look at Table 5 will show that all sixteen of the canoe types of the northern Moluccas[14] are classic double outriggers, in contrast to their total absence in Micronesia. Except for a type from Weda, all have two booms on each side, a trait that likewise supports the Drake documents. All but a few employ bamboo floats, either single or multiple, except for five that employ another material and four that offer a choice of either bamboo or something else, usually light wood. One-piece dugouts rather than planked-up boats are the rule, although it should be understood that in most instances some pieces of timber are added on in the form of endpieces, washstrakes, and so on. Neyret does not report on the finish of the hulls; this may not interest him but it does us, and I shall return to this matter in due course. Nor does he mention the presence or absence of shell ornaments, again a matter that will be held in abeyance for the time being. The table shows that the bows and sterns of each canoe match one another in form, with three moderate exceptions from Ambon and the Sula group. None of the canoes have the kinds of incurving ends described by Fletcher, except for the type from Buli Bay in eastern Halmahera (Figure 26), and I shall have occasion to expand upon its significant sheer a few pages below. It will be noted that most of the canoes are propelled by sail, yet paddles are of course employed when the occasion arises.

The southern Moluccas are not included in Neyret's survey, although we know that Drake stopped at or observed such islands as Nila, Serua, Damar, and either Roma or Jamdena. Judging from the book *De Boomstamkano in Indonesie* (1932) by Christiaan Nooteboom, there is no reason to feel that there is any significant departure from the northern Moluccan types.

Of the Greater Sunda Islands, we have detailed descriptions by Neyret for various parts of Celebes—important because Drake spent so much frustrating time probing its wildly indented eastern coast—and for the nearby island of Buton (Butung) and the port of Raha on Muna Island (Neyret 1970b:6–16). Eighteen canoe types

## Table 5. Traits of Sixteen North Moluccan Canoe Types

CANOE TYPE AND LOCALE

| CANOE TRAIT | IVD1b1—Galela | IVD1b2—Morotai | IVD1b3—Buru | IVD1c1—Galela | IVD1c2—Buli Bay | IVD1c3—Weda | IVD1c4—Batjan | IVD2—Obi | IVD3a—Buru | IVD3b—Buru | IVD4a—Ambon | IVD4b1—Ambon | IVD5a—Ceram | IVD5b—Ceram | IVD6a—Sula Is. | IVD6b—Sula Is. |
|---|---|---|---|---|---|---|---|---|---|---|---|---|---|---|---|---|
| double outriggers | yes | yes | yes | yes | yes | yes | yes | yes | yes | yes | yes | yes | yes | yes | yes | yes |
| booms | 2 | 2 | 2 | 2 | 2 | 3 | 2 | 2 | 2 | 2 | 2 | 2 | 2 | 2 | 2 | 2 |
| cane floats | yes | yes/no | no | yes | yes | yes/no | yes | no | yes/no | no | no | yes | yes/no | no | yes | yes |
| dugouts | yes | yes | yes | no | no | yes | no | yes | yes | no | yes | yes | yes | yes/no | yes | no |
| glossy hulls | — | — | — | — | — | — | — | — | — | — | — | — | — | — | — | — |
| twin ends | yes | yes | yes | yes | yes | yes | yes | yes | yes | yes | yes | no | yes | yes | no | no |
| incurving ends | no | no | no | no | yes? | no | no | no | no | no | no | no | no | no | no | no |
| shell ornaments | — | — | — | — | — | — | — | — | — | — | — | — | — | — | — | — |
| propulsion | p | p | p | s | s | s | s | p/s | s | s | p | s | p | s | s | s |

SOURCE: Neyret 1970c. Table constructed by author.

NOTE: p = paddles, s = sails, — = no information given.

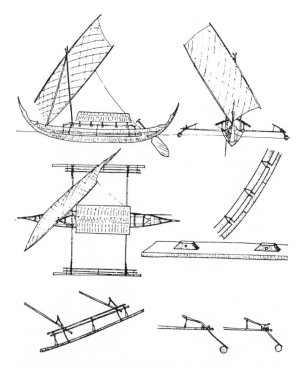

Figure 26. Canoe Type from Buli Bay, Halmahera. This double outrigger is one of the few Indonesian types in which crescentic ends appear in this century. Source: Neyret 1970c:4. (*Courtesy Les Amis des Musées de la Marine*)

are suitable for analysis,[15] and without going into detail it may be said that all but two conform to the classic double outriggers of the East Indies, the aberrant types being single dugouts from Macassar that are believed by Hornell to be an adaptation for better maneuverability in the port. In two other instances, three booms instead of the usual two appear. Neyret's reportage on the floats is incomplete, but it would seem that bamboo floats are employed only half the time. Information regarding the frequency of dugout hulls is also incomplete. Twin endpieces, lacking the incurved form, are the rule. As expected, there is no information regarding the glossiness of canoes or the use of shells as ornaments. Only a few of the Celebes area canoes are propelled wholly by paddle.

We also have Neyret's coverage of another of the Greater Sundas—Java, where Drake stopped for about fifteen days at a harbor on the southern coast—and of the nearby island of Madura

(Neyret 1970d:1–7). But I shall forego a review of these two places because their canoe characteristics present us with no meaningful departures from the usual Indonesian pattern.

Of the Lesser Sundas, we are furnished canoe descriptions by Neyret (1970c:11–16) for the islands of Timor, Lombok, and Bali. Of these, Drake probably passed by Timor or, less likely, Bali. Although there is considerable information regarding the canoes of these islands, it is unnecessary to analyze it as we will have reached a point of diminishing returns. Suffice it to say that the canoes of Timor and Bali are of the general Indonesian type.

I now turn my attention to three traits of Fletcher's canoes that have not hitherto been satisfactorily accounted for: the semicircular ends of great height, the glossy hulls, and the decorative shells.

There is overwhelming evidence that in former times two kinds of high, incurving endpieces were common although not exclusive in the Moluccas.

The first that I discern is one in which the whole canoe profile including the keel presents a crescentlike shape, much as does the Buli Bay canoe mentioned above. The ends are high out of the water and their tips curve gracefully to a fine tapering point. Centuries-old engravings in such books as those of Willem Lodewijcksz (1598), Johann Theodor de Bry (1601), Jacob Cornelius van Neck (1601), and Walter Schultzen (1676) depict such canoes, although one should bear in mind that their engravers often drew on the same source or copied from one another. They appear in lavish profusion in François Valentijn's multivolumed work *Oud en Nieuw Oost-Indiën* (1724–1726), where one finds illustrations of crescentic canoes especially from Ambon and Ceram, and the nearby islands of Buru, Manipa, Nusalao, Oma (Haruku), and Honimoa (Saparua).[16] One of Valentijn's illustrations (Figure 27), engraved by Frederik Ottens, shows the whole Ambon warfleet of *coracora*s, with the inordinate sheer appearing in all but a few of the sixty-six vessels portrayed. The engraving is given authority by Valentijn's many years in Moluccas as a clergyman and scholar.

The other canoe type that I detect is one in which the endpieces alone, rather than the whole canoe profile, curve inward—this time to such an exaggerated extent that they can be described as helicoid. Fletcher undoubtedly observed both this type and the other, without bothering to discriminate between the two. The

Figure 27. Crescentic Canoes at Amboina. The *hongi*, the *coracora* warfleet at Amboina, was under Dutch control in Valentijn's day. Source: Valentijn 1724–1726:II, pl. 43. (*Courtesy The Gross Collection, UCLA School of Management Library*)

helicoid or near-helicoid type appears mostly in the larger canoes, with their high, massive endpieces. It is depicted in several old European works on travel and trade in foreign lands, among them being de Bry's *Petits Voyages*, often referred to informally as *Indiae Orientalis* (1597–1628). One engraving in Neck's book shows over a score of these canoes, all propelled by oars, as they lay off the coast of the island of Ternate (Figure 28). But most interesting of all are the eight helicoid canoes shown in small inserts on various "Drake maps" published soon after the circumnavigation. Thus, the Antwerp map of c. 1581 depicting Drake's global voyage for the first time shows four galleys moored to the *Golden Hind* while it was anchored at Ternate, and four more afloat close by. The Hondius broadside map of c. 1595 in the British Museum has a somewhat similar insert, but the canoes are less distinct and not clearly helicoid. That the helicoid endpieces extended to other parts of the East Indies goes without saying; but its presence in the Philippines should also be noted, for it appears conspicuously in a drawing of a huge Mindanao-Jolo *juangan* in the Alzina manuscript, which mentions it briefly in the text.

The two Moluccan types—crescentic and helicoid—are often depicted side by side, as in an engraving (Figure 29) dramatically depicting a meeting between canoes belonging to the sultans of Tidore and Ternate (Valentijn 1724–1726:I, 363). The event took place in 1692. In the illustration the endpieces of the big canoes rise high above the horizontal plane of the hulls, and they are not always alike. Some of the crescentic canoes are relatively small but others are as large as the great helicoid type. Apparently, there is no indication as to just when and under what circumstances the artist, G. Schouté, drew the picture; but probably the author of the book, François Valentijn, in which the illustration appears, was an eyewitness to the occasion, having been a longtime resident of Ambon. If so, this would give great credibility to the authenticity of the engraving.

If the high incurving endpieces faded away in the course of time, it must have been because they were extravagantly ornamental rather than utilitarian. Some were carved into unusual shapes that demanded considerable expenditure of effort. With the decline in power and importance of the Moluccas as suppliers of spices, and the development of less flamboyant stems and sterns, incurved

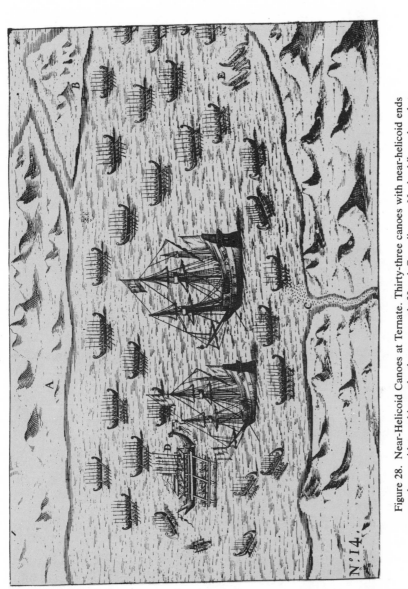

Figure 28. Near-Helicoid Canoes at Ternate. Thirty-three canoes with near-helicoid ends are shown with two ships under the command of Jacob Cornelius van Neck while anchored at Ternate in 1599. They are oar-propelled rather than paddled or sailed. "D" indicates the sultan's *carcolle* (*coracora*). Source: Neck 1601:pl. 14. (*Courtesy The Huntington Library, San Marino, California*)

ends virtually disappeared in Indonesia. However, at least the crescentic type was still in existence when Thomas Forrest was in the Moluccas two centuries ago, for in describing the *coracora* he says it "is a vessel generally fitted with outriggers, with a high arched stem and stern, like the point of a half-moon" (Forrest 1779:23 fn.).

There can no longer be any doubt that when the "Famous Voyage" tells of canoes "hauing a prowe, and a sterne of one sort, yeelding inward circle wise, being of great heigth," and *The World Encompassed* similarly describes the same canoes as having a prow and stern "of one fashion, yeelding inward in manner of a semicircle, of a great height," they did not have Micronesian canoes in mind but rather the crescentic and helicoid endpieces of Moluccan watercraft.

Figure 29. Royal Canoes from Ternate and Tidore. Helicoid and crescentic canoes still prevailed in 1692. Source: Valentijn 1724–1726:I, 363. (*Courtesy The Huntington Library, San Marino, California*)

Explicit proof of another trait of the canoes at the Island of Thieves—glossy hulls—is not as easy to come by and remains a desideratum seemingly incapable of attainment. Such a modern authority as Nooteboom, who has written a whole book on dugout canoes in Indonesia, is of no help. Neyret is silent on the subject, and so are Paris and Hornell; but on the other hand their silence may be construed as auguring well for gloss, because these same three writers are articulate enough when describing the painted hulls of Micronesian canoes and could be expected therefore to make note of painted exteriors if they had known of them for the Moluccas. Lack of paint of course is not synonymous with gloss; it simply serves not to rule it out. Old engravings and descriptions are of no more help than modern authorities except that they imply that carving rather than paint was the prevailing means for decorating watercraft in the East Indies.

As for the "white and glistering shels" that decorated the end-pieces of the canoes at the Island of Thieves, just as shells were once found on the now-vanished *tsukpin* of Yap and the old war and racing canoes of Palau, they were likewise used on some East Indian canoes. Old records do not seem to mention them but a Dutch artist-traveler depicts and describes white cowries attached to the high crescentic prows of canoes he saw in 1918 on the south Moluccan island of Roma (Nieuwenkamp 1925:42, 45), a place that may have been visited by Drake. Indo-Pacific cowries occur in many possible colors and certainly the so-called egg cowries, which are highly prized for decorative purposes, are white. All cowries are notable for their pronounced, porcelainlike gloss. Other islands of the south Moluccas also used cowries to decorate their canoes. For instance, a model of a Jamdena *feestprauw* in the Prins Hendrik maritime museum in Rotterdam has such shells, strung along evenly on the sharp outer edge of the prow piece. Two horizontal rows of shells are evenly spaced at the juncture of the prow piece and hull, and two similar rows are fastened to the juncture of the stern piece and hull. What seem to be shells are suspended by a rope from the stern piece, but this is not certain from the photograph and in any event is not commented upon by the author who reported his examination of the model (Nooteboom 1932:186, photo 93). Jamdena is the largest of the Tanimbar Islands and may have been visited by Drake.

In an earlier chapter, I made reference to John Drake's mention of the oars used by the natives at the Island of Thieves. Older works on the East Indies prove through discussion and illustrations that they were in common use at the time of Drake and the centuries that followed. On the other hand, they were totally lacking in Micronesia, where paddles have been used exclusively as an indigenous artifact. If one were to insist on a clear distinction in formal usage of these terms, Indonesia or the Philippines would have to be the locale of the oars; but such a distinction cannot be maintained for Drake's time. In John's second deposition the Spanish word *remos* was used, and was translated later by Lady Eliott-Drake as "oars." Even though we know that a few centuries ago the Spaniards had words for "paddle," a paddle was viewed as merely a variant kind of oar, just as the English at that time thought of a paddle in the same way, the word being relatively new in the language. Today the distinction between the two is clearly demarcated, the way in which each is manipulated being very different from the other. But since sixteenth-century usage is less discriminating, the words cannot be used as clues in assigning the Island of Thieves to one locale or the other.

This long, and I fear tedious, discussion of Indonesian canoes has, I trust, shown the value of a painstaking scrutiny of the facts. It leads me to the firm conviction that the inconsistent ingredients in the canoe type described in the Drake documents can only be accounted for as coming from the Moluccas and other islands of Indonesia and being incorporated through faulty memory or hasty scholarship when the documents were compiled. Recall that Fletcher said: "Their canowes were made after the fashion, that the canowes of all the rest of the Ilands of Moluccas for the most part are" (Drake 1628:82). He was writing of the Island of Thieves, which seems to suggest that through a mental lapse he was combining a Micronesian island whose latitude he had previously given as 8° N with Moluccan islands whose location at the first island sighted is given by Fletcher himself at about 1° N and whose actual northernmost limits are at less than 3° N. Remember, too, that Fletcher had been at the Island of Thieves for only three days and in the Moluccas for over three months, except when he was in the vicinity of Celebes. It is easy to see which canoe type would have lingered best in his memory.

Moving on to a more general conclusion, my scrutiny of the two published accounts that drew upon Fletcher's manuscript, which he had hoped would be published as a book of his own, discloses convincingly that he did indeed juggle about and combine different experiences. Undoubtedly, he also pursued a little "library research" of his own to fill in lacunae. In connection with these skepticisms I have sometimes wondered if his description of the betel-nut-chewing complex had not been derived from the East Indies, where he stayed for months, and transferred to the Island of Thieves, where he tarried for only three days with some natives who were probably too peoccupied to demonstrate the practice and its accoutrements, however much these might have applied to them, too. However, I am not prepared to accept a recent assertion that the "whole episode of thievery" at Drake's first western Pacific landfall was plagiarized from Pigafetta (Silverberg 1972:321). This allegation fails utterly to make any mention of the two depositions on the subject by John Drake, who not only describes the trading with the warlike Indians but mentions the killing of twenty of their number.

## ✍ chapter ten ✎

# 𝓐𝓷 𝓤𝓷𝓻𝓪𝓿𝓮𝓵𝓲𝓷𝓰

WITH THE MISLEADING Indonesian canoe traits out of the way the determination of the Island of Thieves is narrowed down considerably. The East Indies never entered into the picture except to throw us off the scent by contaminating the clues. The Marianas, lying between 13°14′ and 20°33′ north of the line, are much too high for young John Drake and his 9 degrees, and of course even more impossible for Fletcher and his 8 degrees. By no means could there have been an error in Francis Drake's use of the astrolabe or the cross-staff, whichever was used. Moreover, if there had been a mistake in Fletcher's unpublished account it could scarcely have influenced John in faraway South America, where he had been imprisoned by the Spaniards after having left England with the ill-fated Fenton expedition shortly after his return on the *Golden Hind*. As for Mindanao, its original promise had not turned out as it appeared it might, although it was at least shown to be the locale of the Foure Ilands. This leaves the Caroline Islands as the only place left in which to look for the Island of Thieves.

### TWO AND ONLY TWO

I have, hopefully once and for all, eliminated all Carolinian atolls as possible suspects. Aside from their inability to grow the areca palm tree and the failure of the inhabitants to blacken their teeth, they simply lacked the requisite population to have maintained and manned a hundred or so hostile canoes. In the instance of Ulithi, there is the added impediment of a latitude of 10 degrees.

The total disqualification of the atolls from the standpoint of their canoe features—single outriggers instead of double ones, wooden floats instead of bamboo ones, sewn planks instead of dugouts, lusterless hulls instead of glossy ones, outcurving instead of incurving ends, complete lack of shell ornamentation, absence of paddling canoes except for small boats used for onshore and lagoon work—all these may be overlooked if we regard Fletcher's descriptions as a faulty composite of essentially Malaysian features combined with some possibly Carolinian ones. But, to repeat, the demographic limitation combined with the masticatory and tooth-blackening ones are insurmountable. Even where the two possible exceptions that have earlier been noted exist, they do not intersect on the same atoll.

Only two remaining places could possibly qualify as Drake's island —the high islands of either Yap or Palau. Which of the two was it?

Had Fletcher not so confused the picture by his transference of Indonesian canoe traits to the Carolines, matters might be resolved more decisively. Yet I do not feel that he entirely excluded Carolinian traits in his description. Some features were undoubtedly seen in both areas and therefore overlap. The problem before us is no longer that of separating East Indian canoe features from Carolinian ones but of differentiating between Yapese features and Palauan ones.

### DEADLOCKED TRAITS

In making a decision, certain characteristics may be ignored because they are held in common to about an equal degree by both island groups and therefore offer no basis for discrimination. These characteristics, all well established, are: canoes with twin ends, canoes in large numbers (John says a hundred), deliberately blackened teeth, betel-nut chewing, throwing spears, and the *modus operandi* in attacks on European vessels. All of these, with the exception of the spears and the tactics, are referred to exclusively in the two Fletcher-based publications. The spears are mentioned once by young John alone, and the thieving is mentioned only by *The World Encompassed*.

Although a great concentration of population is not referred to specifically in any of the four source documents, it is an attribute implied by all except John Drake's second deposition, so it is not too discriminating in selecting either Palau or Yap over the other, for both island groups swarmed with inhabitants before depopulation set in during the last century.

It is strange that another shared trait that was held about equally is not mentioned in any of the documents. It is the tattooing of the body, a practice well established by the accounts of various observers who had been to Palau or Yap in earlier times than the later trained anthropologists. Perhaps it did not show up too well among the Palauans, whose skin is noticeably darker than that of the Yapese.

Of another shared trait, one that is indeed reported, I have already chosen to say nothing. It is the use of two booms to support the floats of the outrigger complex. I dismiss this trait because it is so widespread throughout Oceania that it has virtually no diagnostic value. True, the war canoes of the Palauans did have three booms, but this seems to have been overlooked by Fletcher, who does not seem to have been much interested in making fine distinctions in his reportage.

## TRAITS SHARED UNEQUALLY

Additional features are also held in common in both places, but this time with a slight or even strong edge by one island group over the other.

Thus, the Yapese distended their lobes more than did the Palauans. But I must disagree with Krämer as to the significance of this difference, which he uses to try to discredit the claim that Drake had stopped at Palau. On the one hand he minimizes the extent of distention there by using such words as "rarely" and "to a very slight degre," and on the other he cites Captain Henry Wilson, as well as Captain James Wilson who followed him to Palau fourteen years later, to show that the lobes were "bored" and "cut," and he even cites his own field notes to describe various sorts of good-sized ear ornaments (Figure 30).

I think that the reporting on this grotesque kind of mutilation has been very uneven and that we must bear this in mind in weighing the differences between Yap and Palau. If one looks at the literature on Yap itself, some of the first descriptions are hardly any different than those of Palau. In their pioneering article on Yap,

Figure 30. Abba Thule, a Chief of Koror. The ear of Captain Henry Wilson's benefactor in Palau supports a sizable ornament but the lobe is not unduly enlarged. Source: Keate 1793:plate facing p. 55.

Tetens and Kubary (1873) do not even mention long lobes, despite giving an extended description of the physical appearance of the islanders. Our chief authority on Yap, Müller-Wismar, observed the natives more than one-quarter of a century later, and although he described in some detail the ear ornaments worn by the people, he did not single out elongation (Müller-Wismar 1917–1918:I, 24). A contemporary of his, Pater Salesius, did say that the piercing of ears begins at about twelve years of age, and that the subsequent loading of them with all kinds of ornaments gradually leads to the widening and lengthening of the lobe, which hangs down quite loosely and not infrequently even tears it completely apart (Salesius 1906:35). Yet Arno Senfft, another contemporary, while describing matters in similar terms, does not mention either tearing or undue lengthening (Senfft 1903:52). I am not insisting that some observers are right and others wrong, but that they differed in what they saw as important or unimportant. Surely, some Yapese distended their lobes enormously, and I believe Willard Price when he says that he saw a package of cigarettes in the lobe of a youth's ear. Most likely, extreme mutilation was sporadic on Yap, as well as on other Carolinian islands where it has been seen. I raise the possibility that mutilation could have been extreme in Palau in past times (it was acculturated earlier than Yap) but was either not noticed because it was uncommon, or was noticed but unreported because it seemed unimportant. If this seems farfetched, I refer the reader again to the failure of the Tetens and Kubary article to mention it for Yap.

In all the remaining shared features but this one, Palau has the distinct edge. For one thing, the natives of that place constructed canoes whose hulls were complete dugouts, whereas Yapese canoe hulls were (and still are) usually planked and "sewn" (Figure

Figure 31. Yapese Sewn Canoe. In Müller-Wismar's sketch of a *popo* hull from Yap, "a" is the dugout base, "c" and "c" are the endpieces, and "d" and "d" are edge planks. Source: Müller-Wismar 1917–1918:I, fig. 256.

31). Yap does not have timber of as good a quality as does Palau. It is said that in the last century "most of the large canoes of the Yap people were built on the Palau Islands, since their homes [did] not provide them with the splendid wood found in abundance on the Palau Islands" (Tetens and Kubary 1873:92). It would appear, however, that the Yapese persisted in a cultural pattern suited to the poorer timber of the central Carolines and failed to adopt the Palauan dugout.

The edge goes to Palau, too, in its more extensive use of paddles. This was because its men were averse to deep-sea traveling, which required sails, and tended to hug the shores. In contrast, the Yapese were more accustomed to sailing on the wide sea than were the Palauans and used sails on all but their war canoes. An authority on Yap has remarked that the men were "much too lazy to exert themselves to paddle or pole except under absolute necessity" (Müller-Wismar 1917–1918:I, 182). Be this as it may, paddling was the sole or principal means of propulsion in some types of Palauan canoes, notably the giant *kabekl* war canoe, which was moved exclusively by paddle, and the light transport and fishing *kotraol* canoe, generally propelled also in this manner. The heavy cargo canoe called the *borotong* was apparently similarly paddled. But even racing and other types of sailing canoes could be paddled by the Palauans when the occasion demanded.

A significant edge in shared traits again goes to Palau in the use of shells as canoe ornaments—mentioned only by Master Fletcher—because in that island cluster the number and kinds of canoes displaying such ornamentation was greater.

Yap is not known to have used shells on any but the large, specialized, and seasonally restricted *tsukpin* used to catch flying fish, which was dismantled and stored away when not in use. There was something sacred about the canoe and the whole fishing complex, and the crews who manned the flotillas of *tsukpin* were carefully selected and made to observe clearly defined taboos. Inexplicably, the first report on the canoe of which I am aware refers to such boats as *grossen Kriegskähne*, "large war craft" (Tetens and Kubary 1873:19). This would seem to be in error because: (1) the *tsukpin* was a deep-sea sail canoe and therefore not maneuverable enough for fighting, (2) the actual Yapese war canoe was a paddled dugout with symbolic tridentic ornaments at the tips

of its endpieces, and (3) such interested and knowledgeable
fieldworkers as Salesius, Müller-Wismar, Hambruch, and Krämer,
and such canoe specialists as Hornell and Neyret, consistently
refer to the *tsukpin* as a flying-fish canoe. Why no one has ever
bothered to point out the error in typological terminology is
strange, especially since the article in question is well known and
often cited for other reasons, besides which it carries in its Plate 3 a
lithographed reproduction of a photograph of a *tsukpin* sent to the
Museum Godeffroy by Tetens and Kubary.

Curious as to the possibility that Drake might not have been at
the Island of Thieves during the flying-fish season, I combed the
literature and found that the season begins on Yap "in the spring"
and lasts "often a hundred days" (Müller-Wismar 1917–1918:I, 86).
This would have been too late for Drake to have seen these canoes,
as they would have been out of service by then. It will be recalled
that the English captain arrived at his island on September 30, or
what would have been October 10 if the Gregorian calendar reform
had already gone into effect. If Drake saw shells on Yapese canoes,
it was not on the *tsukpin*, the only type of canoe known to have
been decorated with them.

An actual rather than a speculated early visit to Yap was made by
the Dutch—this time before the flying-fish season began. A journal
written by an unknown member of Gheen Hugo Schapenham's
Nassau Fleet, providing the first firm report on Yap, tells how the
Dutch arrived on February 15, 1625, and were greeted by canoes
putting off from shore; but it supplies no information about shells.
This raises the possibility that at that time, as in recent years, even
war and other canoes did not carry the ornamentation. If shells
were seen, the observer may have been too unimpressed to have
mentioned them, especially as the ships stood offshore only briefly.

In all fairness, it should be kept in mind that the first firm report
of our other suspect, Palau, similarly fails to mention shells. When
the *Santísima Trinidad* arrived at the islands in 1710 the Spaniards
were greeted by seven or eight hostile canoes. The ship remained
overnight, after having had a skirmish with the natives. It is always
possible that the Palauan canoes were not decorated with shells at
the time. More likely, Somera and others simply did not think it
important enough to mention them. But the next visitor, Captain
Wilson of the *Antelope*, more than made up for Somera's silence. It
will be recalled that he had not only said that the canoes were inlaid

with shells in different forms, but that when they went out in state the heads and sterns were adorned with a variety of shells strung on a cord and hung in festoons. He and his men had been shipwrecked at Palau in August 1783 and did not leave until November.

Experienced fieldworkers have described the Palauan canoe shells in greater detail and left illustrations in the form of drawings. One such observer was Kubary, who in the last century noted that on the *kaep* sailing canoe, single ovula cowry shells attached to a short cord dangled from the ends of the thwart bars, as well as from the center of the outrigger rope braces and the board seat over the outrigger booms (Kubary 1895:274, 279, pl. LIII, figs. 6, 12). Another fieldworker to depict and describe the hanging egg cowries was none other than Krämer. Fortunately for us, he is strong where Kubary is weak—on Palauan war canoes. The heads and sterns of the *kabekl* war canoes, he says, exhibited a variety of shells strung on cords and hung in festoons, giving a wild appearance to the boats. Snow egg cowry shells were also hung from the ends of the thwart bars, as well as various parts of the outrigger and especially the two projections of the lee stringer (a pole lashed to the booms in a fore-and-aft direction to keep them in position). "[The shells] sway in the wind or swing in accordance with the motion of the sea and thus animate the scene or even render it magical" (Krämer 1926:184, 185). Cowries were also suspended on cords from the endmost thwart bars of the *kaep* sailing canoe (Krämer 1926: 184; figs. 158, 167). Obviously, these hanging shells were less conspicuous than those on the war canoes, but they go to show the extent to which shells were used on Palauan canoes as compared with Yapese ones. Even the head of the *kotraol* paddling canoe used for fishing and light transport had egg cowries suspended from thwart bars (Figure 32) (Krämer 1926: figs. 173a, 173b). In the light of all this, we cannot seriously entertain Krämer's hasty challenge of the possibility that Drake ever went to Palau when, among other reasons equally as poor, he advances the argument that Palauans used only small shell ornaments on their war canoes, whereas the natives of Yap used large shells on their *tsukpin* (Krämer 1917:11).

With respect to the shell ornaments, Palau is not only clearly favored over Yap but over any place in the East Indies of which I am aware. Fletcher's description was not, after all, purely one of Malaysian craft.

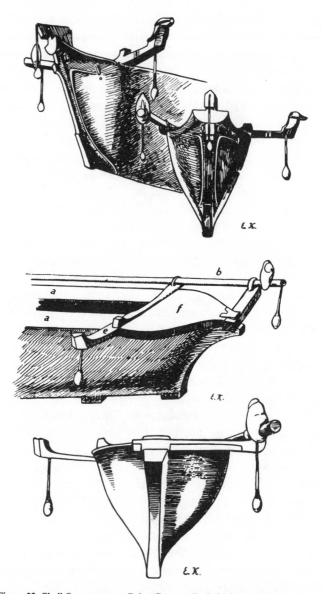

Figure 32. Shell Ornaments on Palau Canoes. Early in the twentieth century, shells were still being hung from Palauan canoes. At the top are two views of a *kaep*, or racing canoe; in the middle and at the bottom are two views of a *kotraol*, or trading canoe. Source: Krämer 1926:figs. 167, 173a, and 173b.

Things tilt still further toward Palau and away from Yap in the matter of nudity, which can be considered a shared attribute if one is willing to accept a broad meaning of the word. The edge that Palau would have in this instance, however, would be that total nudity might have impressed young John Drake and caused him to use the Spanish word *desnudos* in each of his two depositions, whereas incomplete nudity might have been fairly commonplace for him after his experiences with completely nude Indians in California and other parts of the New World. Yapese men invariably wore loincloths (Figure 33).

## UNILATERAL TRAITS

Turning to the unshared as opposed to the shared traits, two favor Yap: the use of the sling and the practice of letting the fingernails grow long. However, neither of these traits is strongly diagnostic, so that their importance is lessened.

My reason for saying this is that with respect to the sling we are not really told that it was in fact used by the thievish islanders. *The World Encompassed* and one of John Drake's depositions refer only to stones, the former saying that they were hurled, the latter saying merely that they were carried. If they were propelled only by hand, then it is not important that the sling has never been reported for Palau except for the relatively aberrant atoll of Kayangel to the extreme north. Incidentally, the "Famous Voyage" and John Drake's other deposition do not even refer to stones, but I do not think this significant. What may be important, however, is the possibility that at the time of Drake the Palauans proper did indeed employ the sling. In this connection there is a statement in a manuscript by Kubary to the effect that on Palau this weapon, called *deliday*, disappeared long ago (Müller-Wismar 1917–1918:I, 191). He gives no evidence for this, and Douglas Osborne, who has conducted two archaeological expeditions to Palau, informs me that he found no sling stones there and knows of no one who ever has. He adds, however, that this may not be significant as Palauans are greatly addicted to hurling stones by hand, even today (Osborne PC, 1973).

As for long fingernails, not mentioned by young John, their presence on Yap has not been established, only inferred by their occasional presence in other islands of the central Carolines. Showing that something does not exist is enormously more difficult than showing that it does. But consider this. Despite giving a detailed description of the physical traits of the Yap islanders, the report based on the materials of Tetens and Kubary (1873) says nothing about long fingernails, and neither does the lengthy

Figure 33. Natives of Yap. Complete nudity was never practiced on Yap. The men wore loincloths, the women "grass" skirts. Source: Tetens and Kubary 1873:pl. 5.

monograph by Müller-Wismar (1917–1918). Just as silent are the reports of Senfft, Salesius, and other field observers. Yet I am willing to admit that a palm-leaf-knot diviner or some other specialist with long nails might have shown up here and there if Drake had been to the Yap islands. To preserve fairness in these matters, I must also be willing to admit that in the old days some Palauan specialists too may have worn one or two of their finger-nails long; but by comparison it does not really seem important whether or not they did, if even on Yap the practice was so restricted that no one ever bothered to reveal it in the literature.

Another unshared trait clearly points to Palau rather than Yap. It is the polish of the canoe hulls. Although I made fleeting mention of this gloss in chapter 5, it is worth enlarging upon because it is the only instance of which I am aware in either the Carolines or the East Indies where attention has been so explicitly drawn to it by firsthand observers. Consider this remark, which I offer in its original French, made by Dumont d'Urville as the result of his observation of canoes at Palau during his second circumnavigation of the globe: "Leurs pirogues sont petites et étroites, mais tres-proprement travaillées: une couleur rouge les recovre; *le poli du bois en est remarquable*" (emphasis added) (Dumont d'Urville 1841–1846:208). Captain Wilson of the *Antelope* had earlier explained how the red color was obtained and the gloss imparted.

> As their mode of applying their paint was uncommon, it may merit being particularly described:— The colours are crumbled with the hand into water, whilst it is warming over a gentle fire in earthen pots; they carefully skim from the surface whatever dry leaves or dirt may float on the top; when they find it sufficiently thick, they apply it warm, and let it dry upon the wood: the next day they rub it well over with cocoa-nut oil; and, with the dry hulk of the cocoa-nut, give it, *by repeated rubbing, a polish and stability that the waves cannot wash off*". (emphasis added) (Keate 1793:316n.)

These remarks are brief in comparison with the detailed reports of two field anthropologists, Jan Stanislaw Kubary of the Museum Godeffroy and Augustine Krämer of the Hamburg expedition. Their technical descriptions appear respectively in *Ethnographische Beiträge zur Kenntnis des Karolinen Archipels* (Kubary 1895:278, 278n.; cf. 1892:201–202) and *Ergebnisse der Südsee-*

*Expedition 1908–1910* (Krämer 1926:112, 113, 185, 190) and may be consulted there by the interested reader. Suffice it to say that these anthropologists found Palauan canoes to have hulls and other parts that were polished by many people using the skin of a ray fish, then painted with two coats of red volcanic earth, followed each time by fine polishing with reeds, after which was applied a varnish made of the oil of nuts of the parinarium tree which had been allowed to become old and resinous.[1]

But what really points most to Palau rather than Yap is undoubtedly its location, a clue that has played a greater part by far than any other in promoting its favored position among the suspect islands. The Palau cluster is within the limits expressed in the two documents derived from Fletcher—7°20' at Koror, 7°44' at Cape Babelthuap, 7°56' at Kossol Reef, and, if one wishes to include some northernmost isles, 8°12' at Kayangel Atoll (Map 11). Yap is too far north of the equatorial line. John Drake's latitude of 9 degrees for the Island of Thieves of course favors Yap rather than Palau; but the young prisoner was testifying from memory when questioned by the Inquisition, so that he could not be expected to be as accurate as Fletcher, who at least had both written records and living survivors of the circumnavigation to consult, though he did not always use them carefully. It must be remembered, too, that John was only about fourteen or fifteen years of age when he left England with his freebooting cousin. With all his faults, Fletcher would have to be considered more reliable on this question of latitude.

## SEA LANES

If it could be shown that there were established or even "natural" sea lanes that brought ships bound for the Philippines and Moluccas nearer to either Palau or Yap, it might help decide which of the two was favored as Drake's island. The truth is that there were not.

Palau was off the beaten track and not positively discovered until 1710 by Padilla and Somera, who had started out from Manila in search of islands to be proselytized. It was next visited involuntarily by the *Antelope*, which was shipwrecked there in 1783 after leaving Macao in China. The Portuguese may have come upon Palau early, but they would have started from the Moluccas.

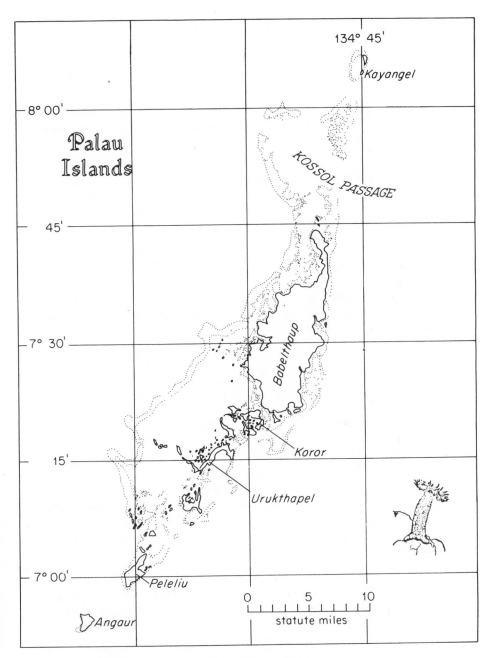

Kayangel

8° 00'

Palau
Islands

KOSSOL PASSAGE

45'

Babelthaup

7° 30'

Koror

15'

Urukthapel

7° 00'

Peleliu

0          5          10

statute miles

Angaur

Map 11. The Palau Islands

Obviously, no westbound sea lanes existed that would have favored the discovery of Palau.

Yap is not much better off. Positively discovered for the first time in 1626 by the Nassau Fleet, which was on its way to the Moluccas via Guam on a westward course across the Pacific, it was actually more off course than Palau if, as often happened, the vessel approached the Moluccan Strait from near the Philippines. Traveling likewise in a westerly direction, when he may have come upon Yap in 1543, was Villalobos, who went from Mexico to Mindanao via the Marshalls and the central Carolines. Other possible visitors to Yap were Portuguese. One was Diogo da Rocha who had started out for Celebes from Ternate, and if it was indeed Yap that he reached in 1525 it was involuntarily and the result of a storm. The other was Francisco Castro, who had been sent out to Mindanao, again from the Moluccas, and fortunately came upon some isles in the Yap area.

Sea lanes are too unreliable a lead on which to base any kind of conclusion. It simply shows that both Palau and Yap remained fairly isolated for a long time. They were off the route of the Acapulco-Manila galleons.


## ONE LAST COMPOSITE

In previous pages I have severely taken composites to task; but I never meant to imply that there is something inherently pernicious about all of them. On the contrary, I feel that a synthesis that is frank and does not masquerade as a straight narrative has a place for itself. Accordingly, in order to draw together all the loose ends of the mystery of the disputed islands in the western reaches of the Pacific Basin, I offer my reconstruction of the story of the crossing of the great ocean by the *Golden Hind*, and of the people and places encountered in one of the more hazy of its episodes. There are some embellishments in my brief narrative but for the most part they are grounded in documentary records and the accumulated knowledge of research workers. At no time have I violated fact in order to fill in a lacuna. For reasons that should be well understood by now, I have had to do some choosing where the historical sources are contradictory to one another, and some interpreting where they are obscure or simply wrong.

Leaving the California coast in the vicinity of the Farallon Islands on July 25, 1579, the *Golden Hind* headed in a southwesterly direction in order to catch the trade winds, and then pursued a course through a great empty area at about 8 degrees to 12 degrees. Drake's chart of the Acapulco-Manila navigation, purloined at sea off the coast of Nicaragua from Alonso Sanchez Colchero, showed him that this was the best latitude for reaching the Moluccas. This took the vessel south of the still undiscovered Hawaiian chain of islands. The sea in these latitudes was an undiluted blue except for the occasional whitecaps whipped up by the steady winds, whose freshness tempered the heat. The trades filled all the canvas of the *Golden Hind* and speeded it onward easily and safely. These northeasterlies did not extend in a belt entirely horizontal with the equator but inclined toward the south. Drake moved gradually toward the line, and at about 4° N he passed between the Marshall and the Gilbert chains of atolls through the only gap through which he could have easily gone without seeing any islands. Unintentionally, he met with "opposing currents"—the counterequatorial current—so before reaching one and one-half degrees he headed west northwest for "China," as the western islands were often called. This enabled him, too, to avoid the doldrum region of light baffling winds that straddle the equator in the western portion of the ocean.

On the sixty-eighth day after leaving New Albion, land was sighted for the first time. It was one of the islands of the Palau group and could be seen clearly because despite overcast skies visibility was excellent and objects could be seen at twenty miles, except within the frequent but scattered torrential rain areas. The humidity was high and the temperature approached ninety degrees. It was the period of the southwest monsoon and the winds were light and variable, with a variety of only six to eight knots. There was no danger of typhoons, for the *Golden Hind* was now south of the average track of typhoon centers, especially at that time of year.

Although the records at times make it appear as if but a single island had been sighted, at others they distinctly spoke of "islands." In any event the landfall was part of a great chain extending in a north-northeast and south-southwest direction for about a hundred miles. The islands were high rather than low, and were variously either volcanic or coralline, with peaks rising a few hundred feet above sea level. They were part of a great ridge in the continental shelf. Although there were eight islands of significant size and over two hundred very small ones—the whole extending from about 6°50' to 8°15' N—only one of them occupied Drake's attention. It might have been Babelthuap, about twenty-three miles long in a north and south direction, for it is the largest of the Palaus and the one farthest north, if one excepts Kayangel Atoll.

The *Golden Hind*, making little way by reason of a scant wind, was soon met by the first of a wave of beautiful, red, "lacquered" dugouts. Some were paddled war canoes without sails. Others were racing canoes and fishing and cargo boats. All except a few of the war canoes had two booms on one side as part of an outrigger complex that included a wooden float. Some war canoes had three booms instead of two. The length of the booms varied with the size of the craft, but in most instances they were over one and one-half yards long. Each end of a canoe rose little above the hull and was a replica of the opposite end—at least for those boats that used sails, for to make tacking possible the craft had to be turned around completely so that the outrigger apparatus was always kept on the weather side. However, under the circumstances there was no need for sails, and in any event the war canoes used paddles exclusively because this gave them greater maneuverability. That is why even the sail canoes were being paddled. No oars were in evidence. White cowrie shells, dangling from cords and hung in festoons, decorated the boats, especially the war canoes, and they presented a lively appearance as they glistened in the light and swayed with the undulations of the sea. The unusual luster of the canoe parts added to the animated atmosphere.

Master Fletcher did not busy himself taking down notes on what he saw of the canoes. Later, when he came to assemble his manuscript in England. he was unable to recall some of their crucial details and substituted instead some traits that he subsequently observed in Indonesia. In Palau he did not see double-outrigger systems or bamboo floats, nor did he see high, crescentic hulls. He could only have seen them in Malaysia. In both places he did see a few similar traits, such as paddles, double booms, and decorative shells. Perhaps Fletcher's errors stemmed from the relatively short and distressing time in which he had to observe Palauan canoes, as compared with the far longer and more tranquil time in which he had to notice Moluccan and other East Indian craft.

The welcomers numbered about eight hundred men and came in about a hundred canoes, in some of which there were only four or six men, in others fourteen or fifteen. In return for beads and trifles they offered the malnourished sailormen fish, coconuts, and "potatoes," as well as some fruits.

The first of the islanders were peaceful and orderly in their dealings, and tried to get the foreigners to draw closer to shore. This aroused the suspicions of the English and it soon seemed to them that their hosts were not what they purported to be. As one group of islanders replaced each of the preceding ones on board the ship, the Palauans showed an increasing reluctance to give up anything in return for the goods they received. The English became so incensed by the one-sidedness of the trading that soon they refused to hand over anything more. This enraged some of the natives and they reached into their canoes for the stones they had stored there, and hurled them against the visitors; but they did not throw the darts they also carried with them. Reaction to this now overt hostility was not late in coming. Drake caused a piece of artillery to be set off to frighten the islanders, who leaped into the water in terror and dived under the keels of their canoes, where they remained until the *Golden Hind* had moved a good distance away from them. Then they climbed back into their boats and hastily made for shore.

However, their fear was short-lived. Soon new groups began to paddle out to the ship, with the same intentions as those of the previous parties. Resorting to guile, they abandoned their tactic of violence and pretended to be ready to trade fairly. All this was only a pretext to enable them to come aboard and steal whatever they could. One Palauan went so far as to pull a dagger and some knives from the belt of one of the sailors, and when he was forced to restore them he only renewed his efforts to catch at more. Meanwhile, the islanders were constantly quarreling with one another, taking the beads and other things from each other, with the strongest among them retaining possession.

The captain-general was unable to shake off these ungracious visitors, so he decided to teach them a lesson. He had his men fire at them, killing twenty, according to the recollection of young John. The English then decided to leave, but not before giving the place the name of the Island of Thieves so that later Europeans would be warned against such ingrates.

John Drake told the Inquisition that the men seen by the English were completely nude, a condition that he had already encountered in both Patagonia and California during his adventures. Master Fletcher recalled that the ear lobes of the men were pierced and enlarged, sometimes to such an extent that they dangled loose against the cheeks. He remembered that some of the men had fingernails an inch long. This must have been a prerogative of rank or an indication of some special pursuit—it is not known. The islanders had jet black teeth, stained by a paste made of burned lime and various herbs; but if the teeth seemed bizarre to the foreigners, they did not to the islanders, who regarded them as beautiful and an aesthetically preferable alternative to the dirty, brownish discoloration imparted from chewing the betel cud, for, these were people completely habituated to the chewing of the mildly narcotic areca nut, and their mouths drooled with a reddish saliva. They easily grew the areca palm which supplied the nut, and had no difficulty in growing the betel pepper tree which supplied the leaf used as a wrapper for the sliced-up nut. The men carried long bamboo tubes, from which they sprinkled burned lime over the nut. The visitors from the British Isles had never before seen anyone chewing this large wad and it left an impression on them. Later, they were to see vast numbers of Indonesians similarly chewing—and spitting—but not making any effort to cover up the dirtiness of their teeth with a black dye.

The aggressive and thieving actions of the islanders were not the result of a sudden transformation of character brought on by the foreigners, who though they were rough and filled with a sense of their own superiority were not shapers of the existing ethos. Palau was a cluster of islands where internal warfare between village-district *rupak* or chiefs was constant, and treachery and deceit an instrument of political policy. The natives already knew about iron because of their proximity to Halmahera and other islands of the Indies, which obtained it from Chinese and European traders. It is even possible that they had acquired iron objects directly from early Spanish visitors, but of this there is no real proof.

More important, however, than their keen desire for iron could have been their interest in the beads the foreigners gave them. The Palauans already knew about beads, which from ancient times they used for money and valued with a deep and all-pervading passion. Coming entirely from Indonesia and the Philippines—and possibly

Figure 34. Palauan Beads. From olden times, beads served as valuables and money on Palau. Shown are a string of red beads (above) and a girdle (below), both made of carnelian. Source: Keate 1793:pl. 3, fig. 1; pl. 6, fig. 1.

ultimately from China, India, and the Mediterranean—vitreous and ceramic beads and other forms of ornaments, fashioned from both glass and clay, entered into the economic, social, political, and religious life of the people, and even acquired an extensive body of mythological tradition (Figure 34). When Captain Wilson was on Koror he took note of the presence of beads and said that some of them, made of green and white glass, had been fashioned from small pieces of broken bottles got out of the wrecked *Antelope* two months before (Keate 1793:176).

Possibly the behavior of the Palauans was motivated not only by their already acquired appetite for foreign artifacts but a feeling that they had not been compensated adequately for the food and water they had turned over to the visitors. We do not know, but given the ethics of the times it may be that it was the foreigners more than the islanders who were the ones to see charity as a one-way street. Had the Palauans seriously intended to harm the English out of some sort of sheer perversity they could have used more than stones. They carried spears with them and did not use them, and if battle had been their original intent they could have used arrows, which they are known to have shot with devastating effect when engaged in fighting.

The *Golden Hind* sailed away from Palau on October 3, three days after its arrival, and continued its course through the Philippine Sea until the 16th, when it sighted the eastern coast of Mindanao at a latitude of 7°5' northward of the line. Here the coast, in the general vicinity of Yaco Point, was separated by small mostly bold and exposed rocky bays. There were no islands in the vicinity. So the ship proceeded in a generally southward direction, passing wide and deep Mayo Bay with its high, rugged shore in the north, and then passing Guanguan Peninsula separating the bay from Pujada Bay to the southwestward. The ship did not stop at Pujada Bay, which indents the coast to a distance of twelve miles in a northwesterly direction. It continued on for about thirty miles to Cape San Agustin, observing that the coast was high, rugged, and rather steep-to with no good anchorage.

It doubled the cape and entered big Davao Gulf, which indents the southeastern coast of Mindanao for a distance of seventy-three miles in a northerly direction and lies between the southern part of the Diuta Range on the eastern shore and the rugged Apo Range on the western shore. It proceeded in a generally northerly direction along the eastern shore until Drake, sighting the large island of Samal in the gulf, steered his ship to the west, skirting both the southern shore of Samal and the small island of Talikud flanking it to the west. Continuing on, the ship anchored on the western side of the gulf, where it took on wood and water.

Even though in the early morning there was no grey mist on the water's face and vision was impeded only occasionally by heavy rain squalls, Drake had no way of knowing he had entered a gulf. From the crow's nest, the head of the gulf could not be seen. Drake thought that he had coasted four islands, not two sides of a gulf and two islands within it.

All the while, from the time the ship had first sighted the eastern coast of Mindanao in the vicinity of Yaco Point, no canoes and no people were seen. Mindanao was a sparsely populated island and the coasts were especially devoid of settlements, except in the southwest where Islam had made its presence felt. The pagan Kulaman, Mandaya, and Bagobo living in Drake's area were essentially hill people, not oriented toward the water. Although the Spaniards had already visited the island, and Arellano and the *San Lucas* had even stayed in the gulf for over a month in 1565, they had not established a foothold there by the time of Drake's visit. True, some Spaniards had come upon people and canoes in the area of what must have been Bislig or Lianga bays, but this was farther north than the point at which Drake first sighted the coast on his way to the Moluccas. As for the canoes and people encountered by Arellano in the gulf, they were met with only after the passage of considerable time, as we have seen.

After coasting the "four islands" of Davao for five days and taking on wood and water, the *Golden Hind* left the gulf and proceeded in a southerly direction. On October 22, as his vessel passed between the islands of Sarangani and Balut off the southernmost tip of Mindanao at Tinaca Point, Drake saw his first natives since leaving the Palau Islands. They were in two canoes and wanted to talk to the foreigners, who wished to respond but could not do so because so much wind arose that it drove their ship southwards away from the canoes.

It is not necessary to trace Drake's subsequent itinerary except in a most general way and as a reminder of the great period of time the captain spent in East Indian waters. Leaving the Sarangani Islands the *Golden Hind* passed Siau and some other small islands before negotiating the Molukka Passage, and on November 3 came in sight of its goal, the Spice Islands. Drake chose to anchor at Ternate, where he concluded a verbal treaty with the sultan and took on some tons of cloves. The ship set sail six days later and began its wanderings through the Molucca and Banda seas, and even touched the Arafura and Timor seas before reaching the south coast of Java. During that time the English had repaired their ship at a deserted island of idyllic beauty, and left Maria and the two other Negroes there when they sailed away. Also during that time the *Golden Hind*, while running southward before the wind, crashed on a reef off the coast of Celebes and barely missed bringing the treasure-laden vessel to a watery end. To continue— leaving Java on March 26, Drake headed across the Indian Ocean for the Cape of Good Hope. After rounding the cape the only stop he made was at Sierra Leone, to pick up food and water, before arriving at Plymouth Sound on September 26, 1580. A plague was raging in the town, and he did not go ashore; his wife came to the ship.

Soon thereafter the queen summoned Drake to London, where he had a long audience with her, and before returning to Plymouth presented her with his diary of the voyage around the world, as well as a letter about it.

The sort of confusion and inaccuracy that attended so much of Drake's circumnavigation extended even to his being knighted. On April 4, 1581, Elizabeth visited the gaily bedecked *Golden Hind* at Deptford, where it had been placed on land for the public to see. As

Figure 35. Queen Elizabeth Knighting Drake. From a drawing by Sir John Gilbert, R. A. (*Courtesy The New York Public Library*)

her guest she had with her the Sieur de Marchaumont, an envoy sent from France to prepare the way for a forthcoming visit to England by the French king's brother. It is commonly supposed that Elizabeth herself performed the ceremony of knighthood, and this is how it is depicted in a well-known drawing (Figure 35) by Sir John Gilbert, the nineteenth-century historical painter and book illustrator. In reality it was carried out at her request, after a lavish banquet on board ship, by Marchaumont, who had been handed a gilded sword by the queen and bidden to knight Francis. It was a thinly disguised public insult to Philip of Spain and his ambassador, and the climax of an amazing and lucrative circumnavigation.

After the knighting one might have thought that a plethora of books on the circumnavigation might have appeared; yet, although pictures and ballads, and perhaps chap books too, were published in the hero's praise, it would seem that among other things accounts of the voyage had been forbidden by the queen. It has been suggested that she feared that too much detail might support the Spanish claims for indemnification, or that in some way some foreign power might benefit from the knowledge. *The World Encompassed* did not appear until a quarter of a century after the queen's death, and the leaves of the "Famous Voyage" had been inserted in Hakluyt's first volume not a good many years before her demise in 1603. Neither was based on the diary and letter presented by Drake to the queen, who may have destroyed them. If they still exist in some hidden recess, state or private, and are ever made known to the world, they could settle a host of vexing questions surrounding the voyage, including the ultimate and irrefutable identification of the Island of Thieves. I have done my best without them.

# *Notes*

1. Possibly there is an ultimate source other than Sarfert for the mistake in date. Krämer, one of the greatest authorities on the Carolines, claims that Edward Cavendish Drake in his *New Universal Collection* mistakenly gives 1587 as the year when Drake left England and 1588 as the year in which he reached the Island of Thieves (Krämer 1917:10, 10 fn.6). In point of fact, however, Drake makes no such mistakes, giving the respective years as 1577 and 1579, the latter date however being unspecified but inferrable by reconstructing on a more or less month to month basis from a specified baseline year. How Krämer arrived at the conclusion that E. C. Drake was off by so many years is not clear, unless the 1770 edition which he cites differs from the 1768 edition I consulted. I do not think it does; the 1770 edition is probably the same as the 1771, which I also consulted. The latter does not have the dates alleged by Krämer.

E. C. Drake was capable of confusing dates because of his failure to convert from the Old Style calendar, in effect at the time of the circumnavigation, to the New Style belatedly adopted in England in 1752. The new year usually began on March 25 according to the Old Style; but Drake's book appeared in 1770, eighteen years after the reform had gone into effect, so there was ample opportunity to bring readers abreast of the times. However, these discrepancies happen to have no application to the question of the year of Francis Drake's arrival at the Island of Thieves. According to both Old Style and New Style, it was 1579.

Chapter Two

1. How it came about that the Portuguese taught the natives a Spanish rather than a Portuguese expression is not clear. The Spaniards had not yet penetrated the area, while the Portuguese had already done so.

2. Marco Polo was writing of Malaya and the islands off its coasts.

3. The Northwest Passage was finally ascertained to be a reality, of a sort, after Roald Amundsen made the transit of the arctic regions through Viscount Melville Sound in 1903–1906, but by then it was already understood to be an impractical means of access from Europe directly into the Pacific.

4. A Spanish agent in London suspected that Drake was going to Scotland to get possession of the Prince of Scotland (Thomson 1972:100). More than three months after the fleet had sailed, the newly appointed Spanish ambassador to England wrote that Drake was going to Egypt for currants (Wagner 1926:426 n.8).

5. Although he was aware of it, Andrews does not use the additional argument, advanced

as far back as the sixteenth century by Hakluyt, that Drake was probably concerned that by now the Spaniards were probably waiting to attack him in the Strait.

6. It required, instead, two observations of the sun, one before noon and the other after it, each time at the same altitude. The mean time between each of the two observations would be the time when the sun would be at its height and therefore its meridian. The compass bearings were taken at each of two observations of the sun and a mean obtained. The error of the compass would be the difference between this mean and the meridian (Hewson 1951:125–126).

7. Although it is generally assumed that the *Golden Hind* was built at Deptford, she has been described as having been built in the French manner and may actually have been constructed in a Biscayan or Channel port.

8. In his article, "The Mystery of the Tonnage and Dimensions of the *Pelican-Golden Hind*," F. C. Prideaux Naish stresses that the discrepancy in the English estimates are probably due to the use of differing tonnage formulas, while the Spanish estimates are purposely exaggerated, especially by Don Francisco de Zárate, who probably wanted to excuse the surrender and pillage of Spanish ships that were superior in size and force to Drake's (Naish 1948).

9. The name *Cacafuego* was actually a nickname for the vessel, and can be translated euphemistically as "Spitfire," which is phonetically close to its actual English translation. The real name of the ship was *Nuestra Señora de la Concepción*.

10. The *Christopher* was not one of the original ships to leave Plymouth. It was a canter which Drake had exchanged with some Portuguese fishermen for his own *Bark Benedict* at Cape Blanco, off the coast of Morocco. Also broken up for firewood before penetrating the Strait was the *Mary*, the name given by Drake to Nuño da Silva's ship, which had been captured and taken along in the crossing of the Atlantic. Thomas Doughty had been placed in command of the *Mary*, but after he was accused of stealing from the cargo of the prize, Drake's brother Thomas was made its captain.

11. Drake professed to be a devout believer and vigorously espoused the cause of Protestantism over Catholicism, expressing his feelings often against the Papists. Much of his attitude toward the plundering of Spanish ships was inspired by his conviction that the religion of the enemy caused them to deserve his depredations. In contrast, his cousin John Drake turned Catholic after being captured and married a Spanish girl.

12. Apparently the sailors of the *Pelican* had fears that Thomas Doughty was able to work black magic and had used it to hurt the voyage. Doughty was a disciple of John Dee, the English occultist, mathematician, and natural scientist. Dee had an interest in crystal gazing and alchemy, and had been accused of practicing sorcery against Queen Mary.

CHAPTER THREE

1. This map was published again around 1595 by Hondius.

2. The map has the word "Virginia" on it, making it unlikely that it could have been made before 1584, the year when Sir Walter Raleigh's expedition returned from America and the area was so named. See Wagner 1926:409.

3. Richard I. Ruggles expresses about the same sentiments when he writes:

Drake's results did not enter geographic literature immediately, as they apparently became state property when presented to the Queen. There is considerable mystery about many of the exploratory findings of Drake, particularly of Cape Horn. It would appear that these new discoveries were suppressed for political reasons, and that Drake was speaking about them only to the Council of State and to the promoters of his voyage. (Ruggles 1967:229, 232)

4. This work is *The principal navigations, voyages, traffiqves, and discoveries of the English nation*, 3 vols., London: George Bishop, Ralph Newberie and Robert Barker, 1598–1600.

5. It has been suggested that he may have been the "Philip Nichols, Preacher," who in 1626 wrote *Sir Francis Drake Revived* (Cove 1963:152). Inexplicably, Morison (1974:657) writes: "Probably written by John Drake, from Fletcher's notes"!

6. A facsimile reproduction of the first (1628) edition of *The World Encompassed* appeared in 1966 (Cleveland: World Publishing Co.). Later I shall discuss other editions.

7. The whole of the "Famous Voyage" was first published in modern times as an appendix in a book on *The World Encompassed* edited by Vaux in the Hakluyt Society series (Vaux 1854), and later appeared in more exact form in Wagner's *Drake's Voyage around the World* (Wagner 1926:245–284). The interested reader may consult either of these two versions or, better still, a more recent facsimile edition published for the Hakluyt Society and the Peabody Museum of Salem (Hakluyt 1965).

CHAPTER FOUR

1. William A. Lessa, "Depopulation on Ulithi," *Human Biology* 27(1955):161–183; William A. Lessa and George C. Myers, "Population Dynamics of an Atoll Community," *Population Studies* 15(1962):244–257.

2. Oxford English Dictionary.

CHAPTER FIVE

1. Kenneth R. Andrews, who may be forgiven because he was writing loosely and had other interests in mind, makes the offhand statement that at about 8° N, "Polynesian islanders came out in canoes to conduct petty trade with the ship" (Andrews 1967:79). The term "Polynesian" has sometimes been used to describe South Sea islanders in general, but this was many years ago.

2. Clain's account is understandably a rough one and contains inaccuracies as well as distortions. As interpreters he used two Carolinian women who had been stranded previously on Samar, and consequently there may have been some errors in communication.

3. Cantova's report, like that of Clain, has inaccuracies, as one would expect under the circumstances. Laddo and Petangras are not names by which we actually know any of the islets of Ngulu. They sound a good deal like Lotho and Potangras in the Ulithi group, from which some of the people of Ngulu are said to have originated. But the atoll does form a triangle, so these names may be authentic. Eilers (1936:209) thinks they refer to the islets of Letyegol (or Ladjogal) and Pigaras, respectively. From all indications, however, only the islet of Ngulu itself was ever a place of settlement.

4. The U.S. Bureau of the Census has published its 1970 census of Ulithi Atoll but I find it so fantastically inaccurate as to be valueless.

5. The land area in square miles for some large Marshallese atolls is: Likiep 3.96, Maloelap 3.79, Majuro 3.54, Arno 5.00, Mili 5.77, Kwajalein 6.33, Ailinglapalap 5.67, Jaluit 4.38. For the Gilberts: Abaiang 11.05, Tarawa 7.73, Maiana 10.39, Abemama 6.57, Nonouti 9.83, Tabiteuea 19.00, Beru 8.15, Nikunau 7.00, Onotoa 5.21. Compare these with the far smaller areas of the atolls listed in Table 1. Space prevents my going into matters of density but my estimates for the Marshalls in 1862 come to only 277.4 persons per square mile for the four atolls of the Radak chain then having the largest populations, and 317.3 for the four atolls of the Ralik chain with the largest populations. Admittedly, the effects of diseases introduced by whaleships had begun to be felt, but there is no indication that the densities were ever high enough to encourage the belief that they, like the Carolines, could ever have come close to the hypothetical densities needed in Table 1.

6. In response to a query, Edwin H. Bryan, Jr., of the Pacific Scientific Information Center, Bernice P. Bishop Museum, informs me that neither he nor Dr. Harold St. John of the University of Hawaii, whom he consulted, have ever "seen either the palm [or] the pepper growing on an atoll. Between us, we have been on numerous atolls. Neither have we seen natives chewing betel on atolls, although that does not prove they do not, if they had the materials to chew." (Bryan PC, 1969).

7. The natives of all the islands in the Yap "empire," and this includes Ulithi, Sorol, and Woleai—but not Ngulu, paid periodic visits to Yap for the purpose of taking tribute and religious offerings to their upper-caste overlords (Lessa 1950). In addition, individuals might go there for extended periods of time in order to build canoes for themselves because of the availability of suitable timber. On such occasions they could easily have acquired a taste for the betel nut.

8. In 1947 I made a complete inventory of all the economically useful plants on Ulithi and had them identified by botanists at the Bernice P. Bishop Museum in Honolulu, but there was no evidence then of either the palm or the pepper tree. However, in 1960 on a subsequent visit I discovered that a betel palm was now growing on one of the islands, but so poorly that it was more an object of curiosity than of nuts.

9. Perhaps Satawal, also known as Tucker's Island, may be added to the list. When Duperrey's ship *La Coquille* was at this coral island in July of 1824, most of the natives were said to be "completely nude" (Lesson 1839:II, 533). However, Captain James Wilson's chroniclers on the *Duff* do not mention nudity for 1797, the year that they were there.

10. Edwin H. Bryan, Jr., already cited in note 6 above, says of the teeth of betel-nut chewers that he "would describe them as a mahogany brown color" (Bryan PC, 1969). He has also called my attention to a study made by Dr. R. W. Leigh, an Army dentist, of the Bishop Museum's extensive collection of rather old Guam skulls, whose teeth he describes as being discolored, but only partially so on account of "tituration of food, frictional influence of tongue, and dilution of saliva" (Leigh 1929: 267). In his report there is nothing even remotely suggestive of blackness.

11. Cf. Kubary 1892:169.

12. Support for my "masking" suggestion would seem to come from the Capuchin mission father Salesius (1906: 52–53), who says that the natives, especially the women, of Yap preferred blackening their teeth, discolored by betel-nut chewing. He describes the paste used.

13. The Trukese were reported as stealing shamelessly from Duperrey's ship, *La Coquille*, in 1824 (Lesson 1839:II, 529).

14. I have more fully discussed the question of native aggression against European ships in my article, "An Evaluation of Early Descriptions of Carolinian Culture," pp. 354–357.

15. Both Best (1923) and Hornell (1932) refuse to concede that the evidence for the double outrigger in Micronesia (or Polynesia, for that matter) has any merit, and argue convincingly against the possibility. They clearly have the upper hand.

16. The stated length of the booms—about a yard and one-half—is too short for the flying proa, for even the small *popo* used in lagoons and along the coasts has booms at least about ten feet in length. Müller-Wismar (1917–1918:I, 183) states that the length of a representative boom to the axis of the float is 3.6 meters. This is all the more reason to question that the canoes described by Fletcher were Carolinian.

17. Mapia, or St. David's Island, lying off the northern coast of New Guinea, has a canoe whose high heads curve in, instead of outward (cf. Kubary 1889:107 and pl. XIV, and Haddon and Hornell 1936–1938:I, 390, 391). The hull is said to appear to be related to the *tsukpin* of Yap, whose endpieces, however, curve outward. Mapia is located at 0°57' N and is out of the question as a candidate. Its older cultural affinities are not entirely clear but to some

or even most authorities they are considered to be Carolinian, although they do not know how far back.

CHAPTER SIX

1. Legazpi says that he himself was surrounded by four or five hundred canoes (Blair and Robertson 1903–1909:II, 198). On the other hand we are told that Cavendish was "met with 60 or 70 sailes full of Savages" (Hakluyt 1598–1600:III, 817), but it is possible that this relatively small number was gradually augmented as the *Desire* began to trade little pieces of old iron for fish, coconuts, sweet potatoes, and plantains. Olivier van Noort's *Mauritius* was sometimes surrounded with two hundred canoes whose occupants bartered foodstuffs for desperately wanted iron (Noort 1602:33). The Nassau Fleet, when it was off the coast of Guam in 1625, was met by 150 canoes bearing fruits and garden products (*Jour. Nass. Vloot* 1631:101).

2. The account of the visit of the Nassau Fleet to Guam in 1625 states briefly that slings, in addition to assegais, were the Guamanian's weapons, and they used them with great dexterity (*Jour. Nass. Vloot* 1631:103).

3. Louis Isidore Duperrey, who was with Freycinet when the latter visited Guam in the last century, provides us with a description of a sailless, single-outriggered canoe made of one piece (Freycinet 1827–1839:II, 459–460). However, I have no reason to think that this was the kind of boat in ordinary use in Guam, where the flying proa reigned supreme. Jacques Arago, who too was with the Freycinet expedition, describes an even larger dugout canoe using "oarsmen" and occasionally sails, but it was obviously influenced by European design (Freycinet 1827–1839:II, 460). When he was in the Marianas, canoe-building had become so decadent that interisland transportation was being carried on by immigrant Carolinians using their own canoes.

CHAPTER SEVEN

1. The Visayas include Samar, Leyte, Negros, Panay, Cebu, Bohol, and Masbate, as well as the smaller islands of Tablas, Romblon, Sibuyan, Ticao, Burias, Siquijor, and a number of still-smaller islands adjacent to all of these. In short, they are the islands between Luzon and Mindanao (Wernstedt and Spencer 1967:444).

2. The paucity of Chinese records may be due to the fact that prior to the Ming dynasty the Chinese made frequent trading visits to the South Seas but did not establish permanent settlements, as did the Spaniards. Nor were they enterprising travelers. One reason for this is that the Chinese were veritably self-sufficient and felt that the outside world offered them little that they did not already possess. Ancestor worship, with its personal obligations toward ancestral graves, further restrained migration. Moreover, those Chinese who went overseas were sent there because they were in trouble at home and were expected to return to their own land with a fortune or die homeless (Wu 1959:119–129).

3. Gonzalo F. Oviédo y Valdés, who is the source of this statement, made use of a report by Padre Juan de Areizaga, chaplain on Loaisa's *Santiago*, whom he met in Madrid in 1535. Areizaga's report has been lost.

4. Sharp (1961:77) uses the word "sling-stones" in describing the Cuniungo incident, but apparently he is taking it for granted that these stones were not hurled by hand. The Spanish originals I have consulted merely speak of the hurling of stones.

5. Sharp does not pinpoint the source for his statement. I have consulted the *Colección de documentos inéditos . . . ultramar* (1885–1932:III, 449–450) for this episode and it has virtually all the details mentioned by Sharp, except that nothing is said of stones and spears.

6. Pigafetta uses the Italian word *tute* or *tutte*, which means "all" or "entirely," a more precise word than the English "quite" used by the translators.

7. The compiler of the book, which is owned by Professor C. R. Boxer, may have been Gómes Pérez Desmariñas, the new governor of the Philippines. The codex seems to have used Miguel de Loarca and Juan de Plasencia as its chief sources for the Philippines, together with what appears to be some original material by Gómez's son, Luis, who spent some time in the Mountain Province and the Cagayan Valley of Luzon, and in the Visayan islands. Of the seventy-five color drawings in the 270-page manuscript, fifteen deal with the Philippines. Unfortunately, none depict the natives of Mindanao. A picture of a pair of Visayans shows them to be "painted" (tattooed) and wearing only loincloths (Quirino and Garcia 1958:pl. 7).

8. Morga is one of the best early sources for the Philippine Islands, especially Luzon. His great work *Sucesos de las islas Philipinas* was published in Mexico City in 1609 and is a very rare book, but fortunately it has been translated into English and made available by the Hakluyt Society under the title *The Philippine Islands . . . at the Close of the Sixteenth Century* (1868). Dr. Morga was the first auditor of the Audiencia or High Court of Law of Manila and drew on original documents in assembling his book. He was a jurist, administrator, historian, and commander who invited great respect, and later went on to become in 1593 the lieutenant-governor.

9. I am supported in this conviction by an admission to this effect in a passage in the Boxer manuscript. Having described the three main ships of the Visayas, it says that "all the rest are small and are called by many different names, and have different shapes, which need not be treated here not being of much importance" (Quirino and Garcia 1958:409).

10. As an interesting aside, it should be mentioned that while Magellan was falling mortally wounded at Mactan, the king whom he was helping in an effort to vanquish an enemy chief stood by in a *barangay*, having been charged by the captain-general not to leave his boat but to stay on it to see how the Spaniards fought (Blair and Robertson 1903–1909:XXXIII, 181).

11. A *fusta* was the name given by Italians to an oar-propelled, flat boat used by corsairs in the Mediterranean, but we need not accept the possibility that therefore the *barangays* were without outriggers; indeed, we know enough about the Philippine boats to know that outriggers were an integral part of their construction.

12. The Alzina manuscript was first called to my attention by Nicholas P. Cushner, S.J., who kindly supplied me from Spain with a microfilmed copy of pertinent pages of the Muñoz copy in the Biblioteca de Palacio, Madrid (MS. No. 2.015). Apparently this copy is the best, and it is being used by Paul S. Lietz of Loyola University, Chicago, as the main source for his preliminary translation of Alzina into English from the Spanish. The Philippine Studies Program of the University of Chicago has generously made available to me the pertinent pages of the preliminary translation, consisting of part I, book 3, chapters 8, 9, and 10. The complicated history of the Alzina manuscript has been traced in detail in two articles appearing in *Philippine Studies*: Evett D. Hester, "Alzina's Historia de Visayas: A Bibliographic Note" (10 [1962]: 331–365); Paul S. Lietz, "More about Alzina's Historia de Visayas" (10 [1962]: 366–375).

13. Elio insists that the modern *baloto*, at least, is a small boat that can carry no more than four or five persons (1972:120–121 n.6). It closely resembles the *bancas* of Manila, except that it is much narrower, with very long outriggers, and is coarsely built with no awnings or shades. "The Boholanos [originally from Bohol] make their long trips to Mindanao, Leyte, Cebu, Iloilo, Romblon, etc." with these small boats.

14. Referring to a *calaluce* seen by members of the Villalobos expedition while they were en route to Sanguin from Sarangani, an editorial note, which spells it *calaluz*, says that this is the name given to a kind of small vessel used in the East Indies with or without oars (*Col. doc. inéd. Indias* 1864–1884:V, 126 n.2).

15. The drawing shows tied to the outrigger or outlayer of this large vessel what is labeled a *batel*, which appears to be a simple dugout with double outrigger and no sail. This is enough warrant to establish the existence of a kind of canoe that roughly approximates that

described by Fletcher, except that it is much too small and lacks incurving ends. Alzina has drawings of other craft, including a *biroc* with a large square sail but no visible outriggers; an indistinct *baloto menor*, with no sail or visible outriggers but at least two paddlers; and a *rambo ó correlan*, which appears to be a tiny dugout without outriggers, being paddled by one man while another pulls in a huge fish off the stern.

16. The Philippine encomiendas were copied from their American counterparts and consisted of grants of natives (rather than land), who worked practically as slaves for those subjects of the king who had received them as royal favors.

CHAPTER EIGHT

1. Bosney is meant for Borneo. Nuttall as well as Fuller-Eliott-Drake seem to have made a mistake in transcribing, because Wagner (1926:500 n.16) found that the original document in the Archivo General de Indias at Seville says "Borney." At any rate, John Drake cannot be used as an authority to prove a voyage by his captain-general to this large island, far to the west of Mindanao and off the course to the Moluccas. No other source mentions Borneo.

2. A guess has been made by Temple (Penzer 1926:liii) that the islands encountered were St. Andrew's (Sonsorol) and Meriere (Merir), but it has so little merit that I shall not take the time to discredit it.

3. W. S. W. Vaux, editor, *The World Encompassed by Sir Francis Drake* . . . (Works issued by the Hakluyt Society, no. 16. London: Hakluyt Society, 1854). Norman M. Penzer edited a later edition, *The World Encompassed, and Analogous Contemporary Documents concerning Sir Francis Drake's Circumnavigation of the World* . . . (London: Argonaut Press, 1926). Using Penzer's very same text, John Hampden incorporates the complete account of the voyage in his recent work, *Francis Drake, Privateer: Contemporary Narratives and Documents* (University, Alabama: University of Alabama Press, 1972).

4. Despite having severely criticized Vaux for his transcription and editing of the Fletcher manuscript, Penzer (1926) nevertheless likewise prints "within" instead of "without," so we must assume that he consulted Vaux rather than any of the old editions of *The World Encompassed*. Hampden (1972), having admittedly copied from Penzer, repeats the same error. The World Publishing Company's 1966 edition, being a facsimile copy pure and simple, is therefore free of error. I have not been able to discover that any version of *The World Encompassed* published prior to Vaux makes the mistake in question, so I must assume it was a typographical error originating with him. Several writers have, over the years, expressed the possibility that an error had been made by Vaux but none of them consulted the 1628 edition to find out. In my own case I not only had the benefit of the exact 1966 facsimile edition but also reproductions of relevant pages obtained from the original at the British Museum through the kind efforts of my friend, Professor C. Scott Littleton, who also furnished copies from the 1635 edition, as well as copies of relevant pages in the 1652 edition of Philip Nichols' *Sir Francis Drake Revived* (London:Nicholas Bourne, 1653 [sic for 1652]), which reprinted *The World Encompassed* in its entirety. None of these editions makes Vaux's error.

5. Some facts concerning these two islands are relevant because they have to do with the question of the visibility of the northern stretch of the gulf connecting the eastern and western arms. Talikud is 4 miles long and about 2 miles wide, being 474 feet high at its highest point. It is heavily wooded. Because fresh water is lacking it is sparsely populated. It is separated from Samal Island to the east by a deep navigable channel about ¾ mile wide. Samal is a much larger island, being 18½ miles long and 8 miles wide, and attains a height of 1,700 feet. It too is sparsely inhabited, with only a few small villages (U.S. Hydrographic Office 1956:421–423).

6. The term "Manobo" is surrounded by confusion. For those so-called Manobo living on the western side of Davao Gulf, I use the designation "Manobo (Kulaman)," and for those

living in the Agusan Valley and the northeastern part of Mindanao I use the term "eastern Manobo." Cole (1913:149) does not think there is justification for considering the Kulaman, as he calls the western Manobo, to be a part of the great Manobo tribe in the east.

7. That the *San Lucas* anchored on the eastern side of the gulf seems supported by Arellano's statement that after hoisting sail to slip away from the seemingly menacing natives, a "southwest" course was set for the island of Sarangani (*Col. doc. inéd. ultramar* 1885–1932:III, 49). Had he been on the other side he would have had to sail south or even south southeast. If the cove had been far up toward the head of the gulf his course to Sarangani would not have been southwest but south.

8. Dahlgren (1916:107) says two-and-one-half months, his computations being for the first half of the eighteenth century.

CHAPTER NINE

1. John Cooke's narrative appears as Appendix IV in the Vaux edition of *The World Encompassed*. It may be found also in Penzer (1926) and Hampden (1972). The original is in the British Museum, Harleian MSS, No. 540, Folio 93.

2. The "Anonymous Narrative" (Wagner's term) appears as Appendix III in the Vaux edition of *The World Encompassed*, where it has been given the title, "Short Abstract of the Present Voyage, in Hand-Writing of the Time." The original is in the British Museum, Harleian MSS, No. 280, Folio 23.

3. These memoranda appear as Appendix II in the Vaux edition of *The World Encompassed*, under the title, "Memoranda, Apparently Relating to This Voyage." The original is in the British Museum, Harleian MSS, No. 280, Folio 81.

4. Indonesian place names in this chapter, although still commonly used in most instances, are sometimes obsolete or have variant spellings. Following is a list of some that might cause confusion, followed by their current names as employed in USAF Operational Navigation Charts:

| | |
|---|---|
| Ambon = Amboina (I.) | Nusalao = Nusa Laut (I) |
| Buton = Butung (I.) | Obi = Obira (I). |
| Celebes = Sulawesi (I.) | Oma = Haruku (I.) |
| Ceram = Seram (I.) | Pugniatan = Panaitan (I.) |
| Galela = Galea (port) | Roma = Romang (I.) |
| Honimoa = Saparua (I.) | Sangir = Sangihe (I.) |
| Java = Djawa (I.) | Siaul = Siau (I.) |
| Macassar = Makassar (port) | Tagulandang = Tahulandang (I.) |
| Menado = Manado (town) | Talaud = Pulau (I.) |
| Molucca Sea = Laut Maluk | Talaud Islands = Kepulauan Talaud |
| Moluccas = Maluku | Tenimbar Islands = Tanimbar Islands |
| Motir = Moti (I.) | Timor Laut = Jamdena |

Although navigational charts now usually use such Malaysian terminologies as Pulau for Island, Kepulauan for Islands, Laut for Sea, Teluk for Bay, and Nusa for Island—these preceding the name proper—I have usually omitted them because they unduly complicate matters, besides which they are less familiar to most people than English versions established through long usage.

5. Hakluyt published a slightly changed version of the "Famous Voyage" in 1600 but the new edition did little to affect the overall quality of the account of the circumnavigation.

6. Sarmiento, one of the greatest Spanish mariners of the sixteenth century, spent consid-

erable time in Spanish America and left an account, compiled from various sources, including his own experiences, "of what the corsair Drake did and the robberies he committed on the coasts of Chile and Peru, and the measures the Viceroy Don Francisco de Toledo adopted against him." This has been translated and published by both Nuttall (1914:59–88) and Wagner (1926:385–395).

7. It is on the basis of Dueñas' report that Wagner (1926:175) felt unconvinced that the English captain really "past betweene two Ilands," where two canoes tried to talk to him. That these islands exist off the southern tip of Mindanao is not in question; on modern maps they bear the names of Sarangani and Balut. Dueñas had visited them in 1581 en route to the Moluccas on official business, and in a report that he prepared for the governor of the Philippines he makes no mention of Drake having been there two years earlier. If he had, reasons Wagner, the natives would have mentioned this to Dueñas. I think that Wagner has too little to go by, and he himself says that Dueñas' report is not always very consistent or reliable. As I indicated in the previous chapter, I think that my identification of the "foure Ilands" makes the sighting of Sarangani plausible.

8. A man named William Caldeira thought that he had picked up the plate in 1933, three years before its discovery by Beryle Shinn, at Drake's Bay. He had discarded it at a point two miles from the spot where Shinn found it, embedded in the ground and partly overlain with a rock. Only after reading in a newspaper about the later find did he suggest that he might have been the original discoverer, but he was by no means sure. See Walter A. Starr, "Drake Landed in San Francisco Bay in 1579; The Testimony of the Plate of Brass," 1962.

9. Although each of these documents has Drake sailing on without landing (the former being very specific on this point), the "Anonymous Narrative" goes into some detail regarding Drake's fruitless search for badly needed water at a bay to the west of the cape. On this point, John Drake is noncommittal in his first deposition but in his second says they "did not cast anchor because they found no harbour nor did the wind permit them to do so," and they then "went on and doubled the Cape" (Nuttall 1914:54). He says nothing about landing until reaching "the Sierra de Leone on the Coast of Guinea."

10. In his second deposition he placed it at 44 degrees.

11. Surprisingly, Wagner, who otherwise finds much fault with *The World Encompassed* and has singled out most of the criticisms being used here, attempts to gloss over this absurdity by saying that the accounts of the sixteenth-century voyages to those regions indicate that the weather there used to be much colder than now and that it is not impossible that the mountains near the coast could have been covered with snow as late as June (Wagner 1926:488). It is true that the Japanese Current can bring uncomfortable temperatures to the north Pacific coast, even during the early summer, but it is too much to accept that this would have bothered Drake and his men, who after all had spent time at the southernmost latitudes of the South American continent.

12. A cony is of course a rabbit. The term rabbit was originally a name for a young cony only.

13. The meaning of the terms "Moluccas" and "Spice Islands" has varied in time. Initially, only the commercially spice-producing islands of Ternate, Tidore, Motir, and Makian, and possibly Batjan, too, were given these designations by the Portuguese. Later, they referred more widely to twelve islands just west of Halmahera. At present they encompass the whole island group between Celebes and New Guinea.

14. Throughout my recapitulation I have omitted a few canoe types that are either European-influenced, too small for outrigger apparatus, or aberrant in some way.

15. Neyret's eighteen types are: IVclbl (Menado), IVclb2a (Menado), IVclb2b (Menado), IVclb3 (Menado), IVclb4 (Menado), IVc2 (northwest coast), IVc3a1 (Macassar), IVc3a2

(Macassar), IVc3b1 (Macassar), IVc3b2 (Macassar), IVc3b3 (Macassar), IVc3c1 (Macassar), IVc3c2 (Macassar), IVc5a (Buton), IVc5b (Buton), IVc5c (Buton), IVc6a (Raha), and IVc6b (Raha).

16. See volume II, plates III, V, IX, X, XI, XII, XIII, XIV, XVI, XVII, XX, XXIIA, XXIV, XXV, XXVI, XXVIII, XXIX, XLII, XLIII.

CHAPTER TEN

1. The German zoologist Karl Semper (1873:55–56n.) gives his version of the preparation and application of the so-called varnish used by Palauans to coat wooden utensils, and says that boiling water would not remove it. However, his account is not entirely accurate.

# Bibliography

Alexander, Philip F., ed. 1916. *The Earliest Voyages round the World, 1519–1617*. Cambridge: University Press.

Alzina [Alcina], Francisco Ignacio. MS 1668. "Historia de las islas e Indios de Bisayas." San Cugat copy.

——. Muñoz text. "History of the Islands and Indios of the Bisayas." Preliminary translation by Paul S. Lietz. MS, Philippine Studies Program, University of Chicago. Part 1, book 3, pp. 132–178.

Anderson, Keith M. 1969. "Ethnographic Analogy and Archaeological Interpretation." *Science* 163:133–138.

Andrews, Kenneth R. 1967. *Drake's Voyages: A Reassessment of Their Place in Elizabethan Maritime Expansion*. London: Weidenfeld & Nicholson.

——. 1968. "The Aims of Drake's Expedition, 1577–1580." *American Historical Review* 73:724–741.

Anson, George. 1748. *A Voyage round the World, in the Years MDCCXL, I, II, III, IV . . . by George Anson, Esq. . . . Compiled from Papers and Other Materials . . . by Richard Walter*. London: John & Paul Knapton. [Quarto edition]

Argensola, Bartolomé Juan Leonardo de. 1609. *Conqvista de las Islas Malvcas*. Madrid: Alonso Martin.

——. 1708. *The Discovery and Conquest of the Molucco and Philippine Islands*. London: n.p.

Barros, João de. 1563. *Terceira decada da Asia de Ioam de Barros: Dos feytos que os Portugueses fizeram no descobrimento & conquista dos mares & terras do Oriente*. Lisbon: Ioam de Barreira.

Barrow, John. 1843. *The Life, Voyages, and Exploits of Admiral Sir Francis Drake*. [London]: J. Murray.

Barrows, David P. 1905. "Population," in Volume I, "Geography, History, and Population," *Census of the Philippine Islands . . . 1903*. 4 vols.; Washington: U.S. Bureau of the Census.

Beaglehole, John C. 1934. *The Exploration of the Pacific*. London: A. and C. Black.

Benson, Edward F. 1927. *Sir Francis Drake*. New York: Harper & Bros.

Best, Elsdon. 1923. "Did Polynesian Voyagers Know the Double Outrigger?" *Journal of the Polynesian Society* 32:200–214.

[Bigges, Walter]. 1588. *Expeditio Francisci Draki Eqvitis Angli in Indias Occidentales A. M.D.LXXXV*. Leiden: Apud Fr. Raphelengium.

Blair, Emma H., and Robertson, James A., eds. 1903–1909. *The Philippine Islands, 1493–1803*. 55 vols. Cleveland: A. H. Clarke.

Blundeville, Thomas. 1594. *M. Blundevile His Exercises*. London: John Windet.

Boulind, Richard. 1968. "Drake's Navigational Skills." *Mariner's Mirror* 54: 349–371.

Bourne, Henry R. F. 1868. *English Seamen under the Tudors*. 2 vols. London: R. Bentley.

Brand, Donald. 1967a. "Geographical Exploration by the Spaniards." In *The Pacific Basin*, edited by Herman R. Friis. American Geographical Society, Special Publication No. 38. New York: American Geographical Society.

———. 1967b. "Geographical Exploration by the Portuguese." In *The Pacific Basin*, edited by Herman R. Friis. American Geographical Society, Special Publication No. 38. New York: American Geographical Society.

British Museum, Department of Printed Books, Map Room. 1927. *Sir Francis Drake's Voyage round the World 1577–1580: Two Contemporary Maps*. Introduction and description of the maps by F. P. Sprent. London: British Museum.

Bry, Johann Theodor de. 1597–1628. *Petits Voyages [Indiae Orientalis]*. 1st ed.; 13 parts. Frankfort am Main: Johan Saur, in Verlegung Hans Dietherich und Hans Israel de Bry [etc.].

Bryan, Edwin H., Jr. June 23, 1969. Personal communication.

Burney, James. 1803–1817. *A Chronological History of the Discoveries in the South Sea or Pacific Ocean*. 5 vols. London: Luke Hansard.

Burwash, Dorothy. 1947. *English Merchant Shipping, 1460–1540*. Toronto: University of Toronto Press.

California Historical Society. 1953. *The Plate of Brass*. San Francisco: California Historical Society.

Camden, William. 1625. *Annales, The True and Royall History of the famous Empresse Elizabeth*. Translated by A. Darcie. London: Beniamin Fisher.

Cantova, Juan Antonio. 1728. "Lettre du P. Jean Cantova, missionair de C. de J. au R. P. Guillaume Daubenton, Mar. 20, 1722." In *Lettres édifiantes et curieuses, écrites des missiones étrangères, par quelques missionaires de la Compagnie de Jesus*. Vol. 18. Paris: N. Le Clerc.

Carano, Paul, and Sanchez, Pedro C. 1964. *A Complete History of Guam*. Rutland, Vt.: Charles E. Tuttle Co.

Carrasco, Francisco. 1881. "Carolinas. Descubrimiento y descripción de las islas de los Garbanzos." *Boletín de la Sociedad Geográfica de Madrid* 10(1):263–279.

Cawley, Robert R. 1927. "Sailors in the Time of Elizabeth; A Study in the Character of the Men Who Composed the English Crews during the Great Age of Discovery." *Princeton Alumni Weekly* 27:977–982.

*Census of the Philippine Islands . . . 1903*. 1905. "Geography, History, and Population." Vol. 1. Washington: U.S. Bureau of the Census.

Cheyne, Andrew. 1852. *A Description of Islands in the Western Pacific Ocean*. London: J. D. Potter.

Choris, Louis. 1822. *Voyage pittoresque autour du monde, avec des portraits des sauvages d'Amérique, d'Asie, d'Afriaue. et des îles du Grand Océan*. Paris: Firmin Didot.

Christian, Frederick W. 1899. *The Caroline Islands: Travel in the Sea of the Little Lands*. London: Methuen & Co.

Christy, Miller. 1900. *The Silver Map of the World: A Contemporary Medallion Commemorative of Drake's Great Voyage*. London: H. Stevens, Son, & Stiles.

Churchill, Awnsham, and Churchill, John, compilers. 1704. *A Collection of Voyages and Travels*. 4 vols. London: A. & J. Churchill.

Clain, Paul. 1700. "Lettre écrite de Manille le 10. de Juin 1697. par le Père Paul Clain de la Compagnie de Jésus au Révérend Père Thyrse Gonzalez, Général de la mesme Compagnie." In *Histoire des Iles Marianes*, by Charles Le Gobien. Paris: Nicholas Pepie.

Clapham, Crochley. 1877. "On the Brainweights of Some Chinese and Pelew Islanders." *Journal of the Anthropological Institute* 7:89–92.

Coello, Francisco. 1885. *La conferencia de Berlin y la Cuestión de las Carolinas*. Madrid: Imprenta de Fortanet.

Cole, Fay-Cooper. 1913. *The Wild Tribes of Davao District, Mindanao*. Field Museum of Natural History, Anthropological Series 12(2). Chicago: Field Museum of Natural History.

———. 1956. *The Bukidnon of Mindanao*. Chicago Natural History Museum, Fieldiana: Anthropology, 46. Chicago: Chicago Natural History Museum.

*Colección de documentos inéditos, relativos al descubrimiento, conquista y organización de las antiguas posesiones españolas en America y Oceanía, sacados de los archivos reino y muy especialmente del de Indias*. 1864–1884. Ser. I. 42 vols. Madrid: Manuel B. de Quiros et al.

*Colección de documentos inéditos, relativos al descubrimiento, conquista y organización de las antiguas posesiones españolas de ultramar*. 1885–1932. Ser. II, 25 vols. Madrid: Sucesores de Rivadeneyra.

Colín, Francisco. 1900–1902. *Labor evangelica . . . de los obreros de la Compañia de Jesvs . . . en las Islas Filipinas*. Nueva ed. ilustrada con copia de notas y documentos por el Padre Pastells, S.J. 3 vols. Barcelona: Heinrich.

Combés, Francisco. 1667. *Historia de las Islas de Mindanao, Iolo, y sus adyacentes*. Madrid: Herederos de Pablo del Val.

Conklin, Harold C. 1963. "The Oceanian-African Hypotheses and the Sweet Potato." In *Plants and the Migrations of Pacific Peoples, A Symposium*, edited by Jacques Barrau. Honolulu: Bishop Museum Press.

Corbett, Julian S. 1898. *Drake and the Tudor Navy, with a History of the Rise of England As a Maritime Power*. 2 vols. London: Longmans, Green, & Co.

———. 1899. *Drake and the Tudor Navy, with a History of the Rise of England As a Maritime Power*. New ed. 2 vols. London: Longmans, Green, & Co.

Costa, Horacio de la. 1961. *The Jesuits in the Philippines 1581–1768*. Cambridge: Harvard University Press.

Cove, Joseph W. [Lewis Gibbs]. 1963. *The Silver Circle*. London: J. M. Dent.

Dahlgren, Erik W. 1916 [1917]. *Were the Hawaiian Islands Visited by the Spaniards before their discovery by Captain Cook in 1778?* Kunliga Svenska Vetenskapsakademiens Handlingar, ser. 2, 57(4): 1–222. Stockholm.

Damm, Hans, ed. 1938. Zentralkarolinen. 2. Halbband: Ifaluk, Aurepik, Faraulip, Sorol, Mogemog. Based on the notes of Paul Hambruch and Ernst Sarfert. *Ergebnisse der Südsee-Expedition 1908–1910*, edited by Georg Thilenius. II. Ethnographie, B. Mikronesien, vol. 10, part 2. Hamburg: Friederichsen, De Gruyter & Co.

Dampier, William. 1697. *A New Voyage round the World*. 2nd ed. London: James Knapton.

Delgado, Juan José. 1892. *Historia general sacro-profana, política y natural de las Islas del Poniente, llamadas Filipinas*. Manila: Eco de Filipinas.

Department of the Navy, U.S. 1944. *West Caroline Islands*. Civil Affairs Handbook. OPNAV 50 E-7. [Washington]: Navy Department.

———. 1951. *Report on the Administration of the Trust Territory of the Pacific Islands, for the Period July 1, 1950, to June 30, 1951*. Washington: Government Printing Office.

Dixon, Roland B. 1928. *The Building of Cultures*. New York: Scribner's Sons.

Drake, Edward Cavendish. 1768. *A New Universal Collection of Authentic and Entertaining Voyages and Travels*. London: J. Cooke.

Drake, Francis, compiler. 1628. *The World Encompassed, by Sir Francis Drake, being his next voyage to that to Nombre de Dios formerly imprinted: Carefully collected out of the notes of Master Francis Fletcher Preacher in this employment, and diuers others his followers in the same*. London: Nicholas Bovrne.

———. [1966]. *The World Encompassed by Sir Francis Drake, 1628 and the Relation of a Wonderfull Voyage by William Cornelison Schouten, 1619*. Historical Introductions by A. L. Rowse and Bibliographical Notes by Robert O. Dougan. Cleveland: World Publishing Co.

Dumont d'Urville, J. S. C. 1830–1834. *Voyage de la corvette l'Astrolabe exécuté par ordre du Roi, pendant les années 1826–1827–1828–1829*. 13 vols. and 7 atlases. Paris: Tastu.

———. 1841–1846. *Voyage au Pole Sud et dans l'Océanie sur les corvettes l'Astrolabe et la Zélée . . . pendant les années 1837–1838–1839–1840. Histoire du voyage*. 10 vols. Paris: Gide.

Dyer, Florence. 1924. "The Elizabethan Sailorman." *Mariner's Mirror* 10: 133–146.

Eilers, Anneliese. 1936. Westkarolinen. 2. Halbband: Tobi, Ngulu. *Ergebnisse der Südsee-Expedition 1908–1910*, edited by Georg Thilenius. II. Ethnographie, B. Mikronesien, vol. 9, part 2. Hamburg: Friederichsen, De Gruyter & Co.

Elio y Sanchez, Vicente. 1972. "The History of Camiguin." *Philippine Studies* 20:106–146.

Forrest, Thomas. 1779. *A Voyage to New Guinea and the Moluccas*. Dublin: Price [etc.].

Fox, Robert B. 1970. *The Tabon Caves: Archaeological Explorations and Excavations on Palawan Island, Philippines*. Monographs of the National Museum, No. 1. Manila: National Museum.

Freycinet, Louis C. D. de. 1827–1839. *Voyage autour du monde . . . exécuté sur les corvettes de S. M. l'Uranie et la Physicienne, pendant les années 1817–1818–1819–1820*. [Section 1] *Historique*. 2 vols. in 5 parts and atlas. Paris: Pillet ainé.

Fuller, Charles Edward. 1955. "An Ethnological Study of Continuity and Change in Gwambe Culture." Ph.D. dissertation, Northwestern University.

Fuller-Eliott-Drake, Elizabeth. 1911. *The Family and Heirs of Sir Francis Drake*. 2 vols. London: Smith, Elder & Co.

Funnell, William. 1707. *A Voyage round the World*. London: printed by W. Botham for J. Knapton.

Galvão, Antonio. [1563]. *Tratado, que compôs o nobre & notauel capitão Antonio Galuão, dos . . . descobrimentos antigos & modernos, que são feitos ate a era de mil & quinhentos & concoente. . . .* Lisbon?: Impresa em casa de Ioam da Barreira.

García, Francisco. 1937–1939. "Vida y martirio de el venerable Padre Diego de Sanvitores de la Compañia de Jesús, primer apóstol de la islas Marianas." Translated by Margaret M. Higgins. *Guam Recorder* 14–16.

Garvan, John M. 1941. *The Manobos of Mindanao*. Memoirs of the National Academy of Science, XXIII, No. 1. Washington: Government Printing Office.

Germany, Reichstag. 1903. "Denkschrift über die Entwickelung der deutschen Schutzgebiete in Afrika und in der Südsee, 1901/1902." *Stenographische Berichte über die Verhandlungen des Reichstages*. X. Legislaturperiode, 2. Session, 1900/1903. VIII. Anlageband, No. 814. pp. 5301–5311. Appendix F II: Missionsberichte, pp. 5482–5484; H: Medizinalberichte VII: West-Karolinen (Dr. Born), pp. 5519–5534. Berlin: J. Sittenfeld.

Great Britain, Admiralty, Naval Intelligence Division. 1943–1945. *Pacific Islands*. [By J. W. Davidson et al.] Geographical Handbook Series. 4 vols. [London].

Guignes, Chrétien L. J. de. 1808. *Voyages à Peking, Manille et l'Ile de France.* 3 vols. Paris: Imprimerie impériale.

Gulick, L. H. 1862. "Micronesia." *Nautical Magazine and Naval Chronicle* 31: 169–182, 237–245, 298–308, 358–363, 408–417.

Haddon, Alfred C. 1920. "The Outriggers of Indonesian Canoes." *Journal of the Royal Anthropological Institute* 50: 69–134.

Haddon, Alfred C., and Hornell, James. 1936–1938. *Canoes of Oceania.* Bernice P. Bishop Museum, Special Publication 27. 3 vols. Honolulu: Bernice P. Bishop Museum.

Hakluyt, Richard. 1582. *Divers voyages touching the discouerie of America, and the islands adiacent vnto the same.* London: Thomas Woodcocke.

———. 1589. *The principall navigations, voiages and discoveries of the English nation.* London: George Bishop and Ralph Newberie.

———. 1965. *The principall navigations, voiages and discoveries of the English nation* (London, 1589). A photo-lithographic facsimile with an Introduction by David Beers Quinn and Raleigh Ashlin Skelton and with a new index by Alison Quinn. 2 vols. Cambridge: Published for the Hakluyt Society and the Peabody Museum of Salem at the University Press.

———. 1598–1600. *The principal navigations, voyages, traffiqves, and discoveries of the English nation.* 2nd ed. 3 vols. London: George Bishop, Ralph Newberie and Robert Barker.

Hambruch, Paul. 1932. Ponape. I. Teilband. *Ergebnisse der Südsee-Expedition 1908–1910*, edited by Georg Thilenius. II. Ethnographie, B. Mikronesien, vol. 7, part 2. Hamburg: Friederichsen, De Gruyter & Co.

Hampden, John, ed. 1972. *Francis Drake, Privateer: Contemporary Narratives and Documents.* University, Ala.: University of Alabama Press.

Harding, Louis A. 1952. *A Brief History of the Art of Navigation.* New York: William-Frederick Press.

Harte, W. J. 1936. "Some Recent Views on Drake's Voyage around the World." *History*, n. s. 20:348–353.

Heizer, Robert F. 1947. *Francis Drake and the California Indians, 1579.* University of California Publications in American Archaeology and Ethnology, vol. 42, no. 3. Berkeley and Los Angeles: University of California Press.

Heizer, Robert F., and Elmendorf, William W. 1942. "Francis Drake's California Anchorage in the Light of the Indian Languages Spoken There." *Pacific Historical Review* 11:213–217.

Hester, Evett D. 1962. "Alzina's Historia de Visayas: A Bibliographic Note." *Philippine Studies* 10:331–365.

Hewson, J. B. 1951. *A History of the Practice of Navigation.* Glasgow: Brown, Son, & Ferguson.

Heyerdahl, Thor. 1952. *American Indians in the Pacific: The Theory behind the Kon-Tiki Expedition.* London: George Allen & Unwin.

Hirth, Friedrich, and Rockhill, W. W. 1911. *Chau Ju-kua: His Work on the Chinese and Arab Trade in the Twelfth and Thirteenth Centuries, Entitled Chu-fan-chï.* St. Petersburg: Imperial Academy of Sciences.

Holden, Horace. 1836. *A narrative of the Shipwreck, Captivity and Sufferings of Horace Holden and Benj. H. Nute. . . .* Boston: Russell, Shattuck, & Co.

Hornell, James. 1920. *The Outrigger Canoes of Indonesia.* Madras Fisheries Bulletin, vol. 12, report no. 2. Madras: Government Press.

————. 1932. "Was the Double-Outrigger Known in Polynesia and Micronesia?" *Journal of the Polynesian Society* 41:131–143.

Horsburgh, James. 1817. *India Directory, or Directions for Sailing to and from the East Indies, China, New Holland.* 2nd ed. 2 vols. London: Printed for the author.

Hunt, Edward E., Jr.; Kidder, Nathaniel R.; and Schneider, David M. 1954. "The Depopulation of Yap." *Human Biology* 26:21–51.

Hunter, John. 1793. *An Historical Journal of the Transactions at Port Jackson and Norfolk Island, with the discoveries which have been made in New South Wales and in the Southern Ocean.* London: John Stockdale.

James, E. O. 1957. *Prehistoric Religion: A Study in Prehistoric Archaeology.* New York: Frederick A. Praeger.

*Journael vande Nassausche Vloot.* 1631. Amsterdam: Hessel Gerritsz ende Iacob Pietersz Wachter.

Keate, George. 1793. *An Account of the Pelew Islands . . . from the Journals . . . of Captain Henry Wilson . . . in August 1783 . . . There Shipwrecked.* Dublin: Luke White.

Kotzebue, Otto von. 1821. *A Voyage of Discovery into the South Sea and Beering's Straits . . . Undertaken in the Years 1815–1818 . . . in the Ship Rurick.* Translated by H. E. Lloyd. 3 vols. London: Longman, Hurst, Rees, Orme, & Brown.

Krämer, Augustin F. 1917. Palau, I. Teilband. *Ergebnisse der Südsee-Expedition 1908–1910,* edited by Georg Thilenius. II. Ethnographie, B. Mikronesien, vol. 3, part 1. Hamburg: L. Friederichsen & Co.

————. 1926. Palau, III. Teilband. *Ergebnisse der Südsee-Expedition 1908–1910,* edited by Georg Thilenius. II. Ethnographie, B. Mikronesien, vol. 3, part 3. Hamburg: L. Friederichsen & Co.

————. 1932. Truk. *Ergebnisse der Südsee-Expedition 1908–1910,* edited by Georg Thilenius. II. Ethnographie, B. Mikronesien, vol. 5. Hamburg: Friederichsen, De Gruyter & Co.

————. 1935. Inseln um Truk: Zentralkarolinen Ost, Lukunor, Namoluk, Losap, Nama, Lemarafat, Namonuito, Pollap-Tamatam. *Ergebnisse der Südsee-Expedition 1908–1910,* edited by Georg Thilenius. II. Ethnographie, B. Mikronesien, vol. 6, part 1. Hamburg: Friederichsen, De Gruyter & Co.

————. 1937. Zentralkarolinen. I. Lamotrek Gruppe, Oleai, Faris. *Ergebnisse der Südsee-Expedition 1908–1910,* edited by Georg Thilenius. II. Ethnographie, B. Mikronesien, vol. 10, part 1. Hamburg: Friederichsen, De Gruyter & Co.

Kroeber, Alfred L. 1925. *Handbook of the Indians of California.* Bureau of American Ethnology, Bulletin 78. Washington: Government Printing Office.

Krusenstern, Adam Johann von. 1819. *Beyträge zur Hydrographie der Grössern Ozeane.* Leipzig: Paul Gotthelf Kummer.

————. 1824. *Recueil de mémoires hydrographiques, pour servir d'analyse et d'explication à l'atlas de l'Ocean Pacifique par le commodore de Krusenstern.* 2 vols. St. Petersburg: De l'imprimerie du department de l'instruction publique.

Kubary, Jan Stanislaw. 1889. *Ethnographische Beiträge zur Kenntnis des Karolinen Archipels.* Part 1. Leiden: P. W. M. Trap.

————. 1892. *Ethnographische Beiträge zur Kenntnis des Karolinen Archipels.* Part 2. Leiden: P. W. M. Trap.

————. 1895. *Ethnographische Beiträge zur Kenntnis des Karolinen Archipels.* Part 3. Leiden: P. W. M. Trap.

Landström, Björn. [1961]. *The Ship.* Garden City: Doubleday & Co., and London: Allen & Unwin.

Lane-Fox, Augustus H. 1875. "On Early Modes of Navigation." *Journal of the Anthropological Institute* 4:389–435.

Le Gobien, Charles. 1700. *Histoire des Iles Marianes, nouvellement converties à la Religion Chrétienne, & de la mort glorieuse des premiers Missionaires qui y ont preché la Foy*. Paris: Nicholas Pepie.

Leigh, Rufus Wood. 1929. *Dental Morphology and Pathology of Prehistoric Guam*. Bernice P. Bishop Museum, Memoirs, vol. 11, no. 3, 1929. Honolulu: Bernice P. Bishop Museum.

Lessa, William A. 1950. "Ulithi and the Outer Native World." *American Anthropologist* 52:27–52.

———. 1955. "Depopulation on Ulithi." *Human Biology* 27:161–183.

———. 1961. *Tales from Ulithi Atoll: A Comparative Study in Oceanic Folklore*. University of California Publications: Folklore Studies 13. Berkley and Los Angeles: University of California Press.

———. 1962. "An Evaluation of Early Descriptions of Carolinian Culture," *Ethnohistory* 9: 313–403.

———. 1969. "The Chinese Trigrams in Micronesia." *Journal of American Folklore* 82:353–362.

Lessa, William A., and Myers, George C. 1962. "Population Dynamics of an Atoll Community." *Population Studies* 15:244–257.

Lesson, René Primavère. 1939. *Voyage autour du monde entrepris par ordre du gouvernement sur la corvette "La Coquille"; par P. Lesson*. 2 vols. Paris: Pourrat Frères.

Lietz, Paul S. 1962. "More about Alzina's Historia Visayas." *Philippine Studies* 10: 366–375.

[Lodewijcksz, Willem]. 1598. *Premier livre de lHistoire de la Navigation aux Indes Orientales, par les Hollandois . . . par G. M. A. W. L.* Amsterdam: Corneille Nicolas.

Lütke, Frédéric. 1835–1836. *Voyage autour du monde exécuté par ordre de sa Majesté l'Empereur Nicolas Ier*. 4 vols. and atlas. Paris: Didot.

Martin, Paul S.; Quimby, George I.; and Collier, Donald. 1947. *Indians before Columbus*. Chicago: University of Chicago Press.

Mason, Alfred E. W. 1941. *The Life of Sir Francis Drake*. London: Hodder & Stoughton.

Matsumura, Akira. 1918. *Contributions to the Ethnography of Micronesia*. Tokyo: University of Tokyo Press.

Meinicke, Carl E. 1875–1876. *Die Inseln des Stillen Oceans: Eine Geographische Monographie*. 2 vols. Leipzig: Paul Frohberg.

Morga, Antonio de. 1868. *The Philippine Islands, Moluccas, Siam, Cambodia, Japan, and China, at the Close of the Sixteenth Century*. Translated from the Spanish with notes and a Preface, and a letter from Luis Vaez de Torres, describing his voyage through the Torres Straits. By the Hon. Henry E. J. Stanley. Works Isssued by the Hakluyt Society 39. London: Hakluyt Society.

Morison, Samuel Eliot. 1974. *The European Discovery of America: The Southern Voyages* A.D. *1492–1616*. New York: Oxford University Press, 1974.

Müller-Wismar, Wilhelm. 1912. "Austroinsulare Kanus als Kult- and Kriegs-Symbole." *Baessler-Archiv* 2: 235–249.

———. 1917–1918. *Yap. Ergebnisse der Südsee-Expedition 1908–1910*, edited by Georg Thilenius. II. Ethnographie, B. Mikronesien, vol. 2, parts 1 and 2. 2 vols. Hamburg: L. Friederichsen & Co.

Naish, F. C. Prideaux. 1948. "The Mystery of the Tonnage and Dimensions of the *Pelican-Golden Hind*." *Mariner's Mirror* 34:42–45.

Navarrete, Martin Fernandez de. 1825–1837. *Colección de los viages y descubrimientos, que hicheron por mar los españoles desde fines de siglo XV*. 5 vols. Madrid: Imprenta Nacional.

Neck, Jacob Cornelius van. 1601. *Le seconde livre, Iournal ov Comptoir, contenant le vray Discovrs et Narration Historique, dv Voiage faict par les huict Navires d'Amsterdam, au mois de Mars l'An 1598, soubs la conduitte de l'Admiral Iagues Corneille Necq*. Amsterdam: Corneille Nicolas, sur l'eaüe Diare. Pour Bonaventure Dacivelle Libraire a Calais.

Neyret, Jean-Marie. 1969. "Pirogues Polynésiennes. III, Micronésie. IIIB. Iles Marshall. IIIC. Iles Carolines." *Neptunia* 93: supplément 17–24.

———. 1970a. "Pirogues océaniennes. IV. Indonésie. IVA. Les Philippines." *Neptunia* 97: supplément 1–12.

———. 1970b. "Pirogues océaniennes. IV. Indonésie. IVB. Iles de Borneo. IVC. Iles de Célèbes." *Neptunia* 98: supplement 1–16.

———. 1970c. "Pirogues océaniennes. IV. Indonésie. IVD. Iles Moluccas. IV. Petites îles de la Sonde." *Neptunia* 99: supplement 1–16.

———. 1970d. "Pirogues océaniennes. IV. Indonésie. IVE Petites îles de la Sonde (suite). IVF. Ile de Java. IVG. Ile de Sumatra et Péninsule malaise. IVH. Madagascar. IVI. Iles Comores." *Neptunia* 100: supplement 1–20.

Nichols, Philip, et al. 1653 [*sic* for 1652]. *Sir Francis Drake Revived*. London: Nicholas Bourne.

Nieuwenkamp, Wijnand O. J. 1925. *Zwerfttocht door Timor en onderhoorigheden*. Amsterdam: Elsevier.

Noort, Olivier van. 1602. *Description dv penible Voyage faict en tovr de l'vniverse*. Amsterdam: Chez C. Claessz.

Nooteboom, Christiaan. 1932. *De Boomstamkano in Indonesie*. Leiden: E. J. Brill.

Nuttall, Zelia, trans. and ed. 1914. *New Light on Drake: A Collection of Documents Relating to His Voyage of Circumnavigation*. Works issued by the Hakluyt Society, 2nd series, 34. London: Hakluyt Society.

Osborne, Douglas. July 20, 1973. Personal communication.

Oviédo y Valdés, Gonzalo F. de. 1557. *Historia general de las Indias. Libro XX. De la secunda parte de la general historia de las Indias*. Vallodolid: Por Francisco Fernandez de Cordoua Impresses de su Magestad.

Pagés, Pierre M. F. de. 1791–1792. *Travels round the World, in the Years 1767, 1768, 1769, 1770, 1771*. 3 vols. London: J. Murray.

Paris, [François] Edmond. [1843]. *Essai sur la construction navale des peuples extra-Européens*. 2 vols. Paris: Bertrand.

Parker, John. 1965. *Books to Build an Empire: A Bibliographic History of English Overseas Interests to 1620*. Amsterdam: N. Israel.

Penrose, Boies. 1952. *Travel and Discovery in the Renaissance, 1420–1620*. Cambridge, Mass.: Harvard University Press.

Penzer, Norman M., ed. 1926. *The World Encompassed, and Analogous Contemporary Documents concerning Sir Francis Drake's Circumnavigation of the World, with an Appreciation of the Achievement by Sir Richard Carnac Temple*. London: Argonaut Press.

Porten, Edward von der. 1970. "Note to 'Drake's Navigation Skills.' " *Mariner's Mirror* 56:258.

Price, Willard. 1936. *Pacific Adventure*. New York: John Day.

Quill, Humphrey. 1966. *John Harrison, the Man Who Found Longitude*. London: John Baker.

Quirino, Carlos, and Garcia, Mauro. 1958. "The Manners, Customs, and Beliefs of the Philippine Inhabitants of Long Ago; Being Chapters of 'A Late 16th Century Manila Manuscript,' Transcribed, Translated and Annotated." *Philippine Journal of Science* 87:325–449.

Repetti, W. C. 1940. "A Continuation of the Early History of Guam." *Guam Recorder* 17:229–231.

Retana [y Gamboa], Wenceslao E., ed. 1895–1905. *Archivo del Bibliófilo Filipino*. 5 vols.

Madrid: [Imp. de la Viuda de M. Minuesa de los Rios].

Robinson, Gregory. 1949. "The Evidence about the *Golden Hind.*" *Mariner's Mirror* 35:56–65.

Rogers, Woodes. 1718. *A Cruising Voyage round the World.* 2nd ed. London: Andrew Bell & Bernard Lintot.

Ruggles, Richard I. 1967. "Geographical Exploration by the British." In *The Pacific Basin*, edited by Herman R. Friis. American Geographical Society, Special Publication No. 38. New York: American Geographical Society.

Safford, W. E. 1903. *Guam and Its People.* Smithsonian Institution, Annual Report for 1902. Washington: Government Printing Office.

Salesius, Pater [Salesius Haas]. 1906. *Die Karolinen-Insel Yap: Ein Beitrag zur Kenntnis von Land und Leuten in unseren deutschen Südsee-Kolonien.* Berlin: Wilhelm Susserott.

Sawyer, Frederic H. 1900. *The Inhabitants of the Philippines.* London: Sampson Low, Marston & Co.

Schultzen, Walter. 1676. *Ost-Indische Reyse.* Amsterdam: Jacob von Meurs und Johannes von Sommern.

Schurz, William Lytle. 1939. *The Manila Galleon.* New York: E. P. Dutton & Co.

Scott, William Henry. 1968. *A Critical Study of the Prehispanic Source Materials for the Study of Philippine History.* Unitas-Filipiana Series. Manila: University of Santo Tomas Press.

Semper, Karl. 1873. *Die Palau-Inseln im Stillen Ocean.* Leipzig: F. A. Brockhaus.

Senfft, Arno. 1903. "Ethnographische Beiträge über die Karolineninsel Yap." *Petermanns Mittelungen aus Justus Perthes' Geographischer Anstalt* 46:49–60, 83–87.

———. 1904. "Bericht über den Besuch einiger Inselgruppen der West-Karolinen." *Mitteilungen von Forschungsreisenden und Gelehrten aus den deutschen Schutzgebieten* 17:192–197.

———. 1905. "Die Karolineninsel Oleai und Lamutrik." *Petermanns Mitteilungen aus Justus Perthes' Geographischer Anstalt* 51:53–57.

Sharp, Andrew. 1960. *The Discovery of the Pacific Islands.* Oxford: At the Clarendon Press.

———. 1961. *Adventurous Armada: The Story of Legazpi's Expedition.* Christchurch: Whitecombe & Tombs.

Silverberg, Robert. 1972. *The Longest Voyage: Circumnavigators in the Age of Discovery.* Indianapolis: Bobbs-Merrill Co.

Somera, Josef. 1715. "Relation en forme de journal, de la decouverte des Iles de Palaos, ou Nouvelles Philippines." In *Letters édifiantes et curieuses, écrites des missiones étrangères, par quelque missionaires de la Compagnie de Jesus.* Vol. 11. Paris: N. Le Clerc.

Spilbergen, Joris van. 1619. *Specvlvm orientalis occidentalisqve Indiae navigationvm, quarum una Georgij à Spilbergen classis cum potestate Praefecti, altera Iacob le Maire auspicijs imperioque directa, annis 1614, 15, 16, 17, 18.* Leiden: Nicolaum à Geelkercken.

Starr, Walter A. 1962. "Drake Landed in San Francisco Bay in 1579: The Testimony of the Plate of Brass." *California Historical Quarterly* 41: September supplement (pp. 1–29).

Taylor, Eva G. R. 1930a. "The Missing Draft Project of Drake's Voyage of 1577–80." *Geographical Journal* 75:46–47.

———. 1930b. "More Light on Drake." *Mariner's Mirror* 16:134–151.

Tetens, Alfred. 1958. *Among the Savages of the South Seas.* Translated by Florence Mann Spoehr. Stanford: Stanford University Press.

Tetens, Alfred, and Kubary, Johann. 1873. "Die Carolineninsel Yap oder Guap nebst den Matelotas-, Makenzie-, Fais- und Wolea-Inseln [bearbeitet von Dr. E. Gräffe]." *Journal des Museum Godeffroy* 1:84–130.

Thilenius, Georg, and Hellwig, F. E. 1927. Allgemeines; Tagebuch der Expedition; (Die

Untersuchung der gesammelten Gesteinsproben by R. Herzenberg). *Ergebnisse der Südsee-Expedition 1908–1910*, edited by Georg Thilenius. I. Hamburg: L. Friederichsen & Co.

Thompson, Laura. 1932. *Archaeology of the Marianas Islands*. Bernice P. Bishop Museum, Bulletin 100. Honolulu: Bernice P. Bishop Museum.

————. 1945. *The Native Culture of the Marianas Islands*. Bernice P. Bishop Museum, Bulletin 185. Honolulu: Bernice P. Bishop Museum.

Thomson, George Malcolm. 1972. *Sir Francis Drake*. New York: William Morrow & Co.

Thrower, Norman J. W. 1956–1958. "The Discovery of the Longitude: Observations on Carrying Timekeepers for Determining Longitude at Sea." *Navigation* 5: 375–381.

Trogneux, Georges V. 1889. *Notice historique sur les divers Modes de Transport par Mer*. Paris: E. Plon, Nourrit & Cie.

Trust Territory of the Pacific Islands. 1959. *Census Report 1958*. Agana, Guam: Trust Territory of the Pacific Islands.

U.S. Hydrographic Office. 1956. *Sailing Directions for the Philippine Islands*. Vol. 3. *Palawan . . . and East and South coasts of Mindanao*. Hydrographic Office Publication No. 92 (formerly H. O. Pub. No. 80). 1st ed. Washington: Government Printing Office.

Valentijn, François. 1724–1726. *Oud en Nieuw Oost-Indiën*. 5 vols. Dordrecht and Amsterdam: Joannes van Bram [etc.].

Vaux, W. S. W., ed. 1854. *The World Encompassed by Sir Francis Drake, Being His Next Voyage to That of Nombre de Dios. Collated with an unpublished manuscript by Francis Fletcher, chaplain to the expedition*. Works issued by the Hakluyt Society, 16. London: Hakluyt Society.

Vollbrecht, John Loudon, ed. 1945. "Ulithi Encyclopedia." Vol. 1. Mimeographed. Ulithi Atoll: Armed Forces Radio Station WVTY.

Wagner, Henry R. 1926. *Sir Francis Drake's Voyage around the World: Its Aims and Achievements*. San Francisco: John Howell.

————. 1970. *Drake on the Pacific Coast*. With an Introduction and Notes by Ruth Frey Axe. Los Angeles: Zamorano Club.

Wallis, Helen M., ed. 1965. *Philip Carteret's Voyage round the World, 1764–1766*. Works issued by the Hakluyt Society, 2nd series, 24. 2 vols. Cambridge: At the University Press.

Ward, Ralph Gerard, ed. 1966–1967. *American Activities in the Central Pacific 1790–1870*. 8 vols. Ridgewood, N. J.: Gregg Press.

Waters, David W. 1958. *The Art of Navigation in England in Elizabethan and Early Stuart Times*. London: Hollis & Carter.

Wernstedt, Frederick L., and Spencer, Joseph E. 1967. *The Philippine Island World: A Physical, Cultural, and Regional Geography*. Berkeley and Los Angeles: University of California Press.

White, Raymond C. 1953. "Two Surviving Luiseño Indian Ceremonies." *American Anthropologist* 55: 569–578.

Wiens, Herold J. 1962. *Atoll Environment and Ecology*. New Haven: Yale University Press.

Williamson, James A. 1946. *The Age of Drake*. 2nd ed. London: Adam & Charles Black.

Wilson, William, et al. 1799. *A Missionary Voyage to the Southern Pacific Ocean Performed in the Years 1796, 1797, 1798, in the Ship Duff, Commanded by Captain James Wilson*. London: T. Chapman. [This printing is by S. Gosnell, whose pagination differs from the 1799 printing by T. Gillet, which was also done for the same publisher.]

Wroth, Lawrence C. 1937. *The Way of a Ship: An Essay on the Literature of Navigation*. Portland, Maine: Southworth-Anthoensen Press.

Wu, Ching-hong. 1959. "A Study of References to the Philippines in Chinese Sources from Earliest Times to the Ming Dynasty." *Philippine Social Sciences and Humanities Review* 24: 1–181.

Yanaihara, Tadao. 1939 and 1940. *Pacific Islands under Japanese Mandate*. Shanghai: Kelley & Walsh, 1939; London and Oxford: Oxford University Press, 1940.

Zúñiga, Joaquin Martinez de. 1966. *An Historical View of the Philippine Islands*. Translated by John Maver. Manila: Filipiana Book Guild.

# Index